JOHN MOSS OF OTTERSPOOL
(1782-1858)

Railway Pioneer   Slave Owner   Banker

Graham Trust

authorHOUSE

AuthorHouse™ UK Ltd.
500 Avebury Boulevard
Central Milton Keynes, MK9 2BE
www.authorhouse.co.uk
Phone: 08001974150

© 2010 Graham Trust. All rights reserved.

No part of this book may be reproduced, stored in a retrieval system, or transmitted by any means without the written permission of the author.

First published by AuthorHouse 6/29/2010

ISBN: 978-1-4520-0444-0 (sc)

This book is printed on acid-free paper.

Acknowledgements

The Author and Publisher would like to thank:

Mr. Charles Gladstone for granting permission to quote from John Moss's 312 letters and other material in the Glynne-Gladstone collection GG452-518, GG370-372 and GG2856-2880 held at Flintshire Record Office in Hawarden, North Wales.

Staffordshire and Stoke on Trent Archive Service for granting permission to quote from John Moss's 109 letters and other material in the Sutherland Papers D593/K/1/3/16-33 of which they are the legal owners, having raised the necessary £2m to save the collection.

I dedicate this book to my wife Chris who endured seven long years of my "Mossing".

Contents	xi
Introduction	1
Chapter 1 Otterspool	5
Chapter 2 The Saga of 1,000 Slaves	11
Chapter 3 The Abolition of Slavery	27
Chapter 4 Apprenticeship & The Indentured Labour Experiment	44
Chapter 5 Emancipation and Beyond	65
Chapter 6 Incessant Banking Avocations	81
Chapter 7 The Liverpool & Manchester Railway	115
Chapter 8 The Grand Junction Railway	156
Chapter 9 Amalgamations	186
Chapter 10 Foreign Railways	203
Chapter 11 The End	217
Appendix A	219
Appendix B	225
Appendix C	227
Appendix D	229
Bibliography	232
Index	239

Contents

John Moss of Otterspool 1782 – 1858

Chapter 1 - Otterspool: his upbringing **5**; enters his father's business (1803) **6**; his inheritance (1805) **6-7**; marries Hannah Taylor (1805) **7**; moves into Otterspool House (1811) **7**; his children **7**; improves the strand at Otterspool **7-8**; skating at Otterspool **8**; his death at Otterspool House (1858) **10**

Chapter 2 – The Saga of 1,000 Slaves: receives William Roscoe's help for securing a slave shipment **12**; inherits Uncle James's slaves (1820) **12**; befriends John Gladstone (1822)**12**; seeks Gladstone's assistance in resuming the slave shipment **13**; obtains licence to continue with the shipment **14**; appoints attorney to purchase Demeraran estates **14**; purchases *Anna Regina* estate (1823) **15**; Moss the absentee planter **15-16**; approves of William Wilberforce's pamphlet and policies **17-18**; laments the outcome of the Demerara Rebellion **21**; attacks James Cropper for allegations of mismanagement of British slave plantations **23**; defends the humane nature of the laws of the Bahamas **24** ; defends the humane nature of his slave shipments (1824) **25**; writes to foreign office regarding 99 slaves marooned on Crooked Island (1828) **26**

Chapter 3 – The Abolition of Slavery: invests in labour saving devices for Anna Regina (1830) **27**; receives the first shipment of the new vacuum pan sugar (1831) **28**; is challenged regarding the enhanced quality of his sugars by a Surveyor of the Kings Dock **29**; hears Thomas Fowell Buxton's motions re the abolition of slavery **29**; supports the election campaign of Lord Sandon (1832) **30**; sees further improvement in the quality and sale price of vacuum pan sugars **30**; recognises poor slave productivity on *Anna Regina* compared to Gladstone's estates **31**; appoints Gladstone's attorney MacLean as his own attorney (1831) **31**; gives MacLean full power over management of *Anna Regina* **31**; seeks Gladstone's help in persuading MacLean to comply with the government's slave initiatives (1832) **32**; witnesses a further motion from Buxton for emancipation **32**; is attacked by the anti-slavery society **32**; examines the results of Tom Gladstone's vacuum pan experiments on Anna Regina **33**; proposes to conduct his own vacuum pan experiments **33**; receives the results of MacLean's first year on Anna Regina **34**; remains adamant regarding the efficacy of the vacuum pan **34**; complains to Lord Sandon re foreign sugars being refined in Britain **35**; endorses Buxton's proposals for emancipation (1833)**35**; goes to London to seek best compensation terms from government for loss of slaves **36**; begs Gladstone to come to London to assist him with negotiations **37**; Anna Regina used in parliament as an example of an estate where maltreatment of slaves occurs **38**; together with Gladstone presents an eleven page plan to government for emancipation and after **38-39**; praises Gladstone for his successful negotiations with Wellington, Peel and Russell **39**; condemns government for the haste with which it drafted the Emancipation Bill **40**; meets EGS Stanley to strike a deal for compensation and apprenticeship **40**; writes telling MacLean of his and Gladstone's support for the government's emancipation measures **41**; again begs Gladstone to come to London to assist him **41**; leaves London for Lord Sandon to complete the work on behalf of the West Indian interests **41**; receives congratulations from Peter Rose on his emancipation negotiations **41**; reflects on his work for the West Indian planters' cause **41-42**; is again attacked by the anti-slavery movement **43**

Chapter 4 – Apprenticeship and the Indentured Labour Experiment: receives letters from MacLean re the satisfactory situation on Anna Regina **44**; worries about the lack of labour which will arise after emancipation **44-45**; rejects Robertson

Gladstone's proposals for importing consenting Africans to the West Indies (1834) **45**; rejects MacLean's advice to purchase further West Indian properties **45**; recruits a Moravian missionary to provide the apprenticed slaves on Anna Regina religious and moral instruction **46**; receives a satisfactory report from Robertson Gladstone on Anna Regina's workers **47**; is informed by James Stephen of the proposed revision of sugar duties **48**; following emancipation, worries about reduced sugar output **45-46**; is heartened by William Ewart Gladstone's appointment as Under Secretary for the Colonies (1835) **49**; makes plans to cut operating costs on Anna Regina and to import more provisions for the apprenticed workers **50**; receives James Stewart's approval of the vacuum pan following some very favourable results **51**; grieves following the death of his daughter Annie and son in law Major Ferrand **51**; accepts £40,000 compensation for the loss of 805 slaves (1836) **52**; lays foundation stone of and donates stained glass window to St Anne's church **52**; receives gloomy report from Cottingham Moss on the supply of willing workers after the apprenticeship scheme finishes **53**; proposes to ship workers from India to West Indies **53**; undertakes to ensure compliance with all government requirements for the shipment of Indian workers (1837) **55**; persuades Gladstone to reduce the Indians' period of Indenture from 7 to 5 years **55**; obtains government approval for shipment of 414 Indians **56**; accuses abolitionists opposed to the shipment of hypocrisy **57**; thanks Gladstone for taking over full responsibility for the shipment **57**; worries that the Indians may be refused entry by Demerara's Governor **58**; worries about the competitive disadvantage the West Indies has against the countries with slave economies **59**; rues the collapse of the Indentured Labour Scheme **63**

Chapter 5: Emancipation and Beyond: urges Gladstone to invest in a trans Atlantic steam packet company **66**; challenges Gladstone's negative view of the steam packet, but agrees with him eventually **66**; rejects workers from the Voluntary Subscription immigration Society **66**; begs Gladstone to press for the resumption of Indian Indenture **68**; finds himself in competition with other estates for workers **69**; considers renting Anna Regina to Mr McKay or selling to Mr Stuart **69**; delighted with a Tory general election victory and by the appointment of William Ewart Gladstone as Vice President of the Board of Trade (1841) **70**; complains of the government's continuing move away from protectionism towards free trade (1843) **71**; in the absence of new workers, sends out a steam engine to Anna Regina (1846) **71-72**; worries that the equalisation of the Sugar Duties will have dire consequences **73-74**; frets about the Irish Potato Famine, bank restriction and free trade **74-75**; suggests the introduction of a regulated "free trade" in African slaves **76**; rejects the notion that Chinese labourers be introduced (1848) **77**; predicts that only half of British Guiana's estates will be in operation in 1849 **77**; bequeaths Anna Regina to his son Thomas (1858) **80**

Chapter 6 – Incessant Banking Avocations: inherits his father's business (1805) **81**; advertises for a banking partner (1807) **83**; forms the bank of Moss, Dales & Rogers **84**; lends money to Thomas Brown of Whitby 84; the debt rises to £35,000 **84**; obtains Brown's mansion Newton House in settlement of the debt **85**; bank survives the commercial crisis of 1809-10 **85**; takes Henry Moss into partnership (1811) **85**; opens new bank premises on Dale Street **85**; bank becomes returners of the Custom House receipts **86**; loses status of returners of Custom House receipts to Arthur Heywood (1822) **86**; seeks the help of Gladstone and Huskisson in the scramble to become returners (1823) **86**; wins back the returners role in partnership with William Ewart **87**; Ewart dies, forcing Moss into dialogue with his rivals **87**; wins the account of John Gladstone **88**; shares the role of returners with 4 other banks (1824) **88**; averts the banking crisis of 1825 using knowledge of previous crises **91-92**; advises Gladstone against entering into a banking partnership **93**; visits London and witnesses the commercial crisis (1826) **93**; returns to find Liverpool in crisis **93**; Holidays in Harrogate and refuses to cash Gladstone's Bills **94**; apologises to Gladstone **95**; meets Duke of Wellington as one of a committee of country bankers **96**; takes Cottingham Moss into partnership (1827) **96**; expresses scepticism regarding joint stock banks (1831) **97**; criticises Bank of England for raising their rates **97**; takes Thomas Moss into partnership **99**; resists the trend of converting to a joint stock bank **101**; averts the 1836 financial crisis **102**; criticises the directors of the Bank of England **103**; averts the financial crisis of 1847 and criticises the joint stock banks **106**; grieves for his daughter Margaret and his brother James **107**; loses nephew Cottingham and brother Henry (1848) **108**

Chapter 7 – The Liverpool & Manchester Railway: authorises William James to carry out a survey of the proposed route **116**; appointed chairman of a Provisional Committee of the railway (1822) **116**; appointed chairman of a Permanent Committee of the railway (1824) **117**; complains to Liverpool Council about the sharp practice of canal proprietors **118**; relinquishes the chairmanship **119**; appointed vice chairman of the railway **121**; questions the practicality of restricting dividend payments to 10% per annum **121**; disposes of shares as a member of a secret committee **122**; a clash of personalities with Lister Ellis (1825)**123**; signs 4,000 share certificates **124**; attends locomotive trials at Killingworth Colliery **124-126**; expresses doubts about the Bill for the railway, but stays in London to assist **126**; leaves London, much to the relief of other committee members **127**; expresses intention to obtain another Bill after the first Bill is rejected **127**; writes to William James and George Stephenson on the same day **128**; upset by the resistance of Lords Sefton and Derby to the proposed new route **129**; attends the opening of the Stockton

& Darlington Railway **130**; more ill feeling towards Lister Ellis **130**; offers Marquis of Stafford 1,000 shares in the railway **132**; confirmed as deputy chairman of the railway **133**; travels to London to help the Bill through parliament (1826) **134**; visits the railway works at Chat Moss (1827) **136**; anxious about his meeting with Robert Bradshaw (1828) **137**; wins various concessions from Bradshaw **138**; expresses contempt for Thomas Telford's report on the railway (1829) **139**; helps frame the conditions for the Rainhill Trials **140**; expresses admiration of George Stephenson's engineering achievements **142**; enjoys a trip along the railway **142**; proposes a railway from Liverpool to London **143**; suggests the Bridgewater Canal be converted into a railway **143**; receives a deputation from 3 men proposing a railway from London to Birmingham **143**; focuses his attentions on the Liverpool & Birmingham railway **144**; is daunted by the magnitude of future new railway projects **145**; journeys along the full length of the Liverpool & Manchester Railway (1830) **145**; receives a congratulatory letter from Lord Derby **146**; meets the Duke of Wellington **146**; assigned to direct the *Northumbrian* locomotive on the opening day of the L&M **147**; airs his views about the death of William Huskisson on the opening day of the railway **151**; tells Gladstone he no longer believes he will become MP for Liverpool **152**; is considered as Huskisson's replacement MP for Liverpool **153**

Chapter 8 – The Grand Junction Railway: becomes involved in the Liverpool & Birmingham railway project **157**; helps prevent the railway's Bill being put before parliament (1829) **158**; agrees to Loch's plans for a bridge at Runcorn **159**; offers the Marquis of Stafford shares in the railway **159**; warns Loch of the importance of a railway / canal alliance **160**; makes a further offer of shares to the Stafford family (1830) **160**; announces the intention to put a Bill before Parliament (1832) **161**; becomes chairman of the Liverpool & Birmingham

Railway **161**; purchases the Warrington & Newton Railway cheaply **162**; gives evidence before a Parliamentary committee of the London & Birmingham Railway **163-164**; becomes chairman of the Grand Junction Railway **164**; resists calls for amalgamation of the GJR and the Liverpool & Manchester **164**; considers resigning from the L&M board (1833) **164**; disposes of L&M shares **165**; refuses to criticise Stephenson harshly **165**; purchases land around Aston Hall in Birmingham (1835) **166**; ill health **167**; gives shareholders an update on the progress of engineering works (1834) **168**; returns home after a continental holiday **168**; accepts Stephenson's resignation **169**; keeps on good terms with Stephenson **169**; recommends GJR shares to Gladstone **170**; accepts an investment of £50,000 from Gladstone **170**; resists efforts of L&M board to bypass their 10% dividend limit (1836) **171**; asks Loch's permission to resign from the L&M boards **171**; proves to have been a capable chairman **174**; praises the GJR engineer Joseph Locke **174**; resigns from the L&M board (1837) **176**; withdraws his resignation **176**; announces the results of the GJR's first few months of trading **176-177**; complains about the poor management of the GJR (1838) **177**; resolves to resign from the L&M but is again dissuaded by Loch **177**; complains about his treatment at the hands of the board members of both the L&M and GJR **178**; informs Gladstone of corruption on the GJR (1839) **179**; declines the offer of a place on the board of the Brighton Railway (1840) **179**; announces the GJR's intention to construct workshops at Crewe **180-181**; following more ill health, reduces his work load **181**; appoints Captain Huish as Secretary and General Manger of the GJR (1841) **181**; holds on to his GJR shares despite market volatility (1842) **182**; rues more ill health and more bickering between the L&M and GJR boards (1843) **182**; is described as a worthy chairman **183**; makes speech at a dinner at the Crewe works **183**

Chapter 9 – Amalgamations: announces the GJR's intention to play a pivotal part in creating a national rail network (1837) **186**; meets Robert Peel and the London & Birmingham and Chester & Holyhead chairmen to discuss the proposed route to Wales (1844) **188**; is scornful of the C&H and its chairman **188**; receives C&H's letter about its intention to purchase the Chester & Birkenhead Railway **189**; withdraws from the proposed alliance **189**; proposes that the L&B and Manchester & Birmingham participate in the Trent Valley scheme **189**; is dismayed by the L&B's duplicity **190**; seeks Gladstone's assistance in securing government approval for the west coast line **191**; recommends that the GJR makes a sizeable investment in the Lancaster & Carlisle Railway **191**; comments on the Railway Mania **192**; boasts about the ruination of some canals **193**; suggests the GJR should become independent of the L&M **193**; thinks amalgamation of the GJR and L&M may be desirable **194**; complains about his heavy work load (1845) **194**; ill feeling towards and mistrust of George Carr Glyn (1845) **195-196**; becomes involved with the Birmingham & Oxford Railway **196**; makes heavy investments in railways during the Railway Mania **198**; announces half year results for 1845 **198-199**; announces his retirement as chairman **199**; recriminations with Glyn **199**; his personality is stamped on the GJR **201**

Chapter 10 – Foreign Railways: notifies Gladstone of an opportunity to invest in French railways **204**; subscribes for 500 shares in the Paris & Rouen (1840) **204**; assures Gladstone there will be no war with France **204**; procures shares for Gladstone **204**; chairs a meeting in Liverpool for the P&R shareholders **206**; releases payment of subscriptions to the French **207**; makes 100% return on his investment **208**; assures Gladstone that the P&R's shares will pay excellent dividends (1843) **209**; becomes involved in the Rouen & Havre railway (1842) **209**; expresses satisfaction with his involvement in the

P&R, R&H and the Great Northern railways (1846) **210**; sells shares in P&R and R&H **211**; reduces his holdings in English railways (1847) **211**; invests in the Dutch Rhenish Railway (1845) **212**; persuades Gladstone to buy shares **212**; expresses pride in the DRR (1846) **213**; complains about the slow pace of engineering work (1847) **214**; notes how receipts have risen since the Emerich line opened (1856) **215**; complains about the shameful mismanagement of the DRR **215**

Chapter 11 – The End: dies before able to collect DRR dividend (1858) **217**; buried at St Anne's church **218**

Introduction

Otterspool Park lies by the River Mersey, in the Aigburth district of Liverpool. I first recall visiting it on a winter's day in the early 1960s when, as a toddler, I sledged down its embankments. In the '70s, during the school summer holidays, I played tennis and golf on its immaculate greens. As a young man, I regularly jogged through Otterspool's wooded hills, and I recall listening excitedly to rock bands performing on the patio in front of the cafe. Never was I made aware that once, in that place, there had stood a splendid mansion, occupied by an outstanding gentleman whose business interests propelled him into the circles of such figures as the Gladstones, William Wilberforce, George Stephenson, the Duke of Wellington and Sir Robert Peel. It was not until 2002, after having purchased a property in Aigburth, that I first became acquainted with the name John Moss. Accompanying the deeds was a copy of Moss's will, which revealed that, at his death in 1858, his estate was valued at just under £120,000 – around £9,000,000 in today's terms.[1] My mother, a member of the congregation at St Anne's in Aigburth, recognised his name as that of the church's founder. I established the date of Moss's death from his mausoleum in the church's grounds, and in Liverpool Central Library, I unearthed the Liverpool Mail's obituary of 9 October 1858, which provided the impetus to write this book.

---

1   equivalent to £9,222,741 in 2008 using the Retail Price Index. Source www.measuringworth.com

It was my great privilege to chance upon a collection of 312 letters at Flintshire Record Office that Moss wrote to Sir John Gladstone (father of the Prime Minister, William Ewart Gladstone). Having read every word of his mercifully legible writings, I was able to put some "meat on the bones" of the Liverpool Mail's obituary. Moss's letters reveal very little about his family life, and there are only scant details about the roles he played in the Conservative Party, the Church of England, the Mechanics Institute, the Botanical Gardens, the Lunatic Asylum, his work as a Magistrate,[2] his charitable works and his work with the various other committees on which he served. I therefore make mention of these topics only in passing, if at all. Nonetheless, I uncovered so many details of other fascinating aspects of his life in business that those omissions scarcely mattered. Although Moss must have been aware that the correspondence of prominent men such as Gladstone might be retained and scrutinised, he was seldom afraid to express a forthright opinion, and his wonderfully frank views litter this book. The correspondence is not continuous, and there are frustrating lapses at crucial times when the two friends may well have refrained from writing at all about matters so sensitive that the risk of their letters being intercepted was too great.

With Gladstone's backing, Moss was able to exert influence both nationally and internationally. He played a leading role in two monumental events which helped shape the modern world; the abolition of slavery and the creation of the railways. As slave owners, he and Gladstone represented the West Indian interest in the debate for the abolition of slavery and, following emancipation, they were the instigators of the Indian Indentured Labour scheme. As the first chairman of the Liverpool & Manchester Railway, Moss was one of the pioneers of a mode of transport which changed British society forever. While chairman of the Grand Junction Railway, his

---

2   On 20 January 1816 Moss was created Justice of the Peace for the County of Lancaster.

vision and drive helped establish a national rail network in the 1830s and 1840s. Thereafter, he assisted in the development of French and Dutch railways. All this was achieved while "keeping up his day job" as the head of Moss & Co, Liverpool's most successful independent family bank. Yet he shunned the spotlight, and his gentlemanly modesty deprived him of enduring notoriety - something he came to regret. When, in 1846, Peel recognised Gladstone's achievements with a baronetcy, Moss felt moved to remind Sir John of some of his own attainments. *"The Liverpool & Manchester, Grand Junction, Paris & Rouen, Rouen & Havre, Birmingham & Oxford all owe their origin to me. So far that I have had the honour of sitting as chairman in starting all, the shareholders, from first to last, have made about twelve millions profit by them...and yet, I believe, some who owe their present situation in life to these rail roads give no credit to me and even doubt if I was the original chairman of the Liverpool & Manchester."*

Now, just over 150 years since his death, it is befitting that we should become reacquainted with John Moss's lifetime of achievement.

Chapter 1

OTTERSPOOL

"...a very pretty place, thought by us children to be one of the finest in England." [1]

Ann Lonsdall Formby - 1879

John Moss was born in Liverpool on 18 February 1782 into a wealthy mercantile family, residing first at Rainford Gardens and later in the highly fashionable St Anne Street.[2] His father Thomas[3] was a timber / general merchant and ship owner. The family's wealth was derived, in part at least, from privateering,[4] slavery and the trade in slaves.[5] By the latter half of the 18th century, Liverpool had become the most important

1   Ann Lonsdall Formby - *Short Sketch of the Life of the Late Doctor Formby*. (1879) From the Bickerton Papers, Liverpool Record Office, H920 FOR
2   John Hughes - Liverpool Banks and Bankers pp191
3   of Whiston (1748-5 February 1805)
4   Hughes, pp190-191. Privateers were armed merchant vessels licensed by the British Government with 'letters of marque' which authorised them to raid enemy shipping and enemy commerce with impunity. The Moss' ship *Jenny*, of 250 tons with 14 guns and 70 men fought *"in the war with America, France, Spain and Holland 1775-1783."* Gomer Williams - History of the Liverpool Privateers and letters of Marque, pp667-668
5   The ship *Ellen* was registered to the brothers Thomas, William and James Moss between 1787 and 1790. At 134 tons she was legally entitled to carry 223 slaves from West Africa to the West Indies. Suzanne Scharz - Slave Captain, p64

centre in the world for the organisation of the slave trade. So integral was it to the town's prosperity that, by 1787, thirty seven of the forty one members of Liverpool City Council were involved in it in one way or another.[6] By 1795, 25% of the ships belonging to the town were employed in the trade. That year, 134 ships were sent from Liverpool to Africa,[7] and Liverpool conducted 63% of Great Britain's trade in slaves.[8] By the time it was abolished in 1807, an estimated 1,360,000 Africans had been transported in more than 5,000 voyages of ships based in Liverpool.[9] Such was the business environment in which Moss was raised.

In 1803, at the age of 21, Moss was taken into partnership by his father, and assumed control of the business upon his death two years later. By then, the forced repatriation of Africans to the Americas had been a normal part of Liverpool enterprise for over 100 years.[10] Although the family still owned extensive West Indian properties worked by slaves,[11] it is likely that they had ceased slave trading by this time. Thomas had fallen under the spell of his brother in law, the prominent abolitionist and *"my friend"* William Roscoe, who acted as executor of his will.[12] In that will Thomas awarded his sons James and Henry £10,000 each. John, the eldest son, was also bequeathed £10,000 (worth over £600,000 in 2007),[13] as well as a warehouse in Peter's Lane , a counting house,[14] yard

---

6   Gail Cameron & Stan Crooke - Liverpool Capital of the Slave Trade

7   London and Bristol despatched only 17 and 5 respectively. C Northcote Parkinson - The Rise of the Port Of Liverpool, p141

8   Michael Craton, James Walvin and David Wright -Slavery Abolition and Emancipation, p58

9   Kenneth Morgan – Slavery, Atlantic Trade and the British Economy, 1660-1800, p88

10   The earliest recorded slaver, *The Blessing*, set sail from Liverpool for Guinea in October 1700. The Norris papers. Liverpool Record Office. 920NOR 2/179

11   Moss's uncle James's will of 1822 reveals that he held extensive estates in the Bahamas and that Moss's brother, also James, was residing at that time in Cuba.

12   Will of Thomas Moss dated 29 November 1804. Thomas refers to him as *"my friend William Roscoe of Liverpool, Banker."*

13   Using the retail price index. www.measuringworth.com

14   Anybody above the status of shopkeeper was considered a merchant and he con-

and shed in Manesty's Lane, off Hanover Street and *"building ground near the Botanic Garden"* on Mount Pleasant. Moss, it can be seen, was handed a splendid start in life, a life he chose to share with Hannah Taylor[15] whom he married at Collegiate Church, Manchester, on 3 September 1805.[16]

Prior to 1811, the Mosses lived on Mossley Hill.[17] In that year they moved into the newly built Otterspool House,[18] *"a handsome Villa residence in the gothic style... pleasantly situated near Liverpool, commanding a fine river view"*[19] where *"the embankments on a summer evening, 'when softe is the sonne', make a delightful spot for rest and contemplation. Here Mersey is nearly at her widest, and the effect of the broad stretch of water, with the green and gentle slopes of Cheshire leading up to the background of the everlasting hills of Wales, the whole lighted up by a glorious sunset, is at once charming and restful."* [20] A traditionally large family was raised at the great house, which stood on the site of the now defunct café in the park.[21] In 1816, Moss purchased the rights to the strand[22] at Otterspool. Thereafter, he stemmed the rate of tidal erosion on the steep clay banks by installing a stone paved slope at the line of high

---

ducted his business in a "counting house", while a mere broker or attorney occupied an "office" for his work. Hughes, p2

15 daughter of Thomas Taylor, Esq. of Blakeley, co. Lancaster. Bernard Burke - A Genealogical & Heraldic Dictionary of the Landed Gentry of Great Britain & Ireland. 1863, p1046

16 Hughes, p192

17 ibid, p195

18 Gorse Directory 1811. He purchased a swathe of land at least a year earlier. "A map of John Moss, Esquire's land in Aigburth" having been drawn up by Edward Edwards in 1810.

19 Edward Twycross - Mansions of England and Wales

20 Hughes, p196

21 Hannah gave birth to 9 children in total. The first surviving son, Thomas, (later Sir Thomas Edwards-Moss) was born on 17 July 1811. A boy also named Thomas, born on 6 January 1810, died in infancy. Three other sons survived into adulthood - John James (1822-1887), William Henry (1824-1859) and Gilbert Winter (1828-1899) as well as four daughters - Anne Jane (died 1835 unmarried aged 15 years), Margaret (died 1846), Hannah (died 1858 aged 44 years) and Harriet Eliza (died 1867). Burke, p1046

22 He paid John Blackburne £500 for interest of the lord of the manor of Garston to the strand at Otterspool.

water, right along the front to the foot of what is now Mersey Road.[23] Such improvements to the river embankments allowed greater access for shipping to his oil mill.[24]

Moss's *Liverpool Mail* obituary laments that *"Multitudes in this great community will long remember the habitual liberality and public spirit with which the fine sheet of water within his grounds at Otterspool was opened to the public for skating and other winter amusements."*[25] There were, in those days, 2 pools on the estate; a small one quite near the shore, and a much bigger one capable of accommodating a large number of visitors around the area where the lily pond is today. The drive to the house then went through a plantation above the pool, following the course of the unadopted Otterspool Road, which leads to the disused railway station. The current pathway came into being around 1862 when the large pool was filled and a road was constructed under the new bridge of the Cheshire Lines Railway[26] (opened in 1864) giving the family access to the house.

In the bitterly cold winter of 1837-38,[27] the local press picked up on Moss's winter sports centre - *"the resort of the more select of the skaiting* (sic) *order."*[28] Entry was restricted to all bar *"respectable applicants"* through the selective issuing of admission tickets. Moss wrote how he had, *"by refusing all except Gents, got some very first rate performers on the ice and the addition of Home made pies and a joint of meat and beer on the ice – has drawn both Ladies and Gents to the place."*[29]

---

23 Transactions of the Historic Society of Lancashire & Cheshire, 1867-68, Vol 20, pp160-162
24 This was co-owned with a George Forwood. Hughes, p195
25 Liverpool Mail, Saturday 9 October 1858
26 Transactions of the Historic Society of Lancashire and Cheshire. Vol 92. 1940, p66
27 "Murphy's Winter" of 1837-38 may well have contributed to the demise, on 7 February 1838, of Moss's 83 year old mother, Betty, from "old age". The following day Moss wrote of *"The illness of a much valued friend and connection who died yesterday..."* Stafford correspondence Moss to J Loch 8.2.1838 (D593/K/1/3/26)
28 Liverpool Mercury, 19 January 1838
29 Stafford correspondence Moss to J Loch 17.1.1838 (D593/K/1/3/26)

In Otterspool House, Moss entertained his wealthy business friends and also some of the less well off. *"He was proverbial for keeping up a sumptuous hospitality within his own extended circle. And his neighbours, from the highest to the humblest, all delight to tell how, whenever sickness and fever visited the district, the poor as well as the rich widely shared the practical sympathies of the kindly family at Otterspool, and how the graperies and hothouses and gardens were always spontaneously laid under contribution to supply choicest fruits to the humblest invalid, without stint, without ostentation, without the semblance of patronizing condescension."* [30] Moss shipped home some exotic specimens from his West Indian plantation to populate the glasshouses and gardens, and Otterspool became renowned for its outstanding collection of orchids.[31]

George Stephenson, the great railway engineer, was among the more celebrated visitors to Otterspool.[32] William Ewart Gladstone, the future Prime Minister, stayed the night on Thursday 10th January 1828.[33] (Gladstone, and Moss's son Thomas, who were born little more than 18 months apart, were contemporaries at Eton and Christ Church, Oxford University.)[34] An offer of hospitality, albeit rather uninviting, was extended to Sir Robert Peel after he led the Conservatives to victory in the general election of June and July 1841. Moss sent his congratulations on 9 July and invited Peel to stay during the visit of the Royal Agricultural Society. *"My*

---

30   Obituary Liverpool Mail, Saturday 9 October 1858
31   Curtis's Botanical Magazine. T.3722. An illustration appeared in an 1839 issue accompanied by the text: *"From the collections of John Moss which, partly owing to that gentleman's extensive South American correspondents and connexions, and partly to the skill of his gardener, Mr James, bids fair to rival some of the many collections of Orchidaceous plants of which this country may well be proud."*
32   Robert Griffiths - The History of the Royal and Ancient Park of Toxteth Liverpool, p113
33   M R D Foot - The Gladstone Diaries, volume 1: 1825-1832, p4. Gladstone was at this time on holiday, having finished his Eton education at Christmas 1827 before going on to University in October 1828.
34   The absence of any further reference to Thomas in Gladstone's diaries suggests they were not close friends.

Carriages and Horses will be at your service to take you where you wish, and should any servant accompany you I have a Bed also at his service." [35] However, the house was undergoing *"considerable alterations"* and Moss asked that Peel *"excuse our being in a very rough state"* [36] It seems unlikely his offer would have been taken up.

Moss died in Otterspool House on 3 October 1858. His eldest son Sir Thomas Edwards-Moss inherited the property, and he too died there, in 1890. Thereafter, it went out of the family's hands. Shortly before the 1914-18 war, William Simpson Cross, an animal dealer and naturalist, moved his menagerie to Otterspool, where buffalo and llamas roamed the grounds freely. Following his death in 1920, the estate passed into the care of his younger brother James Conrad Cross. Six years later, control of the house was passed to Liverpool Corporation. In 1831, Cross became Lord Mayor of Liverpool but, despite this, the city council refused to fund a restoration, and Otterspool House, suffering from dry rot and chronic neglect, was passed over to demolition contractors the same year. [37]

---

35   British Library, ref Add 40485 f.113
36   ibid
37   R Millington - House in the Park, pp69-70

CHAPTER 2

THE SAGA OF 1,000 SLAVES

"These Negroes would be miserable if dispersed. They have lived on an island without one soldier and only seven white inhabitants and been considered as servants, not slaves. My uncle required them to marry and punished every breach of conjugal faith. His Negroes were all armed and protected him and his property against frequent attempts which privateers made to land."

John Moss to John Gladstone – 7th April 1822

In 1818, following a total failure of crops,[1] Moss's uncle James began making plans to abandon his plantation on Crooked Island in the Bahamas. He intended to ship his entire workforce of slaves to Demerara-Essequibo, a British colony on the north east coast of South America. Because the slave trade (but not slavery itself) had long since been abolished, this scheme first required government approval. John Moss enlisted the help of his father in law William Roscoe, a former MP for Liverpool and the town's foremost anti-slavery campaigner.[2] Roscoe wrote on 2 April to the

---
1   Liverpool Courier - 26.12.1824
2   As Whig MP for Liverpool, Roscoe had backed William Wilberforce's 1807 Abolition Bill. Roscoe / Moss family ties were strong - particularly those between

Erratum – William Roscoe was John Moss's uncle

Whigs' most effective Parliamentary debater, Lord Henry Brougham, seeking such *"advice and assistance, either in or out of parliament, as the peculiar circumstances of the case seem to require."*[3] This letter, which Moss delivered by hand, gave him a direct line to the "Saints"[4] at the heart of the abolitionist community and ensured his case was heard favourably - firstly by Brougham, then by William Wilberforce's highly influential "Clapham Sect",[5] and finally, by the Colonial Office, for which Wilberforce's nephew and Sect member James Stephen [6] was legal advisor. On 31 October, the Colonial Office duly granted a licence *"to James Moss to remove his Negroes consisting of about 1,000 from the Bahamas to Demerara on certain terms"*.[7] Having moved only 211 of those slaves, James died at Nassau on 23 October 1820.[8] Unmarried, he bequeathed most of his estate (and the responsibility for completing the slave migration) to his three nephews John, James and Henry.

Matters progressed no further until, early in 1822, Moss turned to his new friend John Gladstone[9] for help. Although

---

the Griffies sisters Betty (Moss's mother) and Jane (Roscoe's wife). After the failure of Roscoe, Clarke and Roscoe's bank in 1816, Betty gave Jane's family much needed financial support. (The Roscoe papers, 2777 – Liverpool Record Office) Rather than let Roscoe's prized book collection be sold off to satisfy creditors, John Moss and other friends purchased a large part of it, and presented it to the Liverpool Athenaeum. (Hughes, p66)

3   The Roscoe Papers, 506 - Liverpool Record Office
4   The "Saints" were the country's leading, and staunchest abolitionists
5   a group of Church of England Evangelicals who campaigned tirelessly for the abolition of slavery
6   Stephen had first been appointed by the Colonial Office, in 1813, to write legal opinions on the validity of colonial laws.
7   National Archives. Colonial Office correspondence, ref PC1/4328
8   Burke, p1045
9   Gladstone's parliamentary career lasted nine years, during which time he represented the constituencies of Lancaster (1818-20), Woodstock (1820-26) and Berwick (1826-27). He was stripped of his Berwick constituency by a parliamentary committee which found in favour of a petition that accused him of obtaining the seat by bribery, treating and other illegal transactions. (SG Checkland - The Gladstones - A Family Biography 1764-1851, p158) Gladstone's parliamentary career was finished. He gave up hope of ever representing Liverpool as an MP and returned to Scotland in 1830, from where he continued to exert his influence on behalf of the town. Moss continued to address him as *"John Gladstone of Liverpool"*

MP for Woodstock, Gladstone had set up home in Liverpool, having arrived from Scotland in 1786 attracted, like thousands of other hopefuls, by the port's booming commerce. In time he came to be regarded as one of England's ablest merchants, and contributed enormously to Liverpool's transition into a major port and commercial centre.[10] As well as owning slave plantations in the West Indies, Gladstone operated a fleet of merchant ships trading all over the world. Enduring friendship arose out of a letter, dated 27 February 1822, in which Moss sought Gladstone's backing in *"a most unpleasant situation"* with the Board of Trade. This concerned a soap manufacturer George Blake who Moss felt *"satisfied is innocent of any intention of fraud."*[11] Gladstone swiftly helped settle the matter in Blake's favour. In return for this and many other acts of assistance, Moss became Gladstone's eyes and ears in Liverpool, rooting out his enemies and supplying some of the excellent market intelligence upon which his astonishing commercial success hinged. He offered Gladstone the assurance that he could *"At all times command my best services here. Obtaining information is attended with no trouble to me for I know many persons of all classes that, without leaving my bank, I can generally get at."* [12]

Moss immediately accepted Gladstone's friendly offer of assistance when wanted, explaining how, following uncle James' death, it was now necessary to obtain a new licence for the removal of the remaining slaves.[13] George Canning, Liverpool Tory MP, had already expressed his reluctance to present Moss's case to Frederick Robinson,[14] President of the Board of Trade.[15] While acknowledging that *"the very subject*

---

10   Moss considered that *"without such gentlemen as yourself and your brother,* (Robert) *Liverpool might have continued a mere fishing town."* Hawarden correspondence Moss to J Gladstone 28.11.1825
11   Hawarden correspondence Moss to J Gladstone 27.2.1822
12   Hawarden correspondence Moss to J Gladstone 6.3.1824
13   via John Backhouse, George Canning's private secretary. Hawarden correspondence Moss to J Gladstone 13.3.1822
14   Frederick John Robinson (later Viscount Goderich) became Prime Minister following Canning's death in 1827
15   Hawarden correspondence Moss to J Gladstone 20.4.1822

of slaves is one which no one likes to meddle with", Moss begged Gladstone to *"prevail upon him to recommend it even if he does not present it."*[16] Gladstone also lobbied Wilberforce,[17] to whom Moss had been introduced by James Stephen. While Wilberforce had always treated Moss with *"the greatest possible kindness"*,[18] Moss found it difficult to get him to consent to any measure because Stephen counteracted all that "*Wilberforce's liberal mind"* [19] had prompted him to do. Wilberforce now regretted ever having approved of the original licence for James Moss. Moss thought it might be wise to be himself *"on the spot"* [20] to answer every question Wilberforce could put without giving Stephen time to intervene. *"I should press the measure upon him as one to benefit the Negroes and not ask his support if I fail to prove that what I asked was an act of the greatest humanity to the Negroes and to refuse it would be absolute cruelty. You know we have the power of sending them for sale to any island and, as the Bahamas cannot find them support, surely it is better to remove them and settle them altogether in Demerara than send them to Jamaica or Trinidad for sale which must be the case if the licence is refused."* [21]

Gladstone's discussions with Canning, Robinson and Wilberforce helped ensure a positive outcome. Licence was granted, on 18 May 1822, to continue with the shipment, but only if the Moss brothers could produce documentary evidence that they owned Demeraran estates "*suitable and sufficient for the employment of the Negroes*" [22] Moss bemoaned this less than satisfactory arrangement. He had now to instruct his Demeraran agents McIvoy & Co to begin the long search

---

16   Hawarden correspondence Moss to J Gladstone 21.3.1822
17   Flintshire Record Office holds many letters from Wilberforce to Gladstone, written in a large, childlike, though legible, hand.
18   Hawarden correspondence Moss to J Gladstone 25.3.1822
19   ibid
20   ibid
21   ibid
22   National Archives. Colonial Office correspondence, ref PC1/4328

for appropriate estates. [23] It took until June 1823 before he committed to purchase, for £30,000 excluding its slaves, *"Anna Regina* [24] *(3 estates from La Belle Alliance) with all the works complete – 200 acres canes, some coffee and abundance of plantains."* [25] Samuel Sandbach[26] (a friend, neighbour and absentee Demeraran planter) helped broker a deal which limited Moss's initial outlay to £10,000; *"the rest to be paid for out of the crops."* [27] Moss felt that he might have driven a better bargain had he held out longer, but *"the Negroes are accumulating (now 600) and the crops will at once come in."* [28] That crop, the main crop of Demerara-Essequibo, was muscovado,[29] a raw brown sugar manufactured entirely within the confines of the plantation. Additionally, rum was made from the sugar by-product, molasses, and treacle from burnt sugar.

Like many other British West Indian property owners, Moss never actually visited his estate. Attorneys and managers

---

23 Hawarden correspondence Moss to J Gladstone 15.4.1822
24 Although Moss always referred to his plantation as being in Demerara it lay, in fact, to the West of the Demerara River, and was therefore in Essequibo, which today, along with Demerara and Berbice, forms the country of Guyana.
25 Hawarden correspondence Moss to J Gladstone 7.6.1823
26 Sandbach, who lived at Woodlands, in Aigburth, served as Mayor of Liverpool in 1831 and was a director of the Bank of Liverpool
27 Hawarden correspondence Moss to J Gladstone 7.6.1823. Moss claimed that *Anna Regina,* which was purchased for £50,000 on 20 June 1823 along with the cotton estate *Lancaster,* was *"of itself fully equal to support and employ one thousand persons."* Another cotton estate *Craig Miln* had been abandoned. Moss to the Colonial Office 6.11.1827. National Archives -Colonial Office correspondence, ref: PC1/4328.
28 ibid
29 The sugar canes were crushed in a mill, and the fluid extracted from them was transported to a factory where it was boiled in a succession of copper receptacles. When the heated sugar was about to crystallise, it was transferred to wooden trays to cool down. Once cool, it was packed into hogsheads which were then mounted on beams in the curing house. The bottom of each hogshead was rifled with bore holes so that a juice residue called molasses, used in the manufacture of rum, could drain freely from the sugar into a cistern. After about a fortnight, the sugar in the hogsheads was rammed down with heavy mallets. The hogsheads were filled to the brim then headed by a cooper, marked with the name of the estate and carted to port for shipment to England. An average hundredweight of muscovado yielded about 70 pounds of pure product and 28 pounds of molasses. William A Green - British Slave Emancipation, p58

were appointed to oversee the running of the plantation.[30] Regardless, he did not enter into this venture lightly. He fully understood that it was not guaranteed to make him money. A Jamaican absentee planter Bryan Edwards warned how a sugar estate *"with all its boasted advantages, should sometimes prove a millstone about the neck of its unfortunate proprietor, which is dragging him to destruction."* [31] In addition to the cost of purchasing the estate, other drains on Moss's resources would be the costs incurred in replacing an ageing and decreasing workforce, the making good of wear and tear on the buildings, the payment of legal commissions to agents and settling an annual tax bill of around £6 per cent, levied in the colony, on the gross value of the sugar and rum produced. That is to say nothing of the devastation which might be caused by fires and by hurricanes, which could destroy, in a few hours, the labours of years. Edwards, at 1791 prices, estimated the gross returns from his estate of 250 slaves to be £4,300 [32] based upon 200 hogsheads of sugar at £15 each and 130 puncheons of rum at £10 each.[33] *"But the reader is not to imagine that all this, or even the sugar alone, is so much clear profit. The annual disbursements are first to be deducted, and very heavy they are;"* Under the headings of *"Negro clothing, tools, food and miscellaneous items"* which could not be procured locally, he made an extensive list

---

30   One attorney might supervise several estates containing thousands of slaves. He was responsible for purchasing supplies, ordering goods from England, handling shipping details in the colonial port and supervising the agricultural management of the estates.

31   Bryan Edwards. The History, Civil and Commercial of the British Colonies, p77

32   £422,583 in 2008 using the Retail Price Index

33   Edward's sugar plantation was made up of 3 parts - land, buildings and stock. The land comprised one third sugar canes, one third pasturage for cultivation of plantains and other crops for consumption by the inhabitants, and one third woodland which supplied building materials and firewood for the boiling and distilling houses. The principle buildings consisted of a mill (water, wind or cattle powered), a boiling house, a curing house, a distilling house with a stone tank or cistern to hold at least 30,000 gallons of water, a dwelling house for the overseer, 2 trash houses, a hospital for sick slaves, a mule stable to hold at least 60 mules, shops for the different tradesmen, viz. carpenters, coopers, wheelwright and smith, and lastly, sheds for the wagons, wains, carts, etc.

of supplies required to be shipped over from the British Isles. (See Appendix B) In addition there was the overseer's salary to pay, the wages of tradesmen and the cost of medical care for the slaves. Then Moss would be obliged to pay Sugar duties based upon the weight and quality of the sugar on its arrival in port. However, evaporation, drainage and spillage on the sea voyage could reduce a hogshead's weight by as much as 16%.[34] It is easy to understand how Moss would have found daunting *"the magnitude of such a purpose"*.[35]

Sugar plantations required vast armies of cheap, readily replaceable labour. While Cuba, Brazil and America continued to be supplied with copious numbers of fresh African slaves, estates in the British West Indies began to suffer from under staffing after 1807, when the trade was abolished. Moss had been extremely fortunate in procuring such a substantial number of workers for *Anna Regina*, (See Appendix C) but just how unfortunate the timing of his entry into Demerara was, would soon become apparent. At this early stage, his views broadly concurred with those of the Anti-Slavery Society,[36] established in the spring of 1823. By way of its relatively moderate aims of protecting slaves from mistreatment and seeking gradual emancipation by reform, it sought to enlist the support of not only hard line abolitionists but also conservatives and even planters. He wrote approvingly of a pamphlet by Wilberforce which *"contains a great deal of sound justice and morality. I have that high opinion of him that I frequently feel disposed to write to ask him to lay down a plan for the treatment etc of our Negroes in Demerara."*[37] In any case, Moss had no need to feel threatened by Liverpool's growing anti-slavery lobby, headed by Roscoe and the Quaker families of Rathbone and Cropper.

34 Green, p41 & p59
35 Moss used these words when his agents earlier identified a property called *Hampton Court*, which *"they consider cheap at £40,000 including the 62 slaves"* Hawarden correspondence Moss to J Gladstone 10.3.1823
36 officially 'The Society for the Mitigation and Gradual Abolition of Slavery throughout the British Dominions'
37 Hawarden correspondence Moss to J Gladstone 3.4.1823

His Bahamian sources assured him that his slaves had always been extraordinarily well treated. "I *believe I may safely say that our Negroes would not accept their freedom. The 100 that are just arrived in Demerara went in a vessel of our own navigated with sailor Negroes and only 2 or 3 white persons on board.*"[38]

Moss hoped that all other West Indian proprietors, too, would "*go hand in hand with Mr Wilberforce in procuring emancipation and indemnity.*"[39] If they failed to do so, he feared the slaves would be freed anyway, and the planters would receive no compensation for the loss of their human livestock. In the event, the West Indian lobby rejected Wilberforce's proposals. He, as the head of an organisation which could only bring them financial ruin, was the object of their hatred. It had been assumed that, after abolition of the slave trade, since the colonists were unable to replace their slaves in the marketplace, they would treat those in their possession better and encourage marriage and child rearing to ensure a continual supply of new labour. It became clear, after the 1819 Slave Registration Act, which enabled reliable information and statistics to filter back to England, that the slaves were still being treated poorly and the population was, in fact, declining.

Parliamentary progress towards emancipation had been almost non existent since 1807. Wilberforce's energies had been fruitfully employed away from the Commons, in the training of missionaries. The greatest practical contribution to the improvement of the slaves' lot arose out of missionaries converting them to Christianity and thereby saving their souls. It was argued that, if the Negro was the white man's equal in the eyes of God, then no man had the right to enslave him. Many colonists viewed missionaries as the tools of the abolitionists, sewing the seeds of discontent and sending home reports of the slaves' unhappy lives. Chapels provided a forum for black self-expression and a life beyond the whites' control.

---

38 ibid
39 ibid

Some were taught to read and write. Such was the case on one of Gladstone's Demerara estates *Success*. A *Success* carpenter slave named Quamina had become a deacon of Bethel Chapel on the adjacent estate of *Le Resouvenir* where the Reverend John Smith of the London Missionary Society preached.[40]

In early 1823 Wilberforce, in failing health, was succeeded as leader of the Parliamentary abolitionists by the more radical Thomas Fowell Buxton. On 15 May, Buxton proposed that measures be taken for improving the slaves' conditions and for the emancipation of children born after a certain date. While rejecting Buxton's calls for emancipation,[41] George Canning, then Foreign Minister, drew up ameliorating resolutions for all colonial governors to implement through their own legislatures at the earliest opportunity:

"Religious instruction was to be provided

Sunday markets were to be abolished

Slave evidence in a court of law was to be admissible

Slave marriages were to be legalised

Slave property was to be protected

Manumission was to be facilitated

Families were not to be separated by sale, nor slaves from the estates to which they belonged

Arbitrary punishment and the corporal punishment of females were to be abolished

The driving whip was to be abandoned

Savings banks were to be established."[42]

---

40 Checkland, p186
41 Liverpool Tory MP William Huskisson noted how *"The government did everything in its power to prevent Buxton's motion altogether...Mr Canning in particular asserted all his personal influence with Mr Wilberforce and others for that purpose."* Checkland, p185 – Huskisson to John Gladstone dated 2 November 1823
42 Sir George Stephen - Anti Slavery Recollections, p90

This Order in Council was discussed by Demerara's Court of Policy on 21 July and 6 August. It proved exceedingly unpopular.[43] The delay in implementing the measures and the suppression of this information caused rumours of emancipation to circulate among the slaves. After chapel on the night of Sunday 17 August, a meeting was held of prominent slaves from *Success*. Foremost among the speakers were Quamina and his son, known as Jack Gladstone. It was decided that a rising would take place at eight o'clock the following evening. Violence would be kept to a minimum, the whites would be locked up, their guns seized and the Governor forced to give the slaves what they believed their legal right - freedom. However, news of the plot leaked out and the authorities were informed of the forthcoming unrest. Next morning, Governor Murray tried unsuccessfully to persuade a large group of already armed slaves to return to work, and then proclaimed martial law.[44] The rebellion's leaders had hoped to incite the entire colony to rise up but, of the estimated 75,000 slaves in Demerara-Essequibo, it is thought that only around 12,000 from about 55 plantations on the east coast took part.[45] Main houses were set on fire, windows were broken and overseers and managers put in stocks. A measure of the restraint shown was that only three whites were killed - two overseers and one soldier.[46] Moss's west coast estate remained undisturbed.

---

[43] Raymond T Smith - British Guiana, p35

[44] *The Times* of 14 October 1823 (it should be remembered that the journey from Demerara to England took about 40 days by sea)

[45] Article from Starbroek News – 21 August 2003

[46] Gladstone, whose information was supplied by his Demerara attorney, Frederick Cort, held a different point of view. *"Wherever any resistance was made the Whites were insulted, beat, and wounded, and many so severely, that the limbs of several have since been amputated."* As for the slaves' supposed restraint he explained that *"The confinement of the rest* (of the whites) *was only meant to be temporary: their final fate remained to be determined when the Negroes should have got possession of the colony. The general conduct of the Negroes, wherever they had the superiority, was most ferocious and brutal; and it is painful to add, that the ringleaders in the insurrection almost wholly belonged to estates which were most distinguished for kind and indulgent treatment."* By this he referred specifically to his own estates. *Liverpool Courier* 5 November 1823

Following a rebellion in 1791, the slaves on St Domingo (modern day Hispaniola) drove their French captors off the island, repelled a subsequent British invasion and, in 1804, set up the independent state of Haiti (now divided into Haiti and the Dominican Republic). The fear of a recurrence of those circumstances perhaps goes some way towards explaining the brutality with which the Demeraran rebellion was put down.[47] In the battles for freedom, the untrained slaves were poorly armed and no match for Demerara's soldiery. Once back in control, the colonists exacted ghastly retribution. Considerably more than 100 died in battle. A number of prisoners were shot after the ceasefire and, by the end of September, 47 had been executed. Brougham explained that *"A more horrid tale of blood yet remains to be told. Within the short space of a week ten were torn in pieces by the lash; some of these had been condemned to six or seven hundred lashes, five to one thousand each; of which inhuman torture one had received the whole, and two almost the whole at once."*[48]

Quamina fled into the bush, but was tracked down and shot dead on 16 September.[49] Six months later, tactfully avoiding mention of Gladstone's plantations, Moss wrote *"I hope the government will direct the gibbets to be taken down in Demerara. I understand that the Negroes who have been hung are exhibited in chains along the east coast. This cannot fail to contribute to increase the bad spirit that exists. Such sights only serve to make the Negroes more cruel and particularly so when we consider that the Negroes were not much to blame."*[50] Quamina's body was one of those hung in chains on a gibbet and left to rot for months on *Success*. One eye witness observed that *"a colony of wasps had actually built a nest in the cavity of the stomach and*

---

[47] The turning point came on the third day of the insurrection when 3,000 slaves confronted the main body of troops under Lieutenant-Colonel Leahy at *Bachelor's Adventure* plantation. Article from Stabroek News - 21 August 2003
[48] Charles Buxton - The Memoirs of, Sir Thomas Fowell Buxton, p147
[49] Article from Stabroek News - 21 August 2003
[50] Hawarden correspondence Moss to J Gladstone 17.3.1824

were flying in and out of the jaws which hung frightfully open"[51]
His alleged confidante, the Reverend John Smith, was promptly arrested and, because he had failed to take up arms against the slaves, was tried before a military court. Although the court's death sentence was overruled from England, he died in prison on 6 February 1824 in dreadful squalor. Reports of Smith's plight and lurid details of the colonists' reprisals against the slaves, served only to bolster the abolitionist cause in Britain. The general populace now began to question the human cost of exotic West Indian imports. The colonists became ever more intransigent, and a vicious circle developed over the ensuing years. As the anti-slavery movement grew stronger, the government was forced to issue more instructions, which the West Indians emphatically rejected.

Liverpool became a hotbed of anti-slavery. One of the movement's foremost proponents was James Cropper who owned plantations in East India using free, not slave labour. Cropper argued that slavery was an inefficient means of production which would die a natural death if only free trade could be established by the equalisation of sugar duties for East and West Indian sugars. Government protection of West Indian produce by way of bounties, drawbacks and differential duties was costing the country about £1,200,000 per annum, an expense that was borne by the taxpayer and the consumer.[52] Cropper's "Society for the Amelioration and Gradual Abolition of Slavery"[53] resolved to fight slavery on the grounds that it was not only uneconomic but also unchristian and unconstitutional. To add anecdotal and statistical clout to his argument, he set about collecting information from the West Indies and the Americas about the condition of the

---

51 Adam Hochschild - Bury the Chains: Prophets and Rebels in the Fight to Free an Empire's Slaves, p330
52 K Charlton - James Cropper and Liverpool's contribution to the Anti-Slavery Movement from Volume 123 of the transactions of the Historic Society of Lancashire & Cheshire , pp57-80
53 founded in Liverpool in December 1822

slaves. Although Cropper was unquestionably sincere in his wish that the slaves be emancipated, Gladstone and Moss considered him vindictive and self interested. A friend said of Cropper *"Give him pen and ink and he will demonstrate that black is white."*[54]

On 28 October 1823, Gladstone wrote how Cropper *"calls upon us only to use East Indian sugar which he will supply us cheap and good (an abominable lie for the price is high, the quality bad and the quantity small) and thus he hugs himself with the hope of raising his fortune by the destruction of the West Indian planter and his property whilst he also is to be passed off for a Philanthropist, a Friend to Humanity!!!"*[55] There then ensued a public correspondence between Gladstone and Cropper amounting to 18 vitriolic letters.[56] Soon Moss was drawn into the argument as one of Gladstone's informants. In one letter, Cropper alleged that poor management of British estates was responsible for the decline in the slave population. Using Jamaica as an example, he noted that it had reduced by 90,000 in the last 30 years, compared with an increase of 854,735 in the United States; this he attributed to good management alone.[57] Moss was furious. *"I cannot read Mr Cropper's statement of Friday without feeling the greatest astonishment that a person of his character should publish for facts things which he ought, and I fear, does know to be absolutely untrue... The truth is that America was the great market for the sale of African cargoes. So long as the African trade existed in England whole cargoes of slaves were sold in Georgia, South Carolina and New Orleans...I am told that after England abolished the trade the Spaniards considered and found Georgia and New Orleans their best market for the sale of Negroes."* Moss was also aware of at

---

54   Sir George Stephen – Anti-Slavery Recollections, p84
55   Checkland, pp192-193. Letter to William Cobbett
56   The correspondence commenced on 31 October. Cropper's letters were printed in the *Liverpool Mercury* and Gladstone's responses, under the pseudonym of *Mercator*, appeared in the *Liverpool Courier*, a newspaper he co-founded in 1808.
57   Hawarden correspondence Moss to J Gladstone 24.11.1823

least 18 Bahamian plantation owners who received permission from the American Government to remove and settle their slaves in America over that same 30 year period. *"So much for Mr Cropper's 'population by good management alone.' "* [58]

Cropper attacked the laws of the Bahamas, a colony on which Moss was far better informed, having in his possession, the *"bound and folioed"* Bahamas Acts. *"Mr Cropper professes to meet the objection of not having been in the West Indies by saying 'Their laws we can understand as well here as there.'"* Cropper cited an extract from the 1784 Act of the Bahama Islands, an Act Moss knew to have been repealed in 1796. The new Act was, Moss argued, of the *"most humane nature"* in regard to the punishment of slaves. Section 9 made the killing of any slave a capital offence. Section 10 stipulated that the wanton or cruel whipping, beating, bruising, wounding, imprisoning (or confinement without sufficient support) of any slave was punishable by a fine and imprisonment. Section 11 decreed that no slave should receive more than 20 lashes except in the presence of the owner, employee or supervisor of the workhouse and, in their presence, no more than 30 lashes. *"Where Mr Cropper got, or fancied that* (the Act) *'meant that the slave should be executed first and the necessity that lead to his crime be enquired into afterwards' I cannot tell. No schoolboy could construe this clause into such a meaning."* [59]

Anti-slavery sentiment was being spread, according to Gladstone, by *"emissaries to almost every manufacturing and market town in the country to stir up the population to meet and sign petitions to parliament"* [60] In the drive to spread the word, Liverpool's anti-slavery society took responsibility for distributing abolitionist material to Cheshire, Lancashire, Yorkshire and parts north, as well as to Ireland and the USA. Cropper set off, in October 1824, on a three month public

---

58   ibid
59   ibid
60   K Charlton, p64

speaking tour of Southern Ireland. As Liverpool's abolitionists became more radical, so too did its opponents in the West India Association.[61] They stressed that the emancipation of their property was out of the question, and suggested the abolitionists' cause would be better served by them helping put an end to French, Spanish and Portuguese slave trading.

A letter appeared in the *Liverpool Courier* on Boxing Day 1824 from a gentleman (almost certainly Moss) with the pseudonym of *Vindex*, writing on behalf of *"those who have had the misfortune to inherit West India property."* He claimed that the imported Bahamian slaves were so content after their first year in Demerara that their population had grown by 2½%. All had embarked on the journey of their own free will. No deaths had occurred at sea. No provision had been deemed necessary to restrain the unruly. Two of the ships had been navigated by sailors who were also slaves. The captain and a young man from Liverpool had been the only white people on board. *"The Negroes might, if they had wished, have carried any of the vessels to St Domingo."* Between June 1823 and December 1824, Moss's brother James had overseen the removal of 512 slaves to Demerara *"leaving about 99 to take care of the buildings and corn crops on the Estates intending to remove them as soon as he could do it with safety."*[62] The transportation of Crooked Island's final 99 was suspended when, at the end of 1824, James was taken ill and, for the benefit of his health, returned to England.[63] There matters rested until 1826, when an incident involving a Henry Moss of Crooked Island caused what appears to be the permanent cessation of the slave shipment. Henry and his wife Helen were imprisoned for causing the death of a domestic slave girl "Poor Black Kate". Research conducted in 1995 by Louisiana State University asserted that this Henry Moss was the nephew of James Moss, the one time President of the

---

61   *"I have found it impossible to talk to West Indians for some time past. They are as unreasonable as the saints."* Hawarden correspondence Moss to J Gladstone 7.12.1824
62   National Archives - Colonial & Foreign Office correspondence, ref PC1/4328
63   ibid

Bahamian House of Assembly. One Henry Moss did serve a 5 month prison sentence in Nassau for his barbarous crime, but he was certainly not John Moss's brother. (See Appendix D)

The saga of the Bahamian slaves was reopened on 16 May 1828, when Moss wrote to John Backhouse of the Foreign Office, stating *"After what has passed, I should let the subject of our Bahama Negroes drop but on their own account, we have about ninety nine remaining in the Bahamas, of these <u>more</u> than fifty are totally useless from old age and infirmity and were left in the Bahamas until the new residences in Demerara were made comfortable for them."* [64] Charles Grant, Governor of the Bahamas, stood in the way of the final shipment. *"If Mr. Grant objects to the removal altogether, we have (as our establishments in the Bahamas are broken up) no alternative but to request those capable of work to look out for kind masters who will purchase them. The old people shall under every circumstance be <u>amply provided and made comfortable for life by us.</u> The expense of the ninety nine now amounts to £200 a year more than their earnings."* [65] The correspondence between Moss and the Colonial Office does not determine whether permission was ever granted.[66]

---

64 ibid
65 ibid
66 On 18 April 1836, in compensation for the loss of his slave property following the abolition of slavery, a Henry Moss was awarded £1,209 11s 6d for 100 Bahamas slaves and £104 15s 2d for the loss of a further 12 slaves. (British Parliamentary Papers of 1837 - "Return to an order of the Honourable House of Commons" dated 6.12.1837 "for an account of all the sums of money awarded by the Commissioners of Slavery Compensation", Birmingham Central Library.)

CHAPTER 3

THE ABOLITION OF SLAVERY

"The rashness with which the government are proceeding is quite dreadful to think of ... Their measures are no wiser than if the Council of the Zoological Gardens were to pass a resolution that all the beasts and birds should be let at liberty under proper arrangements, and yet, before they had made any of the arrangements, had commenced by taking down all fences which separate the strong from the weak."

John Moss to John Gladstone – 8th June 1833

Although significant progress had been made, both in and outside of Parliament since 1823, it was not until the early 1830s that the abolitionists' persistent campaigning finally began to bear fruit, and Lord Grey's Whig government resolved to force the emancipation issue. John Moss and John Gladstone, mindful of the near certainty that slavery would cease, continually experimented and invested in new, quality enhancing, labour saving devices for their plantations. By September 1830, Moss had sent out a new sugar boiler and a new engine with which to work it.[1] The following month,

---

1   Hawarden correspondence Moss to J Gladstone 9.9.1830

a Mr. Hopkins reported from *Anna Regina* that he had seen very good sugar made by *"the new plan."* [2] This plan was to boil sugar using a vacuum pan, a device invented in 1813 by Edward Charles Howard, which had been much improved upon by resident Demerarans such as Benson, Oaks, Shand, Turner and Martino.[3] The existing, "open pan" method was crude and wasteful, particularly in Demerara where climatic humidity reduced the ignition quality of fuel and prevented brisk sugar boiling. This resulted in an excessively high ratio of molasses to sugar. Consequently, Demerara's sugar had to be heated to 240 or 250 degrees Fahrenheit, a temperature which burned it and changed a significant proportion of it to treacle. The vacuum pan was a closed, copper vessel, about 6 feet in diameter, from which a steam powered pump extracted the air and thereby created a partial vacuum. The greatly reduced atmospheric pressure brought down the boiling point of the sugar to just 150 degrees Fahrenheit. As well as improving the sugar to molasses ratio, a better quality sugar was produced, which sometimes aroused British Customs' suspicions. If Customs decided that it was not ordinary muscovado, but a refined product, a significantly higher rate of duty could be charged, potentially rendering the whole enterprise unprofitable. Superior colonial sugars were penalised in this way in order to protect the British mainland's own sugar refineries.

In February 1831, Moss received a consignment of sugar with a *"beautiful straw colour – much better than I expected of the first made."* [4] Hopkins assured him that *"'Benson improves as he goes on and some sugar he has boiled from the worst of canes is superior to any made when I last addressed you.'"* [5] In

---

2   Hawarden correspondence Moss to J Gladstone 12.10.1830
3   Checkland, p266
4   aboard the *Elizabeth John*. Hawarden correspondence Moss to J Gladstone 10.2.1831
5   Hopkins' letter was dated 3 January 1831 - Hawarden correspondence Moss to J Gladstone 26.2.1831

May, a consignment of 10 hogsheads of vacuum pan sugar[6] aroused the suspicions of Mr. Kendal, a Surveyor of the Kings Dock. Moss was obliged to provide a sworn affidavit as to the sugars being made from cane juice. The Surveyor General and the other Surveyors reached the conclusion that these were, indeed, muscovado sugars. Moss was then permitted to sell them on to Messrs Lightfoot & Co, the grocers, after having paid the relevant duty. He was inclined to believe that *"the Refiners and not Kendal are the persons who raise the question."*[7]

Moss took himself off to London in April to listen to Parliament's debate on the slavery issue. Buxton put forward a three fold motion, on the 15th [8]

"1. That slavery is contrary to Christianity and ought to be gradually abolished.

2. That the West Indies have not done what they ought to have done.

3. That the British parliament must take the subject in hand."

Although the motion was not carried, it was now abundantly clear that the West Indians would have to prepare themselves for the end of slavery. Gladstone began lobbying key government figures to ensure the best possible terms for the planters at the conclusion of the debate. On 22 April Moss, having seen the rejection of the first Reform Bill, [9] then witnessed the dissolution of Parliament by William IV, a supporter of the West Indians and of reform. The resulting June general election brought a great victory for the Whig reformers. Moss accepted that the church as well as the West Indies needed reform. With reluctance,[10] he lent his assistance

---

6 which arrived on the *Christina* - Hawarden correspondence Moss to J Gladstone 5.5.1831

7 Hawarden correspondence Moss to J Gladstone 10.5.1831

8 Hawarden correspondence Moss to J Gladstone 12.4.1831

9 Hawarden correspondence Moss to J Gladstone 21.4.1831

10 *"I had made up my mind not to interfere in any Liverpool election again, nor should I, had I not felt that Mr Thornley's sentiments on religion and Church government were such as no friend of the present order of things could support."* Hawarden correspondence

to the campaign of the Liverpool Tory, Lord Sandon, *"a very amiable gentlemanly man...who was more honestly disposed to West India matters than Mr.* (Thomas) *Thornley"*, his Unitarian and abolitionist opponent.[11] In the event, Sandon was elected and, within 12 months, Moss would feel moved to proclaim that *"the West Indians have no such man in the House of Commons as his Lordship"*[12] who *"is an excellent member for the town, more so than Huskisson was."*[13]

The continuing technological progress made on *Anna Regina* began to bear fruit. A fresh consignment of sugars, which had not evaporated on their way home, arrived in May.[14] Although not sufficiently cured (not dry enough), they had been made *"in the worst season ever known – continued rains."* On these Moss netted £20 per hogshead, as compared with £9 for the old kind. *"On the whole I am more satisfied than I was of the value of the vac pans and will persevere."*[15] He hoped that John MacLean,[16] Gladstone's Demerara attorney acting on both their behalves, would rectify the curing problem through further experimentation.[17] When, in June, Moss received a shipment of 130 hogsheads, he was happy to report *"I got a barrel of it home and it appears to me to be perfectly dry...I emptied the barrel out yesterday and it came out more like salt than sugar."*[18]

Moss to J Gladstone 15.6.1831

11 Hawarden correspondence Moss to J Gladstone 7.6.1831. The candidates' campaign expenses were paid by those with most advantage to gain from their election. Moss, who sat on the finance committee with Sandbach and Grant, *"subscribed £100"*

12 Hawarden correspondence Moss to J Gladstone 5.6.1832

13 Hawarden correspondence Moss to J Gladstone 14.7.1832

14 With each hogshead of pure sugar shipped from the colonies the planters were losing enough molasses to produce 4 gallons of rum. Green, p58

15 Hawarden correspondence Moss to J Gladstone 10.5.1831

16 Checkland states the spelling as MacLean, but Moss spells his name McLean

17 As the vacuum pan became increasingly prevalent in the colony, it produced a much higher quality sugar and, consequently, a lower grade molasses from which the Demerarans produced low quality rum. The Jamaicans, who enjoyed a considerable return on their rum, placed greater emphasis on producing a rich molasses through the traditional open pan method. Green, p210

18 Hawarden correspondence Moss to J Gladstone 7.6.1831

MacLean, like other resident West Indians, found the prospect of emancipation difficult to accept. He felt that his implementation of Gladstone's policies against excessive work and punishment ensured fairer treatment of the slaves on his plantations than on many others. On *Vreedenhoop* he had succeeded in obtaining an annual sugar output of 1,955 lb per slave, as compared with the 1,104 lb per slave achieved on *Anna Regina*. [19] Mindful of this discrepancy Moss appealed to Gladstone to *"write a few lines to him expressing your wish that he should go soon to see the estate and take charge of it."* [20] In July, the month Demerara, Essequibo and Berbice were united to form the new colony of British Guiana, MacLean was appointed Moss's attorney. He had his own methods, borne out of many years experience, and resented interference from his absentee masters. MacLean proclaimed himself *"most particular as to punishments, food and clothing, and attention to the slaves when they are sick"* (and) *"I am induced to think, from my knowledge of the Negro character, that they construe what is intended as kind indulgence into an obligation to which they are entitled."* [21] Moss was eventually forced to concede *"I have told Mr. McLean that I shall not again say one word to him about the management of Negroes. I have given him full power, as much as he has over yours."* [22]

As a concession to the abolitionists, an Order in Council of 2 November 1831, designed to tighten the Slave Code, was sent out by the government to all slave colonies. MacLean and most other colonists opposed the order on the grounds that a remote and ignorant government sent out its missives *"without considering that every colony has its peculiarities ...forgetting that*

---

19 From Viscount Howick's speech in the Commons, 14 May 1833. For the years 1829, 1830 and 1831 *Vreedenhoop's* average of 516 slaves produced an annual average of 1,009,916 lbs of sugar. *Anna Regina's* average 793 slaves produced an annual average of 875,766 lbs. Debate on the Resolutions and Bill for the Abolition of Slavery in the British Colonies with a Copy of the Act of Parliament. 1833
20 Hawarden correspondence Moss to J Gladstone 5.5.1831
21 Checkland, p265
22 Hawarden correspondence Moss to J Gladstone 21.11.1832

the experiment is not tried on a machine which can be stopped and thrown aside in case of failure, but upon the minds of many thousands of human beings." [23] Though understandably frustrated by their worsening economic situation, rising costs and rivalry in world markets from slave grown sugars, the West Indians' resistance to government initiatives proved ever more injurious to their cause in Britain. Moss sought Gladstone's intervention. *"I wish you would write strongly to Mr. McLean upon the necessity of the Colony no longer opposing government... Lord Sandon very justly says in a letter I have from him 'it* (the Order in Council) *recognises the right of the planter to compensation in cases of injury inflicted in the course of our experiment for the amelioration of the slaves...It is a step in a just and honest cause.'* " [24]

On a visit to London in April 1832, Moss witnessed Buxton putting forward a motion for *"immediate emancipation with such compensation as the commercial and financial state of the Country can afford!!!...The king added that he was much attached to the WI, fully aware of their importance, that he would do <u>all he could</u> to assist them."* [25] Locally, however, the outlook was far less favourable for Moss. When Gladstone departed Liverpool for good in 1830,[26] he became one of the town's highest profile slave owners and, therefore, a prime target for abolitionists. He wrote, in August 1832, *"The anti slavery society are again on the walls and I am preparing another answer. I am determined not to let their lies remain unanswered whether it does good or not."* [27] In their latest campaign against the planters, the abolitionists organized lectures nationwide. In early September, a series of public debates was held in Liverpool between the abolitionist George Thompson and Peter Borthwick, defender of the planters. The verbal war was

---

23 Checkland, p267
24 Hawarden correspondence Moss to J Gladstone 18.8.1832
25 Hawarden correspondence Moss to J Gladstone 21.4.1832
26 He made his summer home at Fasque, in Aberdeenshire
27 Hawarden correspondence Moss to J Gladstone 18.8.1832

accompanied by one of placards on which Moss's name was prominent.[28] All the local newspapers gave extensive coverage of the arguments. *The Albion* captured the prevailing mood in Liverpool and in the country. *"We think it must now be obvious, even to the West Indians themselves that, so far as the opinion of the great majority of the Liverpool people is concerned, the question of the expediency, the immorality and the inhumanity of slavery is completely set at rest."* [29]

In November, Moss's son Thomas returned to Liverpool after several months of intelligence gathering in the West Indies. He had witnessed *"sugar being made in half a dozen islands"* and was yet to be wholly convinced by the superiority of the vacuum pan. While the time spent boiling was halved, the quantity of sugar produced was greater and it "carried home" better, against this had to be factored the extra costs of the coals and of labour for *"pumping it up."* Thomas cautioned *"that what may do very well on a small experiment may fail if tried on a large scale."* Experiments to carry out the curing process on *Anna Regina* (rather than in England) and to make the sugar white resulted in half being washed out into the still. From there it was fit only for making rum. Washing or liquoring opened the door to robbers. *"There are about a dozen children of 10 to 12 years of age carrying trays of sugar. Others are attending drying it, turning etc. etc and... the deficiency so much complained of, in some degree arises from eating and waste. It is... astonishing to see how much sugar these little fellows will consume in a day."* [30] Moss continued experimenting at home, and entered into dialogue with a British based vacuum pan engineer named Crossley, whose object was to cleanse the sugar in England. A trial apparatus was erected in a small room over Moss's bank for a week so that he could see all with his own eyes. [31]

---

28 Checkland, p272
29 The Albion – 10 September 1832
30 Hawarden correspondence Moss to J Gladstone 7.11.1832
31 Hawarden correspondence Moss to J Gladstone 1.11.1832 and 7.11.1832

The results from the first year of MacLean's management of *Anna Regina* were heartening.[32] Between 1830 and 1832, when vacuum pan experiments were taking place, the number of hogsheads of sugar produced per slave inevitably reduced, but this was somewhat redressed by the higher price obtained for these superior sugars.[33] For the year 1831-1832, *Anna Regina's* sugar yielded £23 10s per acre cut. Samuel Sandbach's sugar plantation *Coffee Grove* was situated only 4 estates away from *Anna Regina*. There they employed purely traditional methods, and the yield was just £16 10s per acre, *"a balance in favour of AR £7...against which is to be set the extra labour and coals."* Yet Gladstone's son Robertson[34] advised Moss that vacuum pans *"will not do!!!"* [35] and MacLean, too, expressed negative views about the new technology, without stating specifics.[36] Perhaps the extra work and expense and an innately human resistance to change were reasons enough. Moss, though, was adamant.

---

32 Hawarden correspondence Moss to J Gladstone 21.11.1832. The sale proceeds from *Anna Regina's* sugars, out of which the entire cost of running the estate had yet to be deducted, for the year ending 1 July 1832, were:

"56 hogsheads sugar in the old way at £12.10   =£ 700
263 hogsheads vacuum pan sugar at £20   =£5,260
247 puncheons rum at £9   =£2,223

                                              =£8,183"

£8,183 is the equivalent of £632,611in 2008. There are approximately 200 gallons to the puncheon

33 ibid

"   Negroes   Made Hogsheads Sugar

1825   614   218
1826   612   320
1827   702   510
1828   745   472
1829   770   704
1830   785   500
1831   800   350"
1832   Presumably still 800 319

34 He visited the West Indies in 1828-1829 - Checkland, p169
35 Hawarden correspondence Moss to J Gladstone 21.11.1832
36 *"No one hesitates to say or to write that vac pans will not answer but no one will fairly meet me and tell me why."* ibid

The facts spoke for themselves, and his decision was final. "*I have given the matter more consideration than ever I did a subject in my life – and the conclusion I come to is to persevere.*"[37]

On 5 January 1833, Moss wrote to Lord Sandon[38] complaining that if the government persisted in allowing foreign sugars to be refined in England, the West Indies would be ruined. Whereas the British planter was obliged to incur the expense of "*increasing the comforts and decreasing the labour of his people*" the price of sugar was effectively being regulated by countries, like Brazil, where such improvements had not even been contemplated.[39] He questioned why, under the Order in Council of 2 November 1831, the labours of an adult Negro should be limited to nine hours a day when, in factories in Britain, it was permissible for children under 16 to be worked for twelve hours. He instructed his attorney in Demerara to inform the slaves of this discrepancy. "*It should show the Blacks what they can expect from British Justice when made free.*"[40]

The great abolition debate was now nearing its finale. The moderate side of the anti-slavery movement (represented in the Commons by Buxton and Lord Suffield) proposed compensation for the planters and apprenticeship for the slaves. The Negro apprentices would have to continue working for their owners as neither freedmen nor slaves, for a set number of years, before being emancipated. Those years would provide a crucial breathing space during which time a whole social, economic and legal infrastructure could be established; one which might encourage the freedmen to remain in the plantation economy. Moss, although "*uneasy at it*", endorsed

---
37 ibid
38 one of a dying, pro-West Indian breed. Hawarden correspondence Moss to Lord Sandon 5.1.1833
39 ibid
40 ibid

this proposal.[41] James Cropper, Joseph Sturge and George Stephen, on behalf of the more zealous, radical side of the anti-slavery movement, urged Buxton to reject any recompense whatsoever for the planters. Opponents of a planter's pay day were closer to home than Moss would have liked; Henry Booth, the treasurer of the Liverpool & Manchester Railway was among them.[42]

In February, Moss traveled to London to help press for the best possible compensation terms for the West Indians. He rebuffed the advice of Secretary at War Edward Ellice[43] who suggested he should see Buxton.[44] Captain Charles Elliot R.N, the former *"protector of the slaves in Demerara"*,[45] was employed by the government to sound out Moss and other planters.[46] Elliot queried what Moss thought a fair rate of compensation per slave. *"I mentioned £50 per head and he said £30 was more likely."*[47] The government appears to have valued the opinion of one of British Guiana's largest slave owners. However, Moss felt out of his depth in his exchanges with the authorities. When, on 26 February, he and Peter Rose (the London based spokesman for British Guianan planters) received an invitation to meet with Under Secretary for the Colonies Lord Howick, he agreed although *"I felt I had no*

---

41 Hawarden correspondence Moss to J Gladstone 31.1.1833

42 ibid. *"I consider Henry Booth's pamphlet one of the most mischievous papers I have ever read. He cares not what injury others incur if he can only carry his own point... What think you of Mr Cropper's? I am more vexed with him than I can express. He is not fair and honest about us. He knows better. I mean, as soon as I feel a little cool, to write to him."*

43 Ellice became a Privy Counsellor in 1833

44 Hawarden correspondence Moss to J Gladstone 20.2.1833. *"'I think you might do good in seeing Mr. Buxton. He is a very rational man himself.' Now I do not know Mr. Buxton and I feel surprised that Mr. Ellice should even hint at my seeing him."*

45 Hawarden correspondence Moss to J Gladstone 12.1.1833

46 Hawarden correspondence Moss to J Gladstone 20.2.1833. Elliot *"asked if we had any objection to receive a communication from government...I was prepared to say that the Demerara people were disposed to meet the government's wishes provided they were brought forward in a fair spirit, and a proper consideration given for the sacrifices demanded."*

47 ibid

right to see him individually to discuss subjects which belonged to a number of gentlemen whom I was not deputed to act for." [48] Moss assured Gladstone, who remained at his Leamington home, that he would be careful not to commit himself or others. He would tell Howick that his opinions were very much guided by Gladstone's. He urged Gladstone to hasten his way to London. *"The crisis I see approaching more rapidly than I think you imagine."* [49] Still, by 1 March, Gladstone had not entered the fray, and Moss was becoming most anxious. He had seen Howick twice to discuss the government's plans. Howick, it appeared, was *"in the temper to meet the views of the Demerarans."* [50]

A stroke of good fortune befell the planters in April, when EGS Stanley (later Lord Derby) was appointed Secretary for War and the Colonies in place of Lord Goderich. The change prompted Howick's resignation as Under Secretary. Crucially, Stanley was considered *"decidedly more conservative than Howick"* [51] and more determined to bring the whole emancipation issue to a speedy conclusion. On 14 May, Stanley proposed that slavery should cease, slave children under 6 should be freed and that adults should be apprenticed to their former masters over a 12 year transitional period before being granted their freedom.[52] As compensation for the loss of their slave property, the planters should receive a loan of £15,000,000. [53] In response to Stanley's 3 hour speech, Howick denounced his scheme as a perpetuation of slavery. He argued that, in the run up to abolition, the planters were putting ever greater pressure on the slaves to increase production. A correlation was made between the rate

---

48 Hawarden correspondence Moss to J Gladstone 26.2.1833
49 ibid
50 Hawarden correspondence Moss to J Gladstone 1.3.1833
51 Hawarden correspondence Moss to J Gladstone 4.5.1833
52 The apprentices would be obliged to work for their ex masters only for three quarters of their normal working day. They would be free to do what they wished for the remainder of the day.
53 Checkland, p273. Equivalent of £1,216,125,270 in 2008 using the Retail Price Index

of output per slave and the slaves' mortality rate. The estates of Gladstone and Moss were used as Howick's prime example. He alleged that the 102 slaves who died on Gladstone's estates *Success* and *Vreedenhoop* between October 1828 and 1833, had been worked to death by MacLean, who he referred to as *'the murderer of slaves'* [54] *Anna Regina*, pre-MacLean, was held up as a relative paradigm. Here a comparatively smaller crop was produced and the slaves' numbers had increased over the 6 years up to 1832. However, in the autumn of 1831, *"for what reason it is not for me to say, as I cannot know the motives by which men are actuated, the manager of Anna Regina was removed"* [55] *and* replaced by MacLean. In Howick's mind the consequences were inevitable. *"In the tax-roll of the Court of Policy for 1831 the estate is entered as having 805 slaves, while the number returned to the registrar, in May 1832, is only 800. Now, Sir, I think this fact throws much light on the causes of that loss of life..."* [56]

In Howick's opinion, pressure to produce results was placed on men like MacLean by absentee planters like Gladstone and Moss who, though no doubt themselves humane, were ignorant of what was being done in their names. MacLean, he suggested, conveyed to his masters little of what really happened, except for output figures.[57] Naturally Gladstone, Moss and MacLean were outraged by Howick's charges. Much of their improved productivity was down to reorganization, rethinking of working methods and the introduction of new technology. Was it not to be expected, they argued, that a slave population with a high proportion of older people would naturally produce higher death rates?

On 30 May, Gladstone and Moss, *"Deputed by the West India interests of Liverpool"*, presented an eleven page *"Plan*

---

54   John Morley - Life of Gladstone, Vol 1, p102
55   Debate on the Resolutions and Bill for the Abolition of Slavery in the British Colonies with a Copy of the Act of Parliament. 1833
56   ibid
57   Checkland, p273

Proposed for the Emancipation and Future Labour of the Negro Slaves in the British Colonies" to Stanley in a private interview.[58] Rather than accept the government's plan for a loan, they urged it to accept their plan to pay the planters compensation of £20,000,000.[59] In addition, they pressed for a loan of £10,000,000, part of it not to be repaid. Sandon presented these proposals to the Commons on June 3, and he was followed by William Ewart Gladstone, newly elected Tory MP for Newark, making his maiden speech in the House.[60] William argued that compensation should be paid by the government because historically, the state had sanctioned and, indeed, encouraged the planters by its laws permitting slavery and through its bounties and preferential duties on West Indian sugar.[61] He insisted that events on his father's plantations were no worse than on any others. He confessed that cruelty would always exist under slavery and that this was *"a substantial reason why the British legislature and public should set themselves in good earnest to provide for its extinction"* [62] In his address, young Gladstone displayed such strong traits of his future oratory genius that Stanley, Sir Robert Peel and even King William IV praised his efforts. [63] Moss acknowledged that it had been a very powerful speech, but insisted that it had been John Gladstone's interviews with the Duke of Wellington, Peel and Lord John Russell,[64] which saved the West Indians. *"Had you not first convinced these three individuals that a great nation durst not be dishonest, an angel from heaven would hardly have persuaded the House of Commons to listen to your son's splendid speech."* [65]

---

58   Hawarden: Ref GG MSS 2876
59   Checkland, p274. This is equivalent to £1,621,500,360 in 2008 using the Retail Price Index
60   Morley, p102
61   Checkland, p275
62   Morley, p104
63   ibid, p103
64   Russell, a prominent Whig and future Prime Minister, had presented the Reform Bill of 1832 to the Commons.
65   Hawarden correspondence Moss to J Gladstone 3.4.1838

After the debate, Stanley instructed James Stephen to draft the emancipation Bill. Remarkably, Stephen produced this complex, twenty six page document in a mere weekend. In the afternoon of Sunday 8 June, Moss wrote from London *"The rashness with which the government are proceeding is quite dreadful to think of ... Their measures are no wiser than if the Council of the Zoological Gardens were to pass a resolution that all the beasts and birds should be let at liberty under proper arrangements, and yet, before they had made any of the arrangements, had commenced by taking down all fences which separate the strong from the weak."* [66] At 11 o'clock that night, Lord Sandon received written notice of the government's intentions from Stanley. They were unsatisfactory. Late though it was, Sandon and Moss went to see Patrick Maxwell Stewart, MP for Lancaster [67] and stopped with him until 2 arranging their plans.[68] All three met again the following morning at 10, and then went to see Stanley at the Colonial Office where they thrashed out a proposed compensation deal consisting of a £20m grant and 12 years apprenticeship.[69] Moss concluded *"Now that all is right and government pledged I am very glad I stopped. I feel that I have been of some use today."* [70] However, the cabinet refused to sanction the deal and the period of apprenticeship offered was reduced to seven years.[71]

The colonial West Indians, who lacked first hand knowledge of the social changes brought about by the Industrial Revolution and the Age of Reform and never witnessed the intensity of anti-slavery sentiment, found the whole emancipation business unacceptable.[72] Moss wrote to

---

66 Hawarden correspondence Moss to J Gladstone 8.6.1833

67 from 1831 to 1837

68 Hawarden correspondence Moss to J Gladstone 9.6.1833

69 The other offers of *"£15 millions grant and £10 mill loan and 12 years apprenticeship or £20 millions grant and a loan, if wanted, and 7 years apprenticeship"* were rejected.

70 Hawarden correspondence Moss to J Gladstone 9.6.1833

71 Hawarden correspondence Moss to J Gladstone 10.6.1833

72 He wrote of MacLean *"A few months in England would show him how necessary*

MacLean stating that both he and Gladstone *"were pledged to support the measures of government."* [73] On 15 July, again working in London, he begged Gladstone for assistance, alarmed that *"the West India merchants of Liverpool are content to let the momentous question be concluded with no one to represent them but myself...I have sent word to Liverpool that they must either appoint someone from the Chartered Colonies*[74] *or withdraw my name, and let me assist the Demerara Gentlemen."* [75] At the end of July, Moss left London because he dared not consent to the seven year apprenticeship period, although he couldn't see how a better deal could be struck. It was left to Sandon to do the best he could.[76]

The Emancipation Bill passed through the Commons on 7 August,[77] and Moss received a letter from Peter Rose, who had been *"mortified"* not to have had more to do with the arrangement,[78] congratulating him on his work. There had also been grudging appreciation of Gladstone and Moss's labours from the West India Committee in St James Street, London whose *"jealousy of us is quite as much as ever."* [79] The failure of the various West Indian factions to put on a wholly united front had weakened their negotiating power. Although relieved that the matter was settled, Moss felt he might have done better. *"The name of an owner of slaves has, of itself in these times, a stigma, and the consequence was we never could collect our interests*

it was to adapt himself to the times which he is not now prepared for." Hawarden correspondence Moss to J Gladstone 4.5.1833
73 Hawarden correspondence Moss to J Gladstone 13.6.1833
74 British Guiana, Trinidad and St Lucia were Crown colonies – i.e. - their laws were received directly from the King who, with the advice of his privy council, decided what was to be done in and by those colonies, and communicated it by governors on the spot, appointed by Him. Chartered colonies had a legislature of their own with the power to make laws which had to be approved by a governor sent out by the British Government. Their laws had to be sent to England for the approval of the King.
75 Hawarden correspondence Moss to J Gladstone 15.7.1833
76 Hawarden correspondence Moss to J Gladstone 27.7.1833
77 Sir George Stephen - Anti-Slavery Recollections: in a series of letters addressed to Mrs Beecher Stowe, p206
78 Hawarden correspondence Moss to J Gladstone 11.6.1833
79 ibid

together to fight with success."[80] The Emancipation Act, given royal assent on 28 August, decreed that after 1 August 1834, slavery would be illegal. Just as Stanley had proposed, children under the age of 6, or born after the Act, were immediately free and all others were to be apprenticed to their present masters for three quarters of their working day, but free to do as they pleased for the remaining quarter. In the case of field hands, the period of apprenticeship was to be 6, not 7 years and, for "domestics", 4 years. Their masters were obliged to provide housing, food and clothing in return for the continued labour of the former slaves. Stipendiary magistrates were to be appointed to carry out these measures, and provision was to be made for the religious and moral instruction of all. It must be stressed that this Act did not abolish slavery throughout the British Empire; it applied to four areas - The West Indies, Mauritius, Canada and the Cape of Good Hope. The Emancipation Act liberated 800,000 slaves.[81]

The planters, in return for the reduced apprenticeship period, won reparations of £20,000,000 which were allocated according to the relative value of slaves in each colony. The British Guianan interest would receive £4,297,117 10s 6½ d [82] for the loss of its 91,300 slaves.[83] With small wonder, Moss considered his representation of the West Indian cause one of his great lifetime achievements.[84] "*I often think of our exertions*

---

80   Hawarden correspondence Moss to J Gladstone 17.8.1833
81   Howard Temperley - British Anti Slavery 1833-1870, p93
82   equivalent to £357,198,061 in 2008 using the Retail Price Index
83   Flintshire Record Office ref GG MSS 2882., although Raymond T Smith, p38, quotes the same remuneration for the loss of 84,915 slaves
84   The compensation was paid on a sliding scale dependent upon the role and status of each individual slave:

Praedial (agricultural slaves)	£	S	D
Head people	87	8	0 ¾
Tradesmen 68	8	0 ½	
Inferior Tradesmen	38	0	0 ¼
Field labourers	64	8	4 ¾
Inferior field labourers	36	0	5
Non Praedial	£	S	D

to reconcile the West Indians to emancipation. The Government would not so easily have settled the question without us." [85] Some were jealous of this seemingly generous settlement. Hard line abolitionists were appalled that it was the planters and not the slaves who were to be compensated, and there was vehement opposition to the apprenticeship system inside and outside of Parliament. Locally, a radical Whig newspaper, the *Liverpool Mercury* edited by Egerton Smith, launched its own campaign. In the town centre the walls were *"placarded by a notice of 4d of Freemens Rights addressed to J Moss esq., Banker"* [86] Moss saw it in the hands of a Tory and was so disgusted by it that he *"let it pass unnoticed."* [87] The author didn't send him a copy, so Moss didn't read the article, not feeling *"disposed to give Egerton Smith 4d for abuse."* [88]

Moss contented himself with the continuing success of his plantation. He had been able to sell 58 casks of brown sugar for £40.12s.6d (another 2 had been detained by Customs).[89] He had also sold rum at 3.s 6d per gallon, *"9d per gallon higher than any I sold last year."* [90] The future looked bright.

Head Tradesmen	68	8	0 ½
Inferior Tradesmen	38	0	0 ¼
Head People employed on Wharfs, Shipping or other Vocations	87	8	0 ¾
Inferior People of the same description	36	15	7
Head Domestic Servants	63	0	1
Inferior Domestics	35	9	10 ¾
Children under 6 years of age on the 1st of August 1834	19	0	0

Flintshire Record Office ref GG MSS 2882
85   Hawarden correspondence Moss to J Gladstone 30.1.1846
86   Hawarden correspondence Moss to J Gladstone 17..8.1833
87   Hawarden correspondence Moss to J Gladstone 29.8.1833
88   Hawarden correspondence Moss to J Gladstone 17..8.1833
89   "Vacuum Pan sugar @ 58/6 netted £22.12s.6d. The Common sugar @ 60 shillings netted £18.10.0 *or in favour of Vac Pan £4. 2. 6.* Hawarden correspondence Moss to J Gladstone 26.8.1833
90   Hawarden correspondence Moss to J Gladstone 29.8.1833

CHAPTER 4

APPRENTICESHIP & THE INDENTURED LABOUR EXPERIMENT

"The next question is where are labourers to be had from? I have enquired almost everywhere. Some will not go. Others are not worth exporting. After mature deliberation I have almost determined to send for 150 people from India"

John Moss to John Gladstone – 10th September 1836

By September 1833, the battle for abolition now over, the planters had turned their attentions to the question of whether the apprenticed adults would fulfill their obligation to continue working for them until 1840. Moss, who had received the most satisfactory letters from MacLean, both as to the crops and the contentment of the slave population on *Anna Regina*, was optimistic.[1] Robertson Gladstone was pessimistic about the apprentice system as a whole and was unconvinced that, after 1840, the freedmen could be relied upon at all. However, he did plant a seed of hope, which might bring about a solution to the anticipated labour shortage, when he queried:

---
1 Hawarden correspondence Moss to J Gladstone 12.9.1833

"What law is there to prevent any individual sending his ship to the coast of Africa...and bringing back with their own consent a number of blacks to Demerara for instance, and on their landing giving security for their support and binding them to himself under the ordinary apprentice law?" [2] Moss was curious but cautious, and fearing an adverse reaction from the abolitionists, doubted *"the propriety of agitating the question now."* [3]

Emancipation brought with it so many imponderables, which troubled Moss. What was to become of the free children if their apprenticed parents could not support them? Would the planter not then be morally obliged to do so, and should the children therefore not become apprentices too? What would be the consequence when, at the end of the 6 year period, one quarter of the people on his estate would be 12 years old or younger? By December, MacLean had become gloomier about the situation, yet he advised Moss to purchase Bellefield estate, confident that the price of land would rise materially. *"I have replied that I dare not do it."* [4] At the turn of the New Year, the people on *Anna Regina* were still *"behaving uncommonly well. The truth is they see the benefits to be derived from the measures to themselves."* [5] A significant ameliorating step was taken by the Demeraran Courts of policy without prompting from the British Government, when regulations were passed abolishing *"domestic punishment"* from 1 March 1834.[6]

The Emancipation Act merely laid down guidelines. It would be left to colonial governors and assemblies, in conjunction with the Colonial Office, to interpret and implement the Act. Special magistrates appointed by the Colonial Office would ensure the measure was fairly and impartially administered. The abolitionists dreaded the

---

2   R Gladstone to J Gladstone, 11.8.1833.Checkland, p276
3   Hawarden correspondence Moss to J Gladstone 21.1.1834
4   Hawarden correspondence Moss to J Gladstone 4.12.1833
5   Hawarden correspondence Moss to J Gladstone 21.1.1834
6   Hawarden correspondence Moss to J Gladstone 1.3.1834

fact that power, other than that vested in the magistrates, remained in the hands of the old ruling class, which had proved so resistant to change in the past. Their concerns were well founded. Grossly overworked and underpaid, many of the magistrates found themselves in need of the hospitality of the planters. With their independence thereby compromised, many judgments were passed unfairly favouring the planter over the labourer. While domestic punishment may have been abolished, corporal punishment remained the penalty for serious miscreants in West Indian (and British) society.[7]

Moss took seriously his legal obligation to provide religious and moral instruction to his plantation workers. He was particularly keen to appoint a Moravian missionary[8] who would place a strong emphasis on practical Christian life rather than on doctrinal thought or church tradition. The Moravian Church[9] first established a mission among the West Indian slaves on St Thomas in 1732 and subsequently spread its doctrine of the oneness of all mankind, regardless of nationality or race, to many other islands. Given their wealth of experience, it is easy to understand why Moss would reject an inexperienced and zealous missionary from the Church of England who might well have wrought havoc. It was not until September 1835 that the minister, his wife and child were installed on *Anna Regina*.[10] The Moravians filed their

---

7   Green, p406. In 1835 Stipendiary Magistrate Delafons sentenced 19 apprentices on *Rome and Houston* estate in Guiana to 20 stripes each for damaging the property of the proprietor by failing to keep the boiling fires alive. Those labourers had been at work for an average of 15 hours a day during the preceding 8 days. The Governor, Sir James Carmichael Smyth, to whom the magistrates were answerable, rebuked Delafons rather than suspend him. Although Smyth took seriously his work as trustee and protector of the apprentices, he showed leniency on the grounds that a replacement for Delafons would have been virtually impossible to find and that he had 12 children who required his support

8   *"My object will be to induce a person to go from one West India colony to Demerara and there to make his own arrangements with McLean."* Hawarden correspondence Moss to J Gladstone 21.1.1834

9   or the Unitas Fratrum (Unity of the Brethren)

10   *"both Stewart (sic) and McKay think they will do good."* Hawarden correspondence Moss to J Gladstone 29.9.1835

1835 attempt under "Unsuccessful Missions"[11], but a further effort was made in 1837. Although Moss expected much from this *"expensive...Moravian settlement"* costing *"...not less than £3,500 first cash and £350 a year"* [12] there is no record as to its success or otherwise.

Early in 1834, Robertson Gladstone was again sent out to the West Indies. His particular mission was to ensure all his father's slaves were properly accounted for in order to achieve the maximum compensation entitlement. While he was there, John MacLean died and was replaced as attorney by James Stuart (sometimes referred to by Moss as Stewart). Although Robertson's opinion of the vacuum pan was lukewarm,[13] he filed *"a very long and very satisfactory"* report on Moss's estate, describing its people as *"the 'most tractable', 'industrious', 'well disposed', 'contented' and 'thoroughly domesticated' and 'best working gang in the whole colony.'"* He had little to say for Stuart, but wrote approvingly of Mr McKay (the manager) - a *"second Mr McLean"* who Moss felt *"the person best fitted to be my second attorney."* [14] Even a poor sugar crop could not dampen Moss's spirits; rather, it presented him with an opportunity to play the market while other West Indian, Mauritian and Brazilian sugar suppliers were experiencing worse difficulties.[15]

By mid October 1834 when, after a seven week continental holiday, Moss returned through London, the outlook had become bleaker. He found *"no one in the Public Offices except* (James) *Stephen* [16] *who is now assistant Secretary for*

---

11   Edward Reichel - Historical Sketch of the Church and Missions of the United Brethren, p96 (1848)
12   Hawarden correspondence Moss to J Gladstone 16.5.1837
13   *"he says to use them will require 30 additional hands and 1½ hogsheads of coals extra a day"* Hawarden correspondence Moss to J Gladstone 12.6.1834
14   ibid
15   Hawarden correspondence Moss to J Gladstone 12.6.1834
16   When he became permanent under-secretary two years later, Stephen's supreme control over the Colonial Office earned him the nicknames "Mr Over-Secretary Stephen", "King Stephen" and "Mr Mother Country"

the colonies." [17] Ominously, Stephen confided that *"The sugar duties are to undergo an entire revision but not I believe until 1836."* For Moss, it was inconceivable that the West Indies should have to compete on an even footing with foreign slave produce, but there was a vocal free trade movement which argued that global market forces, rather than the moral high ground, should dictate government economic policy. Most abolitionists anticipated that a free and happy workforce would prove more productive than the enslaved ones, and moreover, that they would be able to use Britain's successful emancipation experiment as a paradigm in the international fight against slavery.

Despite dire warnings of riot and bloodshed there were no major incidents in the months following the introduction of the Emancipation Act on 1 August 1834. Fowell Buxton wrote *"It is quite amazing, it is contrary to reason, it cannot be accounted for, but so it is."* [18] The apprentices fulfilled their working obligations to their masters, generally performing their tasks between dawn and 2 p.m. Thereafter they were at liberty to perform extra tasks, which could provide them with wages of up to 2s.2d a day. [19] Regardless, by November 1834, two of Moss's fellow West Indians, Messrs Horsfall and Hodgson, had concluded that, after they were finally released from apprenticeship, *"the Negroes will not work on sugar."* [20] Work on sugar plantations was particularly challenging, and Moss began to cast doubts over Robertson Gladstone's glowing report on *Anna Regina*. *"Those who say my people were working well only mean that they are working as usual."* [21] 1834 was a poor year for all Britain's sugar colonies. Due mainly to bad weather, Demerara's crop produced a deficiency of 15,000 casks. Moss felt that unfair blame had been attached to the colony's

---
17 Hawarden correspondence Moss to J Gladstone 18.10.1834
18 Temperley, p30
19 Green, p135
20 Hawarden correspondence Moss to J Gladstone 15.11.1834
21 ibid

governor *"for his continual proclamations"* when the situation was the same in Antigua where the people refused to work, in St Kitts where martial law had been proclaimed and in Jamaica where an apathetic governor had tried to please the planters. *"The experiment has failed because neither the planters nor the slaves were prepared for the great change which has taken place."*[22] Moss's estimate that the quantity of sugar exported over the next 6 years would reduce by only one fifth was more optimistic than other people's.[23] In the event, between 1834 and 1838 West Indian sugar production reduced only slightly from 3.9 to 3.5 million hundredweight, but the trend was worrying.[24]

Matters appeared to take a dramatic turn for the better when the newly elected Tory Prime Minister Robert Peel appointed William Ewart Gladstone Under-Secretary for the Colonies, on 26 January 1835.[25] At just 25 years of age, his rise, after only two years in Parliament, was remarkable.[26] Moss offered Gladstone senior his congratulations. He was sure William would do credit to both himself and his family and that his appointment would prove most satisfactory to the planters. However, he believed William should have remained a Lord of the Treasury one year longer. He worried that the burden of an office once held by Huskisson and Stanley might prove detrimental to his health. More experience in the routine of public business should have been acquired before such responsibility was placed upon him. However, Moss expressed respect and support for young Gladstone. *"I am always afraid of addressing public men and when I go to London, if your son favours me with an audience, I shall, as I do with Backhouse, so long as I am in the Colonial office, keep in mind*

---

22 ibid
23 ibid
24 Temperley, p114
25 William informed his father that Peel *"adverted to my connection to the West Indies as likely to give satisfaction to persons dependent on those colonies, and thought that others would not be displeased."* Morley, Volume 1, p123
26 Peel wrote to John Gladstone predicting *"Wherever he may be placed, he is sure to distinguish himself."* ibid, p124

that I am a merchant, he a secretary of state" [27] Although, no doubt, affording his father access to much useful information, William's stay in office was short lived. Peel's government collapsed on 7 April.

In 1835, Guianan planters introduced English ploughmen with their ploughs and horses, and 429 Portuguese arrived from Madeira. The next year 44 Irish and 47 English labourers were imported and, in 1837, 43 Glaswegian labourers arrived. None of these workers proved of much use. They suffered terribly from tropical diseases, drank excessively or drifted away to find less strenuous and more profitable occupations or a quick route home.[28] In anticipation of a decrease in the numbers of willing, able workers and yet lower productivity, Moss made plans to reduce costs and make better use of the land. *"I am going to destroy all the provision grounds on Anna Regina and convert them into canes and to send from England all allowances required by law… Salt beef and pork from Hamburgh (sic) would cost less money than fish."* [29] This was a matter of cold economics. *"I think if we grow provisions the Negroes will steal them to feed those under 6 years of age. By exporting them they are obliged to purchase and we can take it out in labour and thus give them an insight what must occur when they are free."* [30] In the coming months Moss imported from Bourdeaux 164 hogsheads of Indian corn. The bulk of this and other provisions would be stored at the Kings Locks in Liverpool from where, every 14 days, supplies amounting to about a month's stock would be sent out to Demerara. Moss reasoned that *"Where there is abundance there is generally waste… I doubt much whether a cargo would keep good long there. Insects, climate and population are all opposed to its measuring out."* [31]

---

27 Hawarden correspondence Moss to J Gladstone 18.2.1835
28 Raymond T Smith, pp42-43
29 ibid
30 Hawarden correspondence Moss to J Gladstone 18.2.1835
31 Hawarden correspondence Moss to J Gladstone 6.6.1835

June 1835 saw the final vindication of Moss's dogged adherence to the vacuum pan when James Stuart declared himself in favour of them.[32] While they produced less rum, this was counterbalanced by the advantages. Moss rejoiced at how "*In the wet months of May and June we made from 76 acres canes 108 hogsheads of vac pan sugar and, as fast as they arrive, they sell.*"[33] Stuart recognised that the vacuum pans were chiefly valuable in wet season and, having made 408 hogsheads of sugar from 1 January to 1 August in such conditions, the results had forced him to alter his opinion for good. Moss wrote that he sold the sugar "*as fast as it arrives to a refiner in Sheffield.*"[34]

August and September were months of extraordinary personal tragedy. At the end of August, Gladstone's brother Robert died while visiting him at Fasque. This, at the same time as the sudden death of Gladstone's sister in law, sent his already frail wife Anne into terminal decline, and she died on 23 September. Moss lamented the slow demise of his own, unmarried daughter Anne Jane who expired on 6 September. Hannah had hardly left Annie's bedside in twelve weeks. "*Whilst the child lived she was able to bear up, but when the excitement ceased she began to droop, and I was glad to get her to Harden Grange where we remained all last week with my daughter Ferrand.*"[35] The purpose of this visit to Yorkshire was to offer support for another daughter Margaret following the death of her husband of six years, Major Walker Ferrand, on 20 September.[36]

---

32 Stuart had written on 27 April '*I should be sorry to see them given up now that you have them with pumps complete.*' ibid
33 Hawarden correspondence Moss to J Gladstone 10.9.1835
34 Hawarden correspondence Moss to J Gladstone 29.9.1835
35 ibid
36 ibid. Moss wrote, from Harrogate "*I have also since I last wrote to you lost two near and dear relatives, both of whom, when we all met at Otterspool at Easter were as likely for life as myself... Events like these ought to cause us to reflect and prepare ourselves for joining them... Major Ferrand has left my daughter more than I could have expected... I hope she possesses good sense sufficient to enable her always to bear in mind how much more is required for happiness than riches and that the trials of prosperity are more*

Moss had been aware of the likely extent of compensation for the loss of his slaves since the beginning of the year. With 136 children under 6 years of age on *Anna Regina*, the average payout per slave was substantially reduced.[37] Although not entirely satisfied, he accepted *"uncontested"* the government's award of £40,353 18s 3d[38] for the loss of 805 slaves.[39] Remarkably, this equates to £50 per head; the exact figure Moss had suggested to Captain Elliot, in February 1833, as a fair rate of compensation.[40] These funds no doubt lent impetus to a plan to establish the Anglican church of St Anne in Aigburth.[41] Moss, Josias Booker,[42] John Abraham Tinne[43] and Charles Stewart Parker[44] undertook to contribute £2,000 towards the estimated construction costs of £4,000. The four man *"Building Committee's"* great wealth was, in part at least, derived from slavery, and all had recently been substantially remunerated for the loss of their West Indian slaves.[45] Moss donated 2,070 square yards of land from his Otterspool estate. He laid the foundation stone on 27 March 1836 and presented a stained glass window for the Chancel. Construction proceeded at such an incredible rate that the first

difficult to withstand than those attendant upon adversity." Margaret died on 5 April 1846. (Burke, p1046)

37   Hawarden correspondence Moss to J Gladstone 6.6.1835
38   £3,476,347 in 2008 using the Retail Price Index
39   on 18 January 1836 on behalf of himself and Henry Moss. Parliamentary Papers of 1837 - "Return to an order of the Honourable House of Commons" dated 6.12.1837 "for an account of all the sums of money awarded by the Commissioners of Slavery Compensation", Birmingham Central Library.
40   In respect of the Bahamas, James Moss was awarded £737 0s 2d (£53,366) for the loss of 76 slaves. (ibid) Gladstone's compensation for a total of 2,039 slaves in British Guiana and Jamaica was £95,526, roughly £47 per head His average compensation per Demerara slave was £53 5s 2d; for his Jamaican slaves it was £14 2s 0d. Checkland, p321
41   in the Parish of Childwall, in the diocese of Chester
42   Booker had been resident manager of his family's sugar and cotton estates in Georgetown, Demerara between 1815 and 1826.
43   Tinne, who was born in Demerara in 1807, was a partner in the Liverpool merchant house of Sandbach Tinne & Co, which had extensive West Indian interests. He was married to a daughter of Samuel Sandbach, a founder of the firm.
44   Parker too was a partner in the company and he also married one of Sandbach's daughters.
45   British Parliamentary Papers of 1837. Birmingham Central Library

service was held on Sunday 19 March 1837. Although at that time Aigburth was almost completely rural, the church could accommodate 735 persons.[46] While the founding fathers had anticipated a migration of professional men from the busy town, after only 5 years, the first vicar Reverend William J. Purdom alerted the Trustees to the insufficient number of pews.[47]

Moss's fears for the aftermath of emancipation resurfaced in September 1836, and he determined to allay them. Henry's son Peter Cottingham, *"who is quite a man of business"*, was in Demerara, and he had *"no expectation of the Negroes working well after the apprenticeship... He cannot get them to apprentice their children on any terms."* [48] The seed planted by Robertson Gladstone in August 1833 was now germinating in Moss's mind. It was imprudent to delay matters any longer. A sugar estate required continuous labour, and a cessation of work amounting to more than a couple of months would ruin *Anna Regina*. He had searched for workers *"almost everywhere. Some will not go. Others are not worth exporting. After mature deliberation I have almost determined to send for 150 people from India"* He had received reports from Mauritius, that the East Indians were the best conducted and the cheapest labourers in the world.[49] Between 1834 and 1836, upwards of 2,000 Indians had been despatched to Mauritius under 5 year contracts of engagement with several different parties.[50] Moss intended using the first 150 workers as a trial. Should it prove successful then, if the black people refused to engage on the same terms, he intended importing *"sufficient to supply all their places... Thus I think we may secure labour cheaper than from anywhere else"* [51]

---

46 Alan A Andrews - Parish Church of St. Anne, Aigburth. A History to Commemorate the 150th Anniversary 1837-1987 (New Edition for 2000)
47 ibid
48 Hawarden correspondence Moss to J Gladstone 10.9.1836
49 ibid
50 Letter from Gillanders, Arbuthnot & Co to John Gladstone, 6.6.1836 from "Brief exposure of the deplorable conditions of the Hill Coolies...".by John Scoble, 28 February 1840
51 Hawarden correspondence Moss to J Gladstone 10.9.1836

Gladstone, who had conducted trade with India since 1814[52] had, unknown to Moss, already made enquiries of Messrs Gillanders, Arbuthnot & Co of Calcutta concerning this very matter.[53] He sought around 100 *"young, active, able-bodied people"* for his Demerara estates, and received an encouraging reply, in June 1836. *"The tribe that is found to suit best in the Mauritius is from the hills to the north of Calcutta, and the men of which are all well-limbed and active, without prejudices of any kind... The Hill tribes, known by the name of Dhangurs, are looked down upon by the more cunning natives of the plains, and they are always spoken of as more akin to the monkey than the man. They have no religion, no education, and, in their present state, no wants beyond eating, drinking, and sleeping; and to procure which they are willing to labour."*[54]

The British Government had not permitted Indians to be exported to Mauritius as slaves, and nor would it to the West Indies. These "indentured labourers" were paid workers, bound under contracts of engagement for five years. Early in 1837, in the name of himself and Moss, Gladstone wrote to Sir John Cam Hobhouse, President of the Board of Control of the East India Company, seeking the government's opinion on his plan to operate a similar scheme in the West Indies. Hobhouse

---

52 Following the removal of certain rights of the East India Company, Gladstone's 516 ton ship, the Kingsmill, was the first to leave Liverpool, fully loaded, for Madeira and Bengal. *Liverpool Courier* 8.6.1814

53 On 4 January 1836 he had written seeking *"a proportion of other labourers, whom we might use as a set-off, and, when the time for it comes, make us, as far as is possible, independent of our Negro population."* Scoble

54 Letter from Gillanders, Arbuthnot & Co to John Gladstone 6 6.1836 (Scoble) Although the Negroes were all to be freed by the Emancipation Act, slavery in its various forms, still flourished in the British Empire, most notably in India and Ceylon where the servile population was estimated, at the time, to be around one million., although it may have been as high as 8 million. (Temperley, p94) In the vast subcontinent, a bewildering array of local customs as well as conflicting Muslim and Hindu laws, made any proposal for the abolition of slavery there unrealistic. (ibid, p99) The British had not created East Indian slavery as they had West Indian. This was not a case of one race enslaving another. In fact, much of what passed for slavery might more accurately be described as serfdom. The Charter Act of 1833 therefore set no specific date for East Indian slave emancipation.

assured him there would be no objection to a properly managed migration. Moss recognised that obtaining official approval was of the utmost importance.[55] The abolitionists viewed such schemes with the deepest scepticism. Moss was determined that this proposal be infused with credibility, that it was not seen as an act of slavery. *"It is...important to the labourers themselves that they be imported under Orders in Council because then the Colonial Secretary can regulate the numbers to be carried in each vessel in proportion to her tonnage and he can also stipulate that the vessel has a surgeon on board and that the people be examined before they are shipped, also that the parties who ask for licences to import have estates in Demerara to place the people on."* [56]

Gladstone was eager to press Lord Glenelg the Colonial Secretary for a 7 year indenture, but Moss persuaded him to seek no more than the same 5 year term as existed in Mauritius.[57] On 13 May, James Stephen wrote Moss a *"very satisfactory letter"* which gave the reassurance that government would only intervene with the project if it suspected any abuse. Moss reminded Gladstone that his and Henry Moss's names must be included in any licence to transport *"Coolies"* [58] otherwise Governor Smyth of Demerara would not permit them to land.[59] He was anxious that Lord Glenelg should permit as much male workers as possible to travel. Of the 811 people on *Anna Regina*, there were already twenty to thirty more females than males.[60] There was no intention on Moss's part that the Negroes be abandoned. He would ensure their free children received better *"Religious and Moral instruction."*

---

55 *"Without it I should fear some risk to the vessel which carries the people to Demerara. She might be detained by some English vessel of war and, a short delay with such a cargo would be ruinous. Besides Demerara being governed by an Order in Council the authorities there might ask for our authority to import these people."* Hawarden correspondence Moss to J Gladstone 20.4.1837
56 ibid
57 ibid
58 The word "Coolie" was a corruption of the Tamil word "Kuli", which referred to a porter or labourer
59 Hawarden correspondence Moss to J Gladstone 16.5.1837
60 ibid

Having now received his compensation money he was *"ready to devote considerable time to better the condition of the people, but unless the Government will aid us we shall all sell our estates to managers overseas and others who will only care for the number of hogsheads of sugar made"* [61]

On 20 May Gladstone confirmed the arrangements with the colonial department, and an Order in Council was immediately published permitting the transportation of 414 Indians to the Demeraran estates of Gladstone, Moss, Andrew Colville and Davidson, Barkley & Co.[62] The abolitionist John Scoble contended that this was *"complaisantly granted them by Lord Glenelg, with the concurrence of Sir John Hobhouse"* and that it gave *"carte blanche to every villain in British Guiana, and every scoundrel in India to kidnap and inveigle into contracts for labour for five years, in a distant part of the world, the ignorant and inoffensive Hindoo!"* The Order in Council was brought to the attention of the British public on 3 January 1838 in the *British Emancipator*, which denounced it as giving birth to a new slave trade, despite the documentary evidence which existed to substantiate that these were paid workers with written contracts of employment.[63] Just as in Mauritius, at the end of their 5 year indenture, the Indians were free to stay in the colony or to return home, at their own expense, on a ship provided by their masters.

---

61 ibid
62 Scoble
63 The following is an extract from a contract for Coolies working on Colville's *Belle Vue* plantation; the contracts of all parties are likely to have been very similar, if not identical:

1) We engage to perform willingly and diligently our duty as labourers, with the usual time allowed us for rest and food; and should we be, at any time during the period hereinafter named, unable to perform our duty, from sickness or other inevitable cause, we hereby agree to relinquish all claim upon our master for wages during the time we are absent, provided we are found in food and clothing while so absent from work.
2) As...the natives shall not be a burden to the colony in the event of their leaving their employment, one rupee per month shall be retained from the pay of each individual till there shall be sufficient sum to provide a passage for each to Calcutta, and should no such contingency take place, the money shall be restored at the end of five years. Dwarka Nath -A History of Indians in Guyana, p13

On 13 January 1838, *The Whitby* set sail from Calcutta carrying 249 emigrants for the estates of Colville and Davidson, Barkley & Co. Sixteen days later a 334 ton ship, *Hesperus*, began the same journey with 165 Indians on board. Two thirds of their number was destined for Gladstone's estates, the remainder for *Anna Regina*.[64] Protest meetings were held all over Britain at which were attacked, not only the indentured labour scheme, but also the apprenticeship system. Moss wished to prosecute the author and printer of a paper concerning the Coolies. *"I wish we had some of the rascals who utter such falsehoods on the treadmill."*[65] As for the apprentices, he insisted that working conditions in Demerara were better than at home. *"How thankful would the lower classes of Warwickshire and Lancashire be now if they were like West India apprentices?"* [66] The abolitionists' latest campaign smacked of hypocrisy. *"The anti slavery men want the ruin of the West Indian planters and merchants. They care nothing for the labourers."* [67] Governor Smyth cared greatly for the apprentices and so too for the welfare of any potential immigrants. He had issued a proclamation, in April 1837, which raised the Negroes' food allowances above a level Gladstone felt adequate.[68] Gladstone later appealed to Lord Glenelg on the grounds that this extra cost was injurious to the planters. Smyth successfully argued that Gladstone himself had provided, in his agreement with the Coolies, far more food than he said was needed for the Negroes.

On 12 March, with the Coolies now on the high seas, Moss wrote to thank Gladstone for his *"offer of taking the whole concern from first to last off my hands"* [69] In the event of Smyth refusing them entry, Gladstone had the fallback of landing the Indians on his Jamaican estates. However, Moss advised against

---

64 ibid, p11
65 Hawarden correspondence Moss to J Gladstone 20.2.1838
66 ibid
67 Hawarden correspondence Moss to J Gladstone 24.2.1838
68 Checkland, p323
69 Hawarden correspondence Moss to J Gladstone 12.3.1838

it, fearing that *"the Anti slavery people will say Mr Gladstone has given Bond to take these people to a country where punishment by whipping is abolished and sends them to where it is continued."*[70] By holding to the letter of the law and complying with the wishes of all the relevant authorities, Moss felt assured that, if anything were to go wrong, *"The blame rests with Gillanders and Co and the government at home or India."*[71]

In March, Governor Smyth died and was replaced by the less quarrelsome Henry Light.[72] At this stage, Moss was unaware of Light's more accommodating nature and, with the arrival of the Coolies still 6 weeks away, there was plenty of scope for anxiety. *"I have read the Order in Council carefully over and I do not see how the Governor of Demerara can refuse to allow the people to land, and it should only be in case of their refusal to work that we should have to prove the contract, and if they want to go after 3 years we can get more and we are at all events released from their journey home."*[73] On 6 March, Lord Henry Brougham, (a fierce opponent of Gladstone's since at least 1812)[74] who had condemned the suppression of the 1823 Demerara uprising and opposed the apprenticeship system, initiated a formal debate. The indentured labour system was condemned with such furore in the country and in Parliament that the government bowed, and the Order in Council was revoked, but too late to invalidate the contracts of those already on their way to the colony. The Government of India stopped any further emigration of its citizens.[75]

Moss continued to worry about the prospect of the emancipated West Indies having to compete on an equal footing with slave economies. *"Surely the East Indian anti slavery people and all will write in preventing the admission of Cuba*

---

70 Hawarden correspondence Moss to J Gladstone 13.3.1838
71 ibid
72 Checkland, p323
73 Hawarden correspondence Moss to J Gladstone 19.3.1838
74 Checkland, p324
75 ibid

and Brazil sugars – or any part into consumption here." [76] He spoke to a gentleman who had spent much time in Brazil and alleged that 50,000 slaves had been landed at one port alone in the last year. The Brazilians were using revenues derived, not only from their exports of sugar to continental Europe but also from British manufactured goods such as cottons, to purchase slaves. *"In fact British capital carries on the trade. He says every British House knows how many slaves are landed every night."* [77] With such complex, interlocking trading systems as these, the only way Britain could possibly have distanced herself from slavery altogether, would have been to have withdrawn from trade entirely. Moss had previously complained about this problem 4 years earlier, but little or nothing appears to have been done about it. *"If this is permitted I am confident the civilisation of the West India Negroes will never be accomplished. The supplies of Blacks to the Foreign Colonies will prevent our own planters hiring the apprentices."* [78]

By 1838 the very system of apprenticeship was nearing collapse, having been severely undermined by the reports of Scoble and of Joseph Sturge who had visited the West Indies in 1836. Scoble had posted a negative report on the continuing punishment of apprentices in British Guiana and other colonies in *The Patriot* newspaper in September 1837. Sturge reported on the much more brutal Jamaican regime. Having facilitated Scoble's visit to every part of the colony and given him free access to official documents, the then Governor Smyth felt betrayed. He considered that *"the good which might be gained by the observations of a judicious and impartial traveller, is, in the case of Mr Scoble, neutralised by the haste with which he arrives at his conclusion, and but too frequently upon erroneous and inaccurate information."* [79] By April 1838,

---

76 Hawarden correspondence Moss to J Gladstone 19.3.1838
77 ibid
78 Hawarden correspondence Moss to J Gladstone 17.6.1834
79 Green, p154. Smyth would have found Scoble's accusation that he was a man controlled by planters bewildering. The previous year he had been censured by Lord

250 petitions calling for the scrapping of apprenticeship had reached Parliament.[80] Smyth did not survive to see the debate's conclusion; the system of apprenticeship in all West Indian colonies was to be abolished entirely with effect from 1 August 1838, a full 2 years before the date stipulated in the Emancipation Act.

The Whitby and *Hesperus* [81] both arrived in British Guiana on 5 May. Five of *The Whitby*'s passengers had died at sea, although fatalities at sea on long journeys were common in those times. The survivors were despatched to Colville's and Davidson Barkley's estates. The death toll on *Hesperus* was a more alarming 13, including 2 people who fell overboard during a violent gale. James Stuart explained that the cause of the high mortality rate was not maltreatment but overeating by people whose diet had always been low.[82] *Hesperus's* 152 survivors were distributed between Gladstone's estates of *Vreedenstein* (31 males, 0 females, 0 children) and *Vreed-en-hoop* (63 males, 3 females, 4 children) and to Moss's *Anna Regina* (41 males, 3 females, 7 children).[83]

For the most part the Indians, like other racial groups,

Aberdeen who advised him that the interests of the apprentices could not be served by him alienating the planters. ibid, p150

80   ibid, p157

81   On 17 December 1839 a devastating storm hit the Atlantic coast of North America. 17 schooners were wrecked and 40 lives lost. A 3 mast coastal schooner with the uncommon name of *Hesperus* was wrecked at Boston's Long Wharf, a tragedy which inspired Henry Wadsworth Longfellow to write one of his best known poems, "The Wreck of the Hesperus"

82   Checkland, p325

83   Dwarka Nath, p11. The indentured worker's day seldom lasted more than 8 hours. On *Anna Regina* the monthly remuneration was 16 rupees for superintendents, 7 rupees for headmen, 6 rupees for mates, 5 rupees for labourers and 4 rupees for boys. A rupee was worth 2s 4d in 1838. (ibid, p12) For the Indians these were extraordinarily high wages. They were given a daily allowance of 14 chittaks of rice, (1 chittak = about 2 ozs) 2 chittaks of dal, ½ chittak of ghee or oil, ¼ chittak of salt, 1 chittak of dried fish, 1 chittak of tumeric or tamarind, and ½ chittak of onions and chillies. In addition each of them received an annual allowance of 1 blanket, 2 dhotis, (a loin cloth about 4½ yards long) one jacket, one cap, and one wooden bowl and one brass cup for four of them. ibid, p13

were segregated on the plantations. They were housed either in old slave 'logies' or in new, cramped barrack blocks. The managers communicated with the workforce through interpreter headmen. The office of Immigration Agent-General was created to ensure immigrants were treated fairly and to act as intermediary in disputes between workers and management over pay and conditions. Scoble visited British Guiana again, in January 1839, on behalf of the British Foreign and Anti Slavery Society. Thereafter, he filed a report entitled *"Brief exposure of the deplorable condition of the Hill Coolies in British Guiana and Mauritius, and of the nefarious means by which they were induced to resort to these colonies."* The deplorable fact was that by September 1839, 64 of the 396 people landed in the colony had died.[84] Scoble stated that the Coolies had to be forced on board *Hesperus* that the hatches were bolted down and that one man died from suffocation. He discovered that, in India, *"the trade of kidnapping Coolies had been extensively carried on, and that prison depots had been established in the villages near Calcutta for the security of the wretched creatures, where they were most infamously treated, and guarded with the utmost jealousy and care, to prevent their escape, until the Mauritian and Demerara slavers were ready for their reception."*

Scoble was able to demonstrate that, after their arrival in Demerara, some of the Indians were badly mistreated or neglected. Although Special Justice Mure had reported that the Coolies on *Anna Regina* appeared *"very cheerful and contented"*, two of their number had died. Without doubt, if Scoble could have found any means of implicating the estate's management he would have; so it may be safely assumed that illness was the cause of these deaths. Governor Light subsequently appointed a commission to enquire into their treatment, and this revealed that *Anna Regina's* Indians had been well cared for by their

---

84 These are Dwarka Nath's figures. Scoble's report stated that by November 1839 the number of dead was 67. He stated there had been a total of 437 immigrants. Dwarka Nath refutes this figure and those of others

manager. In answer to some of the questions put to them there were such comments as *"All we get from Mr. McKay is very good"*; *"Our houses are very good"*; *"We are quite happy"*; *"Our manager is very good to us"*; *"What can we say more?"* [85] Moss would have been delighted with the productivity of his happy workforce. *Anna Regina's* output for 1839 was 715 tons of sugar; more than any other plantation in British Guiana where the average production of the 77 estates for which figures were available, was just 104 tons.[86]

There were bigger fish than Moss for Scoble to fry, and he targeted the estates of Gladstone, the architect of the indentured labour scheme. By 1 November 1839, nine people had been reported dead on *Vreed-en-Hoop*, and a further two were missing presumed dead. On *Vreedenstein* eight had died - a mortality rate higher than on *Vreed-en-Hoop*, in proportion to the numbers settled there. The commission had obtained damning eyewitness accounts of floggings meted out to Coolies at *Vreed-en-Hoop*, *"A report having reached the Governor.... that 2 of them, in consequence of ill treatment, had fled from the estate, and had perished in the neighbourhood of Mahaica".* In another incident, five Coolies who had run away were retrieved and flogged.[87] Elizabeth Caesar, a labourer on *Vreed-en-Hoop*, reported that *"The Coolies were locked up in the sick house, and next morning they were flogged with cat-o'-nine-tails; the manager was in the house, and they flogged the people under his house; they were tied to the post of the gallery of the manager's house; I cannot tell you how many licks; he gave them enough. I saw blood. When they were flogged at the manager's house they rubbed salt pickle on their backs."* Will Clay, the foreman of the plantation stated that *"The Coolies were locked up in the sick house; saw them the day after they were flogged; their backs were swollen; they were in the sick house for two days after the*

---

85 Dwarka Nath, p19
86 N Deerr - The History of Sugar Volume 1, p365
87 Report by Thomas Coleman to the Governor, 16 May 1839. Dwarka Nath states that it was a group of between 6 and 10 Indian labourers

flogging." [88] Mr. Stuart explained that the floggings, which had been carried out by a Bengalese headman, were exaggerated and that they arose out of a misunderstanding which would not recur.[89] Matters were so much worse on Andrew Colville's *Belle Vue* estate, where twenty had died. Scoble had seen a wretchedly filthy sick house populated by patients without mattresses to lie on. *"The Coolies in it were not suffering merely from sores; they had mortified ulcers, their flesh rotting on their bones, their toes dropping off. Some were in a dangerous state from fever, and all were in the utmost despondency."* [90]

The indentured labour scheme was condemned in Parliament and, given the evidence, it was indefensible. Although the Coolies carried on working in accordance with their contracts, there was now no prospect of additional workers being obtained. While he considered that the government was being ruled by the Anti-Slavery people, Moss doubted whether, even if the Tories were to come to power, anything would change. *"They would still keep Stephen and listen to the men who will not rest until they have ruined the West Indies."* [91] By the end of the five year indenture period, 118 of the 414 Coolies who had arrived from Calcutta were dead. 236 survivors returned to India and 60 others elected to remain in the colony. In May 1843, thirty five men, three women, five boys and a girl - all from *Anna Regina* - boarded the *Water Ditch* bound for home.[92] Many had actually prospered, and they carried with them on average £37 2s 6½ d per head, compared with an overall average of £24 8s 3½ d;[93] by this

---

88   ibid
89   Checkland, p325
90   Moss attempted to reassure Gladstone. "*I saw Mr Labouchere. Indeed he sent for me through Lord Sandon on the Coolie business. He seemed to consider that Colville's was the only case to condemn. I found him disposed to do what is right, but evidently under control and fearful of the anti slavery men.*" (Hawarden correspondence Moss to J Gladstone 26.8.1839) Henry Labouchere was a Whig who succeeded Poulett Thompson as president of the Board of Trade on 29 August 1839
91   Hawarden correspondence Moss to J Gladstone 29.1.1840
92   Dwarka Nath, pp 20-21
93   The next most successful were those from *Waterloo* plantation who took away an

measure at least, it could be argued that the experiment with the Indians had been a success on Moss's estate.

---

average of £33 12s 2½ d. ibid

CHAPTER 5

EMANCIPATION AND BEYOND

"I have of late been making some calculations, and I am confident nothing can save the West India Colonies to this country but "Free Trade" in labourers, and... allow the West India planter to supply his Estates with labourers from every part of Africa, only registering them as freemen on their arrival in the West Indies..."

John Moss to Lord George Bentinck - 26th January 1848

Across the West Indies, Emancipation Day 1 August 1838 passed off peacefully in worship and jubilation. The former apprentices were now free to seek employment - or not - as they wished. Some squatted on crown lands and estates abandoned for want of labour. Others disappeared into the bush or developed British Guiana's large uncultivated tracts of land. Some freedmen pooled their money to purchase abandoned plantations, and established free Negro villages. Churches and schools became the nucleus of activities in the new villages, imparting European education and culture. In support of these initiatives, a substantial civil service created posts which had to be filled by local people. The British Government began to take a greater interest in the freedmen's education and health. Where once they had been subject to the control and punishment of the planters, they were now subject to the jurisdiction of the courts and police.

Those who remained in plantation society could not be induced to work as regularly as the colonists would have liked and, on 8 October, Governor Light addressed them: *"I hear that some of you, contrary to your duty… go into the field one day and abstain from it the next; that when you have earned sufficient to fill your bellies, like the wild beasts, after satisfying their hunger, you lie down to sleep or idle your time… and then pretend to wonder that you are not paid a full rate of wages."* [1] Such behaviour had, of course, been widely anticipated and that is why, between 1835 and 1838, a total of 5,926 labourers, including the Indian Coolies, Africans captured from foreign traders, Portuguese, English, Scottish, Irish and Germans had been imported.[2] Nearly all were unsuited to the harsh climate and work. The death rate from illness was very high, and those who didn't return home began also to desert the sugar plantations in favour of urban areas or for less strenuous tasks in the rural economy. The same was true of the 209 Maltese indentured labourers who arrived in 1839.[3] The planters were now in greater difficulty than ever before.

In January 1839, with the cost of sugar production inflated by the payment of wages, Moss, as ever in search of greater efficiencies, urged Gladstone to invest in a new transatlantic steam packet company. He had put his name down for 10 shares.[4] If such a service could be established between Liverpool and the West Indies, then the outward journey would reduce from 40 to 16 days. Such a rapid voyage, and constant communication with the colonies, would bring cost savings

---

1 Dwarka Nath, p7
2 ibid, p23 & p26
3 ibid
4 Six months earlier, the *Royal William* had become the first steam packet to set sail for New York from Liverpool.

and might entice more workers to *Anna Regina*.[5] Although Moss's argument was a cogent one, Gladstone was stubbornly opposed to steam packets. He had recently lambasted his son Robertson for having an interest in the proposed Liverpool and New York service, and ordered him to remove his name from the list of subscribers in favour of increasing his capital in Gladstone & Co.[6] Gladstone's resistance left Moss perplexed. *"So you attach no importance to whether it takes 16 days or 40 days to communicate with Demerara…How often have you, for want of hearing of a vessel with coals being lost, had to purchase coals an extra 24 days in the Colony?... The steam engines and vacuum pans are all liable to want repairs and additions and to get them removed to half the travelling distance from their makers is no small advantage… I feel that if Mr Stuart could have written on 10 Aug that my people wanted no more fish, and had I got his letter on the 26th, the last fish from Newfoundland would not be rotting in the colony…It is so seldom I differ from you I cannot help explaining fully when I do."*[7] Gladstone was not to be swayed, and indeed, he dissuaded Robertson and Moss from participating in one of the most exciting prospects of the age, and an initiative which could have provided them a competitive edge.[8]

The Voluntary Subscription Immigration Society, set up in 1839, brought to British Guiana 2,900 labourers from places like Barbados, St Kitts and Antigua, where labour was plentiful, but land scarce.[9] No workers were procured for *Anna Regina* by this means. Moss was not satisfied that the scheme was being properly regulated. 1,000 blacks sailed from Barbados to

---
5   Hawarden correspondence Moss to J Gladstone 24.1.1839
6   Checkland, pp286-7
7   Hawarden correspondence Moss to J Gladstone 26.1.1839
8   *"I quite concur with you that it would be unsafe and imprudent to take any shares in the steam packet company unless a charter is first obtained… I never felt much confidence in it and only took the shares for the purpose of promoting a measure which I thought would be beneficial to my property in Demerara."* (Hawarden correspondence Moss to J Gladstone 13.1.1840)
9   Vere T Daly - A Short History of the Guianese People, p175

Demerara where they were put to work in trenches. A *"horrid report"* was filed with Lord Russell, Secretary of State for the Colonies.[10] By January 1840, Moss was almost at the point of despair. *"The case of Demerara appears almost useless… It is quite clear the government dare not do anything – Exeter Hall rules them. If Sir Robert Peel and his party came in tomorrow I should not expect any change. They would still keep Stephen and listen to the men who will not rest until they have ruined the West Indies…"* [11] He begged Gladstone to exert his influence in reopening the East Indian traffic in Coolies.[12] This was, however, a forlorn hope.

Had it been necessary for the West Indian colonies to compete on equal terms with Brazil and Cuba, the consequences of emancipation would have been disastrous. However, the emotive connection between sugar and slavery led the British Government to abandon any notion of free trade, and punitive duties were imposed on foreign sugars. Curiously, such stringent protectionist measures were not applied to other slave produced goods like cotton and coffee. The duty on British produced sugar varied according to its quality, but was generally around 24 shillings per hundredweight compared with 63 shillings for foreign sugars. Since the average cost of West Indian sugar on the British market, after duties had been paid, was around 65 shillings this was more than enough to keep foreign sugars out.[13] Despite this, Moss complained, in June 1840, that the crops hardly covered expenses, and there would be dreadful consequences for the planter, the labourer and the grocer.[14] However, even if Demerara were to go to the wall, he was confident he could do without the income,

---

10   Hawarden correspondence Moss to J Gladstone 9.6.1840
11   Hawarden correspondence Moss to J Gladstone 29.1.1840
12   *"I hope you will aid to get the Coolies on any terms. If such men as these and persons like Colville's manager when the Coolies went down, are to have the emigrants we shall all suffer by it."* Hawarden correspondence Moss to J Gladstone 9.6.1840
13   Temperley, p139
14   Hawarden correspondence Moss to J Gladstone 12.6.1840

and neither he nor Gladstone had mortgage interests to pay.[15] In fact, Moss even found cause for optimism in September, believing a great reduction in the price of sugars would soon take place. A price fall to 26 shillings per cwt (20 shillings nett to the planter) would *"ruin every colony but Demerara and Jamaica and then we shall have labour as cheap as we had slave labour. I may be wrong but I am strongly impressed with the opinion that Demerara will in the end beat Brazil."*[16] However, the competition came not just from the slaving nations but also from British planters eager to obtain the right workers at the right price. In consequence, wages were being pushed higher, and *Anna Regina's* labourers worked extra time in neighbouring estates.[17] Despite *Anna Regina "doing very well",* Moss was prepared to consider renting it off to Mr McKay for £4,000 per annum, and had even written to Mr Stuart about the possibility of selling but, in the end, he took up neither option.[18] In December 1840, following an unknown indiscretion, a new resident attorney and manager was sent out from Liverpool superseding Stuart.[19]

The abolitionists' hope that the British West Indian worker's higher productivity could be used as an example to the slaving countries as to the viability of emancipation was dashed. In fact, production fell while that of the slave economies rose. Between 1831 and 1841 British Guiana's sugar production slumped from 58,757 tons to 30,657 tons per annum.[20] In 1815, Cuba had produced 42,000 tons of sugar, but by 1841 she was exporting 160,000 tons, compared with the 100,000 tons exported by the entire British West Indies. Excluding

---

15 ibid
16 Hawarden correspondence Moss to J Gladstone 8 .9.1840
17 In the run up to harvest, despite Moss having given *"positive orders to employ our people at over work",* forty of them were working their extra time on the adjoining *Richmond* estate. Hawarden correspondence Moss to J Gladstone 5.12.1840
18 *"On 29 Dec 1839 Mr McKay wrote to say that he was determined to rent an estate – that Rome & Euston had been let for £2,500."* ibid
19 ibid
20 Walton Look Lai - Indentured Labor, Caribbean Sugar, p273

duties, the cost of the West Indian sugar imported into Britain was over £9,000,000. The same quantity of foreign sugar of the same quality, on the world market, would have cost only £4,000,000.[21] Inevitably, the high price of sugar to the British consumer was a source of ongoing, heated debate. Although all parties were in favour of free trade in principle, in practice most abolitionists were opposed to any tariff reduction as this would encourage imports of 'blood stained' produce. Such a measure would prompt the slave economies to import even more slaves to meet the increased demand. Conversely, the more radical free traders asserted that protectionism benefited just the West Indian planters at the expense of the rest of the community, and Britain owed the planters no debt of gratitude. In May 1841, Lord John Russell argued that it was absurd for Britain to pay a bounty of several million pounds to idle West Indians living in luxury while Britain's population was on the verge of starvation. A motion to reduce the tariff to 36 shillings was proposed but defeated and, within two weeks, Lord Melbourne's Whig government, following a motion of no confidence, resigned. Even within the abolitionist movement, opinion was now beginning to turn against protectionism.[22]

Moss was heartened by the result of the July general election (a Tory majority of 91). To his relief, Peel's government pledged its support for the existing sugar tariff system and, on 31 August, he appointed William Ewart Gladstone as Vice-President of the Board of Trade.[23] William could have had no better grounding in the field of commerce than that provided by his father. Moss, though, was not convinced by the suitability of the appointment. *"Your son has talents of a higher order than are, in my humble opinion, required for trade. I would much rather leave my bank to your management than*

---

21 Temperley, pp138-9
22 On 19 June, Richard Caton, secretary of the Bradford Anti-Slavery Society wrote to the London committee stating '*sugar* (is) *nearly beyond the reach of our actually famishing population at home where our charity should begin.*' ibid, p147
23 a position John Gladstone considered '*a quiet seat*' and '*a step to a higher position ere long.*' Checkland, p345

his. Still I should be proud to see him MP for Liverpool [24] *and a secretary of state."* [25] William was the mastermind behind Peel's great budget of 1842 in which duties were reduced on 750 items and income tax reintroduced as a means of recovering lost revenue.[26] He was a great success in his role.[27] John Gladstone's approval of his son was now at its height, but his continuing movement away from protectionism towards freer trade alarmed Moss, who wrote, in January 1843 *"I have seen, with monopoly times, industrious individuals flourish in every branch of business, large fortunes made and comfort and happiness dispensed to all connected with them. All is now changed, prudence and moderation expelled and no one branch of trade flourishing. Protection withdrawn from one branch of commerce after another and those who have anything left dreading the meeting of parliament because they feel that no property is safe whilst parliament are sitting…I see property depressed and persons of real industry reduced to a pitiable state."* [28] William was appointed President of the Board of Trade in May and entered the cabinet of what Moss considered a *"conciliating government"* which would no doubt let slave grown sugar into the country through the equalising of the sugar duties.[29]

At the British and Foreign Anti-Slavery Society meeting in May 1844, a sizeable and growing minority within the movement expressed the desire to overthrow slavery through complete free trade with all nations. The mainstream opinion was for free trade to be conducted only in free-grown sugar from places such as Java, Manilla and Indo-China. By the budget of 1844, the government announced a reduction of the

---

24   William had been re-elected as MP for Newark. He never represented Liverpool as an MP.
25   Hawarden correspondence Moss to J Gladstone 7.10.1842
26   Checkland, p346
27   Peel wrote to Gladstone extolling his son's virtues. *"At no time in the annals of parliament has there been exhibited a more admirable combination of ability, extensive knowledge, temper and discretion."* ibid, p347
28   Hawarden correspondence Moss to J Gladstone 5.1.1843
29   Hawarden correspondence Moss to J Gladstone 10.7.1843

tariff on free grown sugar from 66 shillings per hundredweight to 36 (only 11 shillings above that at which colonial sugar was admitted).[30] William had been a major contributor to this budget despite the protestations of his father. However, the relaxing of the duties proved ineffectual and, by 1845, foreign free grown sugar accounted for only 3% of total sugar imports.[31] The abolitionists blamed Peel's government for succumbing to the influence of the monopolists.

Government and abolitionists, ever mindful of the West Indian planters' desperate need for labourers, were still in favour of an indenture scheme, but only for voluntary emigrants who were fully aware of the nature of the undertaking and of the conditions laid down. In July 1842, Parliament had voted in favour of Lord Stanley's measures to reopen the traffic between India and Mauritius, and this same privilege was eventually extended to British Guiana's planters in 1845. In that year, 816 Indians arrived in the colony – a woefully inadequate number.[32] With the planters' plight worsening, Moss was prompted to exercise an even more cautious approach towards his investment in *Anna Regina*. Peel's suggestion, in January 1846, that colonial sugars could bear 3 shillings 6 pence less protection forced Moss to abandon plans to send out a *"much*

---

30   Temperley, p160
31   ibid, p164
32   Dwarka Nath, p33. Stanley's measures to safeguard the Coolies' interests were:

1) immigration would be financed by means of a grant from the West Indian Assembly and responsibility placed in the hands of government agents, not private speculators who had been responsible for past abuses.
2) imposition of a strict limit on the number of emigrants embarking on ships according to the ship's tonnage.
3) Coolies would be allowed to bring their wives and children free of charge.
4) Coolies could choose their own employer upon arrival in the colony.
5) contracts would be limited to periods of not more than one year.
6) immigrants would be able to earn the same wages as free labourers.
7) free return passage would be provided after 5 years.
8) those who wished to leave the colony at an earlier date could do so at their own expense. Temperley, p131

wanted" new steam engine.[33] Worse was to come. The debate over the Corn Laws [34] was brought to a head by the first appearance of potato blight in Ireland. Government responded by purchasing enormous quantities of American maize. It was hoped that this would reduce the price of bread to within the reach of the Irish peasantry, and so replace the potato as its staple diet. Peel and William Gladstone were convinced the Corn Laws should be repealed and, on 16 May 1846, they were. This highly contentious decision caused the Conservative party to split in half and, in June, Peel's hopelessly divided government resigned from office.

Events now moved quickly. On 2 July, Lord John Russell took office at the head of a Whig cabinet and, on 20 July, he put forward a plan which only a few years previously would have been unthinkable. He proposed admitting all foreign sugars, regardless of origin, at a uniform rate of 23 shillings and 4 pence, as compared with a duty of 14 shillings on British sugar. The foreign duty would then be reduced in annual stages until, by 1851, all sugars would be admitted at the rate of 14 shillings.[35] In the Commons, opposition to the Sugar Duties Bill was left to the Tory MP Lord George Bentinck and a group of die hard protectionists. Of those connected with the West and East Indies, only five voted against the motion, the majority being in favour of putting an end to the uncertainty which was discouraging investment. On 18 August 1846, the Sugar Duties Act passed into law.[36] Moss was devastated. *"I am strongly impressed with the opinion that before three years a man will be as much ashamed of having been*

---

33 Hawarden correspondence Moss to J Gladstone 30.1.1846
34 The Corn Laws were import tariffs which had been imposed since 1815 for the purpose of protecting British farmers and landowners against cheap foreign grain imports. The British aristocracy, whose political power was derived from landownership and crop production, feared the removal of the Corn Laws would reduce both their income and their influence. In direct opposition to them was a national Anti Corn Law League, founded in 1839 by a group of Manchester free traders.
35 William Law Mathieson - The Sugar Colonies and Governor Eyre, p48
36 Mathieson, p48

a Free Trade supporter as if he had patronised the slave trade." [37]
5 months later, the situation had deteriorated further. *"I do wish you could inoculate Sir Rob & Lord John so as to let us be governed by men of a little common sense. There will be a frightful reckoning for all this free trade."* [38]

The economic effect of the new measure was just as Moss had predicted. 1846 had been a year of extreme drought in the West Indies, and this contributed to the alarming consequence that, by 1847, approximately 20% of the sugar consumed in Britain was of foreign origin - the bulk of it from Brazil and Cuba.[39] Brazil's production leapt from approximately 30,000 tons in the mid 1830s to 60,000 in 1848, and Britain consumed 17% of this crop.[40] Between 1846 and 1848, the price obtained for West Indian sugar fell from 34 shillings and 5 pence to 23 shillings and 3 pence.[41] Worse still, ever more Negroes were carried from Africa to the non-British New World,[42] and soon foreign sugars accounted for a quarter of Britain's consumption.[43] Having failed to stamp out the foreign slave trade and having then purchased its blood stained produce, Britain had lost the moral high ground.

1847 was a year of economic crisis. In April, the effect of large calls on railway shares was aggravated by a break in cotton prices and a drain of gold to pay for imported food. The potato famine in Ireland was nearing its worst. In Britain, the prospect of an unexpectedly good harvest halved the price of wheat. Moss wrote to Gladstone on 8 April *"What extraordinary times we live in. The next 12 months will test the repeal of the usury laws, bank restriction, free trade in corn and*

---

37   Hawarden correspondence Moss to J Gladstone 10.12.1846
38   Hawarden correspondence Moss to J Gladstone 14.1.1847
39   Temperley, p163
40   ibid
41   ibid
42   Curtin, Phillip D - The Atlantic Slave Trade, p234. An estimated 600,000 Negroes were carried between Africa and the New World between 1839 and 1863.
43   Temperley, p163. This figure was reached in 1851.

cattle, foreign sugar and East India Rum and it possibly may be accompanied with a requirement of 10 millions of gold for food in Ireland and here!!! You and I could hardly venture an opinion on such matters. Yet I see all around me going at rail road speed and acting without thought."[44] Disaster struck at the end of August when 18 West Indian houses failed, among them Barton, Irlam and Higginson, which had been Liverpool's largest. Although the plummeting price of sugar had been caused mostly by the financial crisis, the planters ascribed it entirely to the Sugar Duties Act. Bentinck, speaking in February 1848, argued that not one of the, by then, 48 bankrupt houses would have failed had it not been for that Act.[45]

Between 1841 and 1848 British Guiana imported 50,144 indentured workers - 16,047 from Madeira, 12,898 from the West Indian Islands, 12,237 from India, 8,654 from Africa and 278 from other countries.[46] On the face of it, this should have bolstered plantation productivity massively, but the influx was tainted by a major flaw, and James Stephen's hand was behind it. By an Order in Council of 1 March 1837 it was decreed that, as of 1 August 1840, (the date it was then anticipated Negro apprenticeship would be terminated) contracts for labour made outside the colony would be null and void. Another Order in Council of 7 September 1838 (framed by Stephen), besides requiring that all contracts be entered into on arrival at the colony, decreed that the validity of a verbal contract would be just 4 weeks. A written one was valid for 3 years for immigrants, and one year for persons already residing in the colony. A great many of the immigrants refused to enter into written agreements. Most of the Indians had been picked up in the bazaars of Calcutta and Madras, and were unaccustomed to field work and the vicious heat of the tropical sun. After the first 4 week period, the immigrants

---
44   Hawarden correspondence Moss to J Gladstone 8.4.1847
45   Mathieson, p54-55
46   Dwarka Nath, p36. The Madeirans, whose staple crop was the potato, fled their island in the same way the Irish did theirs during the 1840s and 1850s.

began to desert the plantations to live a wandering life and, in the case of the Madeirans, to fulfill the need for shop keepers. The Negroes, too, continued to abandon the estates. A "rough census" taken by Police in December 1848 stated the number of resident labourers on the estates was 34,622, and more than half of these were immigrants - 8,000 Indians, 6,000 Africans and 5,000 Madeiran Portuguese. The majority of the emancipated Negroes - over 40,000 - had become peasant proprietors, settled in villages.[47] Of the 46,625 immigrants who had been brought to British Guiana at the public's expense, only 19,122 were recorded as still residing on the estates.[48]

Outside of Parliament, some free-traders were suggesting the establishment, by means of properly negotiated treaties with Africa, of a regulated slave traffic along the lines of the present unregulated one, with strong safeguards to prevent overcrowding on vessels and other unnecessary hardship.[49] After all the frustrating years of reduced or non existent profit, this was a scheme which Moss endorsed. In January 1848, the colony's Negroes went on strike after refusing to accept a 25% reduction in wages. Despite their inferior physicality, the Portuguese and Indians performed the only estate labour until April, at which point the freedmen generally resumed work at a reduced rate of pay. On 26 January, clearly at the end of his tether, Moss wrote to Bentinck [50] proclaiming that *"the West Indies are doomed. Protection against slave grown sugar would do them no good unless they are supplied with African labourers."* [51] He offered a solution to the continuing shortage of suitable labour. *"I have of late been making some calculations, and I am confident nothing can save the West India Colonies to this country but "Free Trade" in labourers, and I conscientiously believe that*

---

47 Mathieson, p70
48 ibid, p80
49 Temperley, p178 quoting from an article in the Economist of 26.2.1848
50 chairman of the Select Committee on Sugar and Coffee Planting between 1847-48
51 Between 1838 and 1865 13,355 such Africans went to Guiana as contract labourers. Smith, p44

no hope is left for them, or existence for the wives and children of planters, unless they join the "Free Trade" party, and aid them in forcing Government to give up the present expensive Naval force on the coast of Africa, to allow the West India planter to supply his Estates with labourers from every part of Africa, only registering them as freemen on their arrival in the West Indies..." [52] In response to suggestions that Chinese labourers be brought to the colony, Moss was adamant *"Chinese will not do, they were tried in Trinidad, besides there is no money left in the West Indies, nor credit here for them. I am glad the crisis is come. I would not join in a Bond to send back Chinese."* [53]

Moss's prognosis for British Guiana was poor. *"I can hardly imagine that more than half the Estates will be at work in 1849. In short, I fully expect that present prices will cause all but favoured Estates to give up sugar cultivation, this induces me to persevere another year; by that time if I am not greatly mistaken, the manufacturing and agricultural interests will feel the pressure and either insist upon an Equitable adjustment or unite to protect the little property that will then be left."* He observed a similar effect in other free economies. *"The present price of sugar has stopped the works in India and will decrease sugar cultivation*

---

52 The bill for the fleet patrolling the West African coast was footed by the taxpayer. It was estimated that, between 1815 and 1845 Britain had spent £21 million in its vain attempts to suppress the slave trade while the condition of her poor had been almost entirely neglected. An argument was put forward that government should abandon the trade to the laws of supply and demand. Once the demand had been satisfied, the supply would cease. In some circles it was felt that the cost of the fleet and the protectionist measures afforded the West Indians had been a waste of taxpayers' money. Temperley, pp176-177

53 Moss to Bentinck 26.1.1848. Nonetheless, 811 Chinese set sail for British Guiana in 1853 but none were employed on *Anna Regina*. (Walton Look Lai, p292) By 1912 the number of Chinese had risen to 14,189, a mere drop in the ocean when compared to the near quarter of a million Indian immigrants. (Smith, p44) Again, history proved Moss right. The Chinese were expensive, costing about £10 more than Indian immigrants. (Cecilia McAlmont. Article in Stabroek News, 31 January 2003. British Guyana's immigration dilemma: The Chinese Experiment - Part 2) Although the initial influx of Chinese were hardworking they were far from submissive. They, more than any other category of immigrant, understood the terms of their contracts; and they proved a thorn in the planters' sides by exploiting any loopholes to the full

in Mauritius and Java."[54] His dire pessimism was prophetic. In 1849, forty one Guianan sugar estates (nearly a quarter of the whole) were either sequestrated in preparation for sale, or actually sold.[55] The value of estates collapsed. Plantation *Windsor Forest* which was valued at £85,000 during slavery, was sold (without slaves) for £45,000 in 1840, but fetched just £2,000 in 1849.[56] Only with the aid of the immigrants, particularly in the sparsely populated area on the west side of the river Essequibo where *Anna Regina* was situated, had cultivation been maintained. Without their efforts a large part of the 1849 crop would not have been harvested at all.

In June 1848, Lord John Russell had, in response to the Bentinck committee's reports of doom, agreed to postpone the final equalization of the sugar duties until 1854. Bentinck's hard work, up until his death in September 1848, helped secure a guaranteed loan of £500,000 for the West Indians to finance immigration, roads, railways and drainage.[57] Also, Africans rescued from foreign slave ships were to be conveyed to the colonies at the expense of the government. These benefits came on top of the lowering of the duty on rum from 1 shilling to 9 pence in 1847 and the reduction in wages caused by the influx of immigrant labour. The repeal of the Navigation Act in 1849 permitted the colonies for the first time to use cheaper, non British ships to deliver their produce. The conditions for a recovery had been laid down. Lower sugar prices had the positive effect of increasing Britain's consumption from 15 lb per capita in 1840 to 25 lb in 1850.[58]

Between 1841 and 1851, despite British Guiana's sugar exports having increased from 30,657 tons to 38,577 tons, the value of this produce had reduced from £953,113 to

---

54   Moss to Bentinck 26.1.1848
55   Mathieson, p72
56   Green, p235
57   ibid, p239
58   Temperley, p163

£643,134.[59] Nonetheless, the corner had now been turned and, in November 1851, Governor Henry Barkly acknowledged that the colony's position was better than it had been for many years. *"I entertain no manner of doubt that British Guiana in the course of a few years will be able to furnish an unlimited supply of tropical produce in successful competition with any country in the world."*[60] Between 1851 and 1852, imports of British produced sugar to the motherland increased by 1,250,000 cwt. At the close of 1851, the Chancellor of the Exchequer, Benjamin Disraeli, in light of the improving situation, reiterated that protection was to be allowed to run out in 1854, and Lord Stanley declared that Ministers had *"no intention at present or hereafter of renewing that differential duty which was shortly to expire"* and neither did they.[61]

It was principally Indian immigration which had resolved the labour shortage. While the Creoles performed the heavier seasonal tasks, the Indians provided the consistent labour required to keep the plantations alive. From the 1850s onwards, a much tighter regulatory structure was put in place by the Colonial Secretary, Earl Grey, (formerly Viscount Howick) to protect the planters' interests. Upon arrival in the West Indies, immigrants were required to enter into 3 year contracts, and unless they made a payment of £2 10s per year, they were obliged to work another 2 years under indenture. The planters were no longer obliged to provide them with a free homeward journey. After working out their indentures, most Indians entered into new contracts for estate labour, encouraged to do so by the planters' payment of a substantial bounty.[62] Along with their riches, those Indians who returned home took with them stories of British Guiana which, judging by the extent of future immigration, must have been extremely favourable. Between 1838 and 1865 53,652 Indians were

---

59   Look Lai, p273
60   Mathieson, p84
61   ibid, pp64-65
62    $50 according to Alan H Adamson - Sugar Without Slaves, p111

imported to British Guiana - almost double that of the next largest group of immigrants, the Madeirans, who numbered 27,413.[63] The colony's annual average sugar production which, between 1839 and 1846, had been 31,865 tons, increased to 41,790 between 1847 and 1856 and then, between 1857 and 1866, it soared to 61,284.[64] By 1917, when the indentured system ended, aggregate Indian immigration had risen to 238,960.[65] Today 50% of Guyana's population is described as East Indian, and 36% black. The religion of 50% is Christian, 35% Hindu and 10% Muslim. As well as English, other official languages include Hindi, Urdu and Creole.

Having survived those dark years in the 1840s, Moss never relinquished ownership of *Anna Regina*. Upon his death in 1858, his eldest son inherited a half share of the plantation and bought out the shares of his brothers Gilbert Winter, William Henry and John James.[66] Thomas held on to *Anna Regina* until at least 1871.[67]

---

[63] Green, p284
[64] ibid, p246
[65] Smith, p44
[66] Second codicil to the Will of John Moss, 1857. Moss made it clear that Thomas was entitled, *"at any time within twelve calendar months after my death....to purchase the one fourth shares of my said sons"*
[67] Edward Jenkins - The Coolie, His Rights and Wrongs, p281

CHAPTER 6

INCESSANT BANKING AVOCATIONS

"Banking requires more than common care, and no one is fit for a Banker until he has seen and felt bad times"

John Moss to John Gladstone - 16th June 1825.

Upon his father's death in 1805, John Moss inherited a thriving general merchant's and ship owner's business.[68] Soon he seized upon an opportunity for expansion created by the great war, begun in 1793, between Britain and France. To pay its troops and its European allies, the government sent so much of the country's gold abroad that, by 1796, the Bank of England was experiencing difficulty obtaining the gold coins it was obliged to pay, on demand, to the bearers of its bank notes. The lack of confidence caused by the war resulted in a run on the provincial banks as businesses sought to offload all types of money other than coinage. Matters were made worse by the general public hoarding their coins. In February 1797, as ever greater numbers of bankers turned to the Bank

---

68 Moss did not inherit the timber merchant aspect of Thomas's business. That was taken over by his father's partner, Richard Houghton. Hughes, p191

of England for coin, ("specie") there was a run on the Bank itself. It could satisfy demand only by paying out in silver sixpences. At the end of the month, with disaster looming, the government produced an Order in Council, in effect, declaring Bank of England notes legal tender in themselves, and no longer redeemable in gold or silver. This "Restriction Period" resulted in the establishment of a great many provincial banks - "country banks"[1] - which provided capital to business in their own localities and thereby played a crucial role in stoking the fires of the industrial revolution. The suspension of cash payments had been intended only as a temporary measure, but in fact, it continued until 1821.

The Bank of England at this time was a public bank with loyalties only to its shareholders, the British Government and its correspondent commercial bankers. It neither viewed itself as the "lender of last resort"[2] or in any way responsible for determining the quantity of money in circulation. It was under no obligation to supply money for the public's everyday needs. The lowest denomination Bank of England note in common usage was £5. Around the country, small payments, such as wages, were typically settled either in coin or in low value notes of £1 or £2, issued by the country banks themselves. In Lancashire, there was a deep suspicion of country bank notes, caused in no small part by the *"rash and wicked proceedings"*

---

[1] All banks outside of London were, until 1826, country banks, and the law restricted these to a maximum of 6 partners, each one of whom was personally liable to the full extent of his resources. The only joint stock bank in the country was the Bank of England. In theory anyone could become a country banker but, in practice, they were mostly general merchants whose long-standing wealth and integrity inspired the less wealthy with the confidence to deposit money with them. The only restrictions the law placed upon the country bankers were an obligation to register at the Stamp Office and to pay a stamp duty upon their bank notes. Every country banker (or "correspondent") held an account with, and paid commission to a London private banker (or "agent") who worked with Bank of England notes, received deposits, discounted bills and lent on securities. E V Morgan - The Theory and Practice of Central Banking 1797-1913, pp10-11

[2] Nowadays the Bank of England, as was witnessed in the banking crisis of 2007-09, can and does take responsibility for preventing the collapse of the banking system by extending credit to institutions when no one else will.

of the *"Banking bankrupts"*, Livesey, Hargreaves & Co, in 1788.[3] In that county, small payments were mostly made in specie or in the £1 and £2 Bank of England notes which were, uniquely, freely available.[4] The larger debts of the business community were often settled by way of bankers' drafts and transfers through the London agents,[5] but in Lancashire, the bill of exchange[6] was the principal means of settling, or part settling, such debts.

Moss announced his eagerness to become a country banker through an advertisement placed in *Billinge's Liverpool Advertiser*, in 1807. *"A gentleman, possessing a large disposable property, in correspondence with the very first house in London (Barclay & Co) would treat with one person, of known property, to establish a Bank at Liverpool, upon the most solid and permanent basis, by which the Public will be guaranteed against any fortuitous event."*[7] That same year the banking partnership

---

3   The words of "Country Banker" in 1793. L S Pressnell - Country Banking in the Industrial Revolution, p174

4   ibid, p179

5   J W Gilbart - Elements of Banking, p5 (1860) "Every country banker opens an account with a London banker. If then, a person lives at Penzance, and wants to send a sum of money to Aberdeen, he will pay the money into the Penzance bank, and his friend will receive it of the Aberdeen bank. The whole transaction is this: the Penzance bank will direct their agent in London to pay the money to the London agent of the Aberdeen bank, who will be duly advised of the payment. A small commission charged by the Penzance bank, and the postages, constitute all the expenses incurred, and there is not the least risk of loss"

6   This piece of paper was issued by a banker to his customer in exchange for a deposit of money. The bill could either be retained by the customer or used by him to pay a third party for goods or services. The banker was obliged to return the money with interest to either the customer or the bearer of the bill at a specified date in the future, usually anything between 90 days to 42 months. (Hughes, p41). Typically, the banker would "discount" the bill. So, having received a deposit of, say £9 and 19 shillings, he would issue a bill with a redeemable face value of £10, the difference of 1 shilling representing the interest payable. The recipient of a banker's bill implicitly expressed confidence that the banking house would still be solvent by the time the bill matured. The more the bill circulated the safer it was likely to be, carrying, as it did the guarantee of the names of the merchants and industrialists written upon it. Lewis Loyd, (sic) a Manchester banker, said he had seen bills of exchange for £10 with more than one hundred names on them: Pressnell, p173. 1826 Evidence to a Select Committee of the House of Lords.

7   Hughes, p192. Hughes attributes this to Moss though the advert does not make

of Moss, Dales and Rogers opened for business in offices at 4 Exchange Buildings. The Dales - Roger Newton Dale and George Edward Dale - were already married to Moss's sisters, Margaret and Ellen, respectively. The other partner was Edward Rogers, a Liverpool merchant, who also operated an insurance and brokerage business.[8]

Thomas Brown was one of Moss's earliest customers. This formidable character, who fought in the American Revolution on behalf of the British, was introduced to Moss by his uncle James.[9] Brown had left America in 1785 for the Bahamas, where he soon became the island's largest proprietor of slaves; James Moss was second only to him in this respect.[10] Brown returned to his native Whitby in 1802, and purchased an impressive mansion, Newton House, in the township of Ugglebarnby.[11] Six years later, he borrowed £20,000 from John Moss, and pledged to him his lifetime half-pay as lieutenant colonel. However, by 1810 the debt had risen to a staggering £35,000.[12] Between 1812 and 1814, Brown served a 2 year prison sentence for a land fraud committed in St Vincent, West Indies. By the time of his release, the debt had fallen to a still unmanageable £31,943. An agreement was struck whereby, if

---

that fact absolute.
8 ibid, pp193-194
9 Brown left Yorkshire for a new life in Savannah, Georgia in 1774; just two years before the declaration of American independence. A staunch Loyalist, he refused to sign an oath of allegiance to America. The following year, 140 American rebels surrounded his house where, after a fire fight, he was overpowered and beaten senseless. He was scalped in three places, tied to a tree and the soles of his feet burned. The Americans took Brown to Augusta where he was tarred and feathered and paraded through the town in a dung cart. Miraculously he escaped to South Carolina where he got up a force of 300 men to fight on behalf of the British, as King's Rangers. Over the final 7 years of the American Revolution, Brown took part in 17 actions in which he sustained 14 wounds. Although he rose rapidly to the rank of lieutenant colonel, his war record was horribly blemished when, at the siege of Augusta in 1778, he vindictively hanged 17 rebel prisoners and turned several others over to his American Indian allies to be burned alive. Sandra Riley - Homeward Bound: A History of the Bahamas to 1850, p120
10 as at 1802. (ibid, p190)
11 Edward J Cashin - The King's Ranger, p190
12 ibid, p202-203

this was not reduced to £15,000 by the end of June 1817, then Brown would be obliged to hand over his legitimate properties in St Vincent to Moss. However, before deadline day, he had decided that, rather than remain in England living way beyond his means, he would return to St Vincent, where his sugar plantations could provide him a decent standard of living. Instead, in settlement of the debt, Moss took possession of Newton House. A furious Brown wanted no more to do with *"that scoundrel, Moss"*. [13] Moss made good use of what he described as *"a little estate I have near Whitby"*,[14] and the house *"in the midst of the moors"*[15] was his holiday home until at least 1835.

Despite the death of Roger Dale in 1809, the fledgling bank's three remaining partners survived the commercial crisis of 1809-1810 when, it is estimated, half of Britain's traders became bankrupt.[16] In September 1811, Moss's youngest brother Henry was admitted to the partnership and, later that same month, a new building, housing the bank of *Moss, Dale, Rogers & Moss,* was completed. It stood almost opposite Liverpool town hall in Dale Street, next door to *Clarke's and Roscoe's Bank* which sat on the corner of Dale Street and Castle Street.[17] The partnership of Moss, Rogers and Moss continued to flourish after the death of George Edward Dale in 1815.[18] In the same year, following the defeat of Napoleon at Waterloo, the country's economy changed from a war time to a peace

---

13 ibid, p215
14 Hawarden correspondence Moss to J Gladstone 8.1.1825
15 Stafford correspondence Moss to J Loch 10.10.1835 (D593/K/1/3/23)
16 Hughes, pp18-20. The root cause had been the opening up of trade links with Spain and Portugal's American colonies. Vast amounts of English goods had been exported, causing shortage and price inflation at home. In many cases the goods were exported speculatively. Mercantile confidence was undermined and prices on the London stock market began to fall. Then prices of commodities began to fall and panic set in.
17 On 16 September a press notice described the structure. *"A small but very fine specimen of Doric architecture, remarkably well executed in choice freestone, is now exhibited in the building just erected at the top of Dale Street... Such structures as these, in the middle of a great town... reflect honour on the taste and spirit of their proprietors."* Hughes, p195
18 ibid, p196

time one, and the amount of money in circulation was vastly increased. This excessive supply, in turn, caused prices to spiral downward, resulting in the ruin of many businesses. Once again, Moss's bank survived the scare while others of higher repute, notably Roscoe, Clarke & Roscoe, failed.[19]

One of the functions of the more privileged banker was that of government revenue official. In Moss's case he had, for some time up until 1821, been responsible for remitting, via his London agent, taxes raised by Customs and Excise at the port of Liverpool. Prior to remittance, while these monies were under his control, he could lend out and earn interest on the vast sums raised. Before 1821, due to their own shortcomings, other Liverpool bankers had failed in the quarter yearly struggle to wrestle the position of "returners" of the Custom House receipts from Moss.[20] In that year, however, four other bankers did pose a serious threat, and the five competing bankers gave security against excise to the value of £235,000 in all.[21] In March 1822, in partnership with Ewart, Myers & co,[22] Moss, Rogers & Moss were forced to concede defeat to their largest local banking rivals, Arthur Heywood, Sons & co.[23] In the scramble to become returners in June 1823, Moss and Ewart, Myers enlisted John Gladstone's help and that of William Huskisson MP,[24] and their combined might overwhelmed the opposition.[25] At the next round of bidding, in September, Leyland & Bullins stepped up the competition

---

[19] A commission in bankruptcy was issued against William Roscoe, John Clarke and William Stanley Roscoe in January 1820. (Hughes pp64-66) By this time Roscoe had already been obliged to sell not only his enormous collection of books, pictures and prints but also Allerton Hall, his luxurious home with 153 acres of land. Although close family ties ensured a compassionate response by the Mosses to the Roscoes' misfortunes, John Gladstone, unconstrained by such bonds, unleashed a typically vitriolic attack on William Roscoe. Checkland, p193

[20] Pressnell, pp67-68

[21] ibid

[22] Its 2 partners were William Ewart and William Myers

[23] Hawarden correspondence Moss to J Gladstone 13.3.1822

[24] Hawarden correspondence Moss to J Gladstone 21.6.1823

[25] *"We can afford to do it jointly on lower terms than any other house."* Hawarden correspondence Moss to J Gladstone 25.6.1823

in a manner Moss considered suicidal. He feared that Thomas Leyland, whom he held in contempt,[26] would offer to remit the public monies to the Exchequer after 10 days. Moss considered that anything less than 15 days would render the whole exercise unprofitable, and he once again appealed to Huskisson for assistance. Huskisson was, by now, thoroughly tired of tedious banking bickering. *"Nothing since my political connection with Liverpool has given me half so much pain as the misunderstanding or whatever it be that occasioned the discussion on this subject."* [27] On 4 October, the Treasury finally ruled in favour of Ewart & Moss on the basis that, *"Of the three parties with whom that engagement was made, one alone (Ewart & Moss) was punctual and constantly efficient in the fulfilment of it. Of the two others, one has remitted scarcely any part of the Revenue and the other a very small proportion."* [28]

The matter lay settled only for a few days. The unexpected death of William Ewart on 9 October forced Moss into immediate dialogue with his banking rivals.[29] Several meetings were held, mainly at the behest of Heywood's Bank, at which it was proposed that the returner's role be shared among the town's leading bankers. Heywood's pressed Moss *"most strongly not to persevere in a contest the object and end of which, to use Mr Thompson's* [30] *frequent expression, was 'to cut our own throats'... Whatever may be the result I feel that I have done all I could to*

---

26 *"Whenever he feels piqued he will do anything to perplex and create difficulties... Customs, Excise stamps, Receiver General and Post Office... how pleased he would be to create confusion in all these branches...He has a personal dislike to Mr (Samuel) Staniforth (the stamp remitter) and he tried hard to crush poor Falkner the Receiver General a few years ago and would have done if had not some of us interfered. It is not pleasant to transact business for nothing but I should feel mortified to be entirely displaced by Mr Leyland."* Hawarden correspondence Moss to J Gladstone 18.9.1823

27 Letter to John Bolton 6.10.1823. C R Fay - Huskisson and His Age, p373

28 Herrie's ruling from the Treasury. ibid, p374

29 *"With Mr Ewart in connection with us I felt that no department of business connected with Liverpool was improperly entrusted to our charge for I considered him second to none in talent, in respectability and in security."* Hawarden correspondence Moss to J Gladstone 9.10.1823

30 Samuel Thompson had been a partner in Heywood's Bank since 1800. Hughes, p97

conciliate (and I begin to think too much so)."[31] One important consequence arising from Moss's handling of the Custom House receipts is that it, and his general conduct, so impressed Gladstone that, in December 1823, he appointed Moss his banker. Procuring the business of this famous capitalist not only enhanced the credibility of the bank but also cemented their friendship.[32]

The squabbling and intrigue continued into 1824. In April, Moss wrote of Leyland *"I am confident that he would do anything to injure his new allies Messrs Heywood & Co. He never could bear Mr H."*[33] The Hawarden correspondence on this matter, from hereon in, is repetitious and exceptionally tedious. The conclusive point to be made is that Liverpool's remittance was shared among five banks.[34] Moss informed a Select Committee of the House of Commons that, between them, they remitted around £3,500,000 in Customs and Excise duties and Post Office revenue in 1825. The Gross Profit yielded on this sum was around 6½% or £227,500.[35] In that year, however, another matter took precedence over the ongoing saga; one which would ultimately settle the question once and for all. The financial crisis of 1825 is considered by banking historians as relevant to today's policy issues because it is the first example of an emerging market-induced financial crisis and an early lesson on the importance of "lender of last resort" to the monetary authorities.

After the "Restriction Period", Britain was set up on a "gold standard", meaning that the issuers of bank notes

---

31 Hawarden correspondence Moss to J Gladstone 30.10.1823
32 Hawarden correspondence Moss to J Gladstone 8.12.1823. Moss wrote "*I never felt more gratified than I was to have your account opened with us…I assure you I cannot write what I feel for this additional mark of your good will towards me.*"
33 Hawarden correspondence Moss to J Gladstone 15.4.1824
34 Pressnell, p65. From the evidence of John Moss to a Select Committee… into… the Circulation of Promisory notes (1826). Pressnell does not state the names of the other four banks.
35 ibid

guaranteed to redeem them in a fixed weight of gold so that, for instance, the bearer of a £1 note could exchange it, on demand, for one gold sovereign, worth £1. Between 1823 and 1825, the value of banknotes in circulation increased from £26,588,000 to £41,049,000.[36] £26,069,000 were those of the Bank of England but, at the beginning of 1825, it possessed coin and bullion valued at only £8,779,000.[37] The remaining £14,980,000 of notes were those of country banks, who were at liberty to issue as many as they saw fit, without lodging any security for their ultimate payment. The excess of supply over demand caused the debasement of the currency; the £1 notes of one country bank were openly sold at 15 shillings.[38]

The over supply of money helped finance a boom in exports of English goods to the newly independent states of Latin America. Prices and profits were pushed higher and higher and, after 1823, there sprung up on the stock exchange, 532 companies (many of which were dubious and some fraudulent) eager to relieve the public of its new found wealth.[39] *"The shopkeeper ceased to toil, that he might become suddenly rich. The merchant embarked his capital and his credit; the clerk risked his reputation and his place to obtain a share of the broad golden stream, which waited to be drunk."* [40] In March 1825, apparently in an attempt to contract the amount of money in circulation, the Bank of England sold a very large block of Exchequer bills, and this caused jitters in the money market.[41] By April, the stock market boom had reached its peak, and the subsequent collapse of share prices triggered

---

36 John Francis - History of the Bank of England...from 1694-1844, p200
37 ibid, p202
38 ibid, p193
39 with a nominal capital of £441,649,600. The needs of England's industrial revolution are reflected in the numbers of mining companies (74), of gas companies (29), of railway and canal companies (54) and of steam companies (67). ibid
40 ibid
41 Exchequer Bills were a common investment used by country bankers who sold them for cash when the time came for them to remit taxes to government departments. They were usually welcomed by merchants as a secure, interest bearing, transferable, paper investment.

commercial failures.[42]

In November, panic set in and the banks were besieged by customers wishing to obtain gold in exchange for their paper money. The *Morning Chronicle* warned *"that if all persons rush to the banks to draw out their balances, which the bankers must pay instantly, while they cannot compel their debtors to pay the balances due to them, the consequences must be very serious indeed."* [43] Alarmingly, between the end of February and the beginning of December 1825, in order to honour the loans of foreign countries, £6,612,000 of coin and bullion was subtracted form the Bank's coffers, leaving it with only £2,167,000 against a paper circulation of £17,477,000.[44] Desperate country bankers begged the Bank to lend them gold to satisfy their customers' demands, but the Bank refused to act as lender of last resort. It lent selectively, and even then, only partially to the *"highest houses, equal in stability to the Bank."* [45] As a result, the country banks were the first to fall, among them the York house of Wentworth & Co, which was believed to have issued £200,000 of its own notes.[46] At the end of November, Sir William Elford's Plymouth Bank failed, with sorry consequences. *"The holders of notes crossed and jostled each other in all directions. There was literally a whole population, with food in abundance staring them in the face, unable to procure it, as nothing but gold would be taken."* [47] The failure of Pole, Thornton & Co of London, on 5 December, spelt disaster for the forty country bankers whose accounts it held. Only now, with a catastrophe on its doorstep, did the Bank begin to act, but too late to prevent 70 of England's 770 banks in town and

---

42   Moss first wrote of the impending crisis at the end of September. *"Several Houses have failed in Manchester, amongst them the House of Mr Buckley & Sons. I have not heard of any Liverpool news."* Hawarden correspondence Moss to J Gladstone 30.9.1825
43   Francis, p195
44   ibid, p202
45   ibid, p192
46   ibid, p193
47   ibid, p194

country suspending payment by Boxing Day.[48]

Country bankers from all over England visited their London banks to secure cash in anticipation of a run on their houses. The London banks turned to the Bank of England, and hundreds of thousands of sovereigns were sent to the provinces. New coins from the Royal Mint and gold from abroad were constantly arriving at the Bank. From 11 to 17 December, the country's incessant demand for gold put the Bank itself in danger, but its unhesitating readiness to pay out gold as fast as it was demanded ensured that public confidence was quickly restored and, by the 17th, the tide had turned. However, one Bank official later disclosed how close the country had come to bankruptcy. *"Another such week and the bank could not have stood it"*[49] By the 24th, its holding of coin and bullion amounted to just £1,024,000.[50] With the banking aspect of the crisis now beyond its peak, it was recognised that the want of small change, not the need for gold, had been the root cause of the problem. As if by magic, the Bank discovered a box of one million of its own £1 notes. These were despatched around the country and were received with delight by holders seeking a secure small currency. Almost immediately, these notes halted the run on the country banks. Mr Harman, another Bank official, stated *"They worked wonders; as far as my judgement goes, they saved the country."*[51] The country bankers returned hundreds of thousands of sovereigns to the Bank, unpacked and untouched. Yet the Bank of England's failure to satisfy the country's need for £1 and £2 notes was not blamed for the crisis; instead the country banks were pilloried and held universally accountable.

It is remarkable that, even by late December, Liverpool had been virtually free of crisis. Moss wrote how *"we have not*

---

48   ibid, p197
49   ibid, p201 quoting a Mr Richards.
50   ibid, p202
51   ibid, p203

had the slightest run upon us, but for the sake of being prepared for the worst we have kept by us three times our usual stock of cash and I do not mean to part with it until London recovers from its present feverish state." [52] However, if disaster were to strike, he would be ready for it. The collapse of Roscoe's and Aspinall's banks some 10 years ago, after which Moss had paid away £80,000 of money in two days, had taught him "*a good lesson...I consider no prudent banker in Liverpool should ever be without Bills and Cash by him sufficient to meet every balance he has in his hands."* [53] With such prudence, Moss could legitimately call his establishment "a bank", unlike those 63 other country bankers whose houses failed in December, and never resumed payment.[54] A morning journal of the day decreed "*If a house fails, and pays 15 shillings in the pound, a foolish cry is raised that a little reasonable help would have saved it. Saved what? A house that was, in relation to its debts, one quarter worse than nothing... Even if a banker pays 20 shillings in the pound and has no surplus afterwards, he is not a legitimate banker; he is trading without a capital, and the least mishap... may...make him insolvent."* [55]

John Gladstone had spent most of 1825 in Gloucester. In December, the Gloucester country bank of Thomas and John Turner became a victim of the crisis and suspended payments. Gladstone, having investigated its affairs, decided it was a sound concern, and was considering becoming a sleeping partner in a four way partnership with the Turners and another, each providing £10,000 of the £40,000 capital. Although the

---

52 "*Here we have all been in a state of astonishment the whole week to see the whole Commercial part of the country in a state of distress and confusion whilst we were in the most perfect composure. The only difficulty which we have had was to retain the sovereigns which the town absolutely requires...and when the Country Bankers from Yorkshire and Manchester etc etc found they could not get all they wanted from the Bankers they went to our customers and got them to give Checks upon us – which caused some little differences but upon the whole the thing went off very well. I suppose about £40,000 was spared from the Town...*" Hawarden correspondence Moss to J Gladstone 17.12.1825
53 Hawarden correspondence Moss to J Gladstone 30.12.1825
54 Francis, p203
55 ibid, p199

potential profits were enormous, so too were the potential losses in the event of failure as, in that circumstance, each partner would be held personably liable. On 30 December, Moss urged the utmost caution. *"I could not help feeling anxious that you should pause before you trusted your name and property in a business of all others the most dangerous and least profitable. I assure you I durst not remain a banker unless I could give it constant and increasing attention."*[56] The Turners, excited by the prospect of such a high profile partner, announced the agreement prematurely. In early 1826, an indignant Gladstone, now back in Liverpool, withdrew his support, and the scheme collapsed. Gladstone never became a country banker.[57]

Moss spent the first three weeks of February 1826 in London observing the ongoing crisis.[58] Although the rate of country bank failure had slowed to a trickle, the effects continued to reverberate elsewhere in the economy, where a lack of credit brought all manner of the nation's businesses down. As a consequence of falling and stagnating markets, duty payments to the Treasury had come down to *"almost nothing."* [59] The crisis had now reached Liverpool, from where Moss had heard *"the most gloomy accounts. The tradesmen cannot get their money from the Country...what a few Exchequer Bills would do at this moment."* While no banking house of any consequence had stopped payments, the distress of the town exceeded anything Moss could have imagined. On the 26th, upon returning home, he found that confidence had completely gone, and that many merchants would be unable to make their payments in March. *"The government will feel it themselves in the next quarter – our Custom House receipts are dwindled to nothing, certainly not one half of what they were."* [60]

---

56   Hawarden correspondence Moss to J Gladstone 30.12.1825
57   Checkland, pp182-183
58   Hawarden correspondence Moss to J Gladstone 6.2.1826 & 9.2.1826
59   Hawarden correspondence Moss to J Gladstone 16.2.1826
60   Hawarden correspondence Moss to J Gladstone 26.2.1826

The whole country was now in a deep depression. The government, via Prime Minister Lord Liverpool, William Huskisson and George Canning decreed that the monetary crisis had been caused by the *"mad speculation"* of the previous two years, and that *"that speculation has been mainly fostered by the vast increase in the issue of country bankers' notes...and they are chargeable with all of the disasters which have ensued."*[61] Lord Liverpool remarked, disparagingly how *"Any petty tradesman, any grocer or cheesemonger, however destitute of property, might set up a bank in any place."*[62] He was at pains, however, to point out that his comments were not directed at *all* country banks. He acknowledged that there were many as wealthy, as well established, as respectable and as solvent as any London bank. The Liverpool banks of Moss & Co, Leyland, Bullins & Co and Heywoods were, at that time, ranked amongst the greatest of the country banks.[63] Regardless, it was time for government to act. The Bank of England's coffers were refilled with coin and bullion by the sale of enormous numbers of Exchequer Bills. By April, Moss was able to detect a slight improvement in confidence.[64]

In light of the continuing lack of money, on 22 September 1826, whilst holidaying in Harrogate, Moss had the audacity to rebuff Gladstone's request to convert some Bills (no doubt amounting to a considerable sum) to cash. He suggested he send the bills to Richardson & Co who, he thought, would be able to supply the cash on better terms.[65] Gladstone's response was immediate and, apparently, ferocious. On the 27th, still in

---

61 Francis, p202
62 E V Morgan - The Theory and Practice of Central Banking 1797-1913, p11
63 Pressnell, p177
64 Hawarden correspondence Moss to J Gladstone 6.4.1826. *"Money is certainly much easier than it was, but by no means what can be called plentiful – sovereigns have been very abundant which cause persons here who know nothing of the transactions of a Banking House to suppose that it is very abundant. As far as I can judge from our own customers I should say they are not full of money and the acceptances we are now paying are considerably heavier than they were this time last year."*
65 Hawarden correspondence Moss to J Gladstone 22.9.1826. *"I beg you will not hesitate to get your cash wherever you can get it cheapest."*

Harrogate, Moss was forced into a grovelling retreat. *"I regret particularly that the effect of the Harrogate water should be to make me write to you when I was in a disturbed state...In replying to your letter I thought it necessary to give some explanation of the reasons why we did not comply with your wishes or rather proposal. I fear I have done it in too serious a manner......I am very much obliged to you for your observations about your account and nothing can be more satisfactory than the manner in which you keep it and I consider the respectability of having such an account as yours quite as valuable as the commissions."*[66]

It was hoped that a permanent solution to the country's "boom and bust" economy would be found by the Banking Act of 1826. A squeeze was put on the nation's country bankers. The Act forbade the issue of any new £1 and £2 notes by them or by the Bank, and all existing Bank notes of those denominations were to be removed from circulation by March 1829. It permitted the formation of note issuing, joint-stock banks, anywhere outside a 65 mile radius of London. Although liability was still to be unlimited, the number of partners among whom the risk could be spread would no longer be restricted to just 6. With liability potentially spread among hundreds of shareholders the risk of failure would be substantially reduced. For the convenience of public and government alike, the Act also authorised the establishment of provincial branches of the Bank of England. Thereby gold and Bank notes could be made more readily available, and consequently Lancashire's traditional circulation of bills of exchange would be discouraged. The Bank's first Liverpool branch opened in 1827, taking over the remittance of all revenues (including the Customs House receipts) and directly crediting them to the government's London account. Furthermore, the branch stole much of the private Liverpool bankers' business by discounting at 4% as against the Liverpudlians' 3½%. Neither did the Bank's branches charge customers a commission on

---

66 Hawarden correspondence Moss to J Gladstone 27.9.1826

their transactions. The country banks begrudgingly abandoned that practice too. Moss sneered. *"Banking is very pleasant in good times but there are occasional storms which require experience to get through, such as the Governors of the Bank know nothing."* [67]

In May 1828, with the 1833 renewal of the Bank of England's charter up for discussion, Moss met the Prime Minister as a member of a concerned Committee of Country Bankers. The Duke of Wellington granted them an audience of nearly half an hour. In light of the problems caused them by the 1826 Bank Act, they sought reassurances against future acts of discrimination. *"He seemed well disposed towards us and promised that our interests shall be attended to when the Bank Charter expires."* [68] The committee stated that, if government intended to make the country bankers responsible for holding gold reserves equivalent to their note issues, then they would relinquish their issue altogether. The other major matter they brought to the Duke's attention was that the Bank's branches held a particularly unfair advantage over the country bankers in regard to payment of stamp duties on bills of exchange. [69] These were soon equalised.

With Moss heavily involved in other projects, most notably the Liverpool & Manchester Railway, (for which his company were bankers) his time in the bank's offices was limited; its day to day running was now Henry's responsibility.[70] Henry's son Cottingham had, in 1827, been taken on as the fourth partner.[71] By 9 September 1830, with the opening of the railway imminent, it appeared the 1826 initiatives had

---

67 Hawarden correspondence Moss to J Gladstone 27.1.1827
68 Hawarden correspondence Moss to J Gladstone 13.5.1828
69 Equalisation was delivered by Act 9 George IV. cap 23 (1828), prior to which the cost of a circulation of £10,000 a year in £20 bills of exchange was only £35 to the Bank, but £650 to the country banker. Hughes, p33
70 *"I have written this while looking at Business for I have charge of the Bank to-day. Henry Moss is at Southport."* Hawarden correspondence Moss to J Gladstone 23.10.1830
71 Margaret Davies & CN Ward-Perkins - "Country Banks of England and Wales", pp340-341

brought about the desired economic stability. Moss observed that *"Trade is increasing very rapidly and all doing well. I never saw it in my mind more healthy, and merchants are not so fearful of changes."*[72] This was but a brief moment of calm in the general economic chaos of the times. On 16 May 1831 the Bank of Liverpool, the first joint stock bank with its Head Office in the town, opened its doors onto this volatile world, under the chairmanship of William Brown.[73] Moss, sceptical of all joint stock banks, commented *"They will do no good to the shareholders but some injury to us. The joint stock bank at Manchester has just made bad debt of £12,000 – and I am told the one at Birmingham has lost £50,000."*[74] He wrote disapprovingly, of the Bank of England and its branch, too. *"The Bank have raised their rates. In some instances this should not be. No man is safe while the Bank raises and falls its price of money – for the value of money affects every aspect of commerce."*[75]

In 1832, before a House of Commons Select Committee, the Committee of Country Bankers went on the offensive, criticising the *"cumbrous"* joint stock banks for lacking the *"accommodating spirit of private banks...in times of distress."*[76] They argued that such accommodation could only be provided by the country bankers, based on their intimate knowledge of the character of their customers. City bankers were criticised too, for their same lack of accommodation.[77] The country bankers highlighted the *"objectionable mode*

---

72 Hawarden correspondence Moss to J Gladstone 9.9.1830
73 Barclays Bank - 150 Years of Banking in Liverpool (1831-1981), p2. The Manchester and Liverpool District Bank had been the first joint stock to commence trading in Liverpool, on 1 December 1829 - Hughes, p34
74 Hawarden correspondence Moss to J Gladstone 17.5.1831
75 ibid
76 House of Commons Secret Committee on the Bank of England Charter (published 1833) - "A Digest of the Evidence of the Bank Charter, taken before the committee of 1832", pp150-151
77 ibid. *"Loans, on personal character, sustained by a belief in the responsibility of the borrower, are seldom made by London bankers, who do not usually advance upon the personal security of the individual, without other security, nor for an undefined period, as country bankers do."*

of acquiring business by joint stock banks" [78] which tempted customers by transferring bank shares to their name and by transacting business at unsustainably cheap rates. With the Bank's provincial branches also undercutting them, the profits and viability of country banks were undermined, and the consequence for the nation, they argued, could only be further economic distress. The Bank itself was accused of being in cahoots with the joint stocks. By law they could not draw a bill on London for less than £50; could not make their bills payable in London or draw on a firm immediately connected with them in London *"but, in practice, The Bank of England allows these restrictions to be set aside."* [79] The supposed stability provided by the joint stocks' spread of risk was a fallacy. *"When such companies become insolvent, they throw every legal obstacle in the way of their creditor."* Resistance to a claim might be put up for 18 months or 2 years, so that creditors unable to meet the expense of litigation would go without payment.[80] They believed all such companies to be bad *"but the banking joint stock companies are the most mischievous of all. They are peculiarly liable to abuse and mismanagement."* [81] In the event of a joint stock failure, its business would have been so ill conducted, they argued, that it would be very difficult for another bank to take up its accounts.[82] The proposed withdrawal of country notes would greatly impede industry in the provinces, and the Bank would find it impossible to make up that lost circulation.[83] If the Bank of England were to become the sole issuer of notes, then *"the minor channels of circulation would be greatly impoverished, and small transactions embarrassed"* [84] as it was proposed that there should be no intermediate note or coin between £5 and silver coin.[85] While not advocating

---

78   ibid
79   ibid, p152-153
80   ibid, p151
81   ibid
82   ibid, p153
83   ibid, pp148-149
84   ibid, p154
85   ibid, p159. Despite this, nine out of ten country bankers were opposed to the

equilibrium, the committee considered it dangerous, too, for the Bank to hold so low a proportion of gold to paper as it did.[86] Furthermore, the secrecy of its banking system had excluded country bankers from important information.[87] If, in future, they were to be informed of the amount of gold coming into and out of the country, then they might be able to help avert disaster by contracting their issue.[88] It became apparent to Parliament that the country bankers were a responsible, prudent body deserving of far greater respect than previously afforded them.

In early 1833, with his Oxford education at Christ Church complete, at the age of 21, Thomas Moss joined John, Henry and Cottingham in the now exclusively family run bank. Mr Rogers, who had been very unwell for some time, retired.[89] It was apparent that Gladstone approved of the appointment. Moss wrote, on the 17 January, *"I am much gratified with your remarks about my son. He certainly is the steadiest person I ever met of his age. Besides he will always have me and Henry at his elbow."*[90]

The Bank Charter Act of 1833 imposed no additional restrictions on the country bankers.[91] Although the Bank was obliged to pay gold on demand, the Act made its notes legal tender. It became the Bank's responsibility to maintain a metallic reserve equal to one third of its liabilities; a responsibility

---

Bank issuing notes under £5 on the grounds that, *"from experience...all great demands upon the banks have commenced through the demand for small notes, and been created by their holders, who were the first seized with alarm."* ibid, p160

86   Perhaps, they suggested, it would be preferable for silver to be made the standard of value *"because people would not rush for it with avidity, and it is not so portable, or easily kept, or fashionable, and it is more easily obtained."* ibid, p159

87   ibid

88   The availability of more and better information would help create *"a sort of identity of action between them."* ibid, p158

89   Hawarden correspondence Moss to J Gladstone 12.1.1833

90   Hawarden correspondence Moss to J Gladstone 17.1.1833

91   The Bank of England's charter was renewed until 1855, but the government granted itself the power to suspend the Bank's privileges any time up to 1 August 1844, on giving one year's notice.

it struggled to fulfil.[92] The country bankers interpreted this aspect as absolving themselves of any duty to maintain the gold reserve. To aid management of the economy, the Bank was now obliged to provide the Treasury exact accounts of the amount of its bullion, the number of notes in circulation and of the total of its deposits. Amongst other measures, the Act also permitted the establishment of none note issuing joint stock banks in London, a measure viewed by the Bank as a threat to their business. Although joint stock banks were slow to achieve success, by 1833 their number had grown, nationally, to 32.[93]

The three years following the Act were a time of great prosperity, and Moss's Grand Junction Railway (for which Moss & Co were bankers) benefited from the great speculation in new companies, many of which, as in 1825, proved entirely futile. With abundant harvests and competition from the joint stock banks, credit was made available at lower rates of interest. The important distinction between 1825 and the latest boom was that, initially, the investment was almost entirely made in British and Irish enterprises, (particularly mining and railway companies) so that there was little drain on the nation's bullion. This all changed in 1835 with an explosion in speculation in South American, Spanish and Portuguese bonds. In addition, the decision of the United States to establish a metallic currency assisted in draining the Bank's bullion reserves from an average of £10,900,000 in October 1833 to £6,150,000 in June 1835.[94] Yet, in August, by reducing its rate of discount (in essence its interest rate) from 4% to 3½ %, the Bank actually gave stimulus to the frenzy.

The boom in stock market speculation reached its height in the spring of 1836. By August of that year, the Bank had

---

92 On 9 September 1834, for example, the reserve was £7,010,000 against liabilities of £31,058,000. A Andreades - History of the Bank of England, pp261-265
93 E V Morgan, p17
94 Francis, p240

raised its rate of interest to 5%, causing too sudden a contraction of the currency and panic in the country. At the same time, the Bank reduced its loans by refusing to discount the bills of joint stock banks whose proliferation it cited as the cause of the expansion of credit and of the manic speculation. Between 1832 and 1835 thirty four new joint stock banks had been established and, in 1836 alone, a further 44 more commenced trading; in total there were now 200 such banks with 670 branches.[95] Of the seven private Liverpool banks in existence in 1830, one had, by now, failed and two had converted themselves into joint stocks. The remaining four showed astonishing vitality and resisted the popular nationwide wave of conversion.[96] Moss wrote, on 10 September *"I am told we must either make ours a joint stock bank or secede. I intend to wait and see, as you say, the result."* [97]While Leyland had lost the prized account of Sir John Tobin (an eminent merchant and ship owner) to the Royal Bank, Moss had not lost any significant account to joint stock banks. Although, many customers threatened to move to a joint stock when Moss asked them to relieve their accounts, only a few (of the worst kind) actually defected. *"They have got two or three from me which I think they would now willingly return if they could."* [98]

The Bank of England was now refusing to discount an immense number of bills drawn from America, a measure Moss supported despite the fact that Lancashire's commercial houses were particularly highly involved in American investments.[99] To do so would have fuelled the crisis and *"The American Houses would soon have sent all the gold out of the country."* [100] With Henry absent from Dale Street due to illness, Moss viewed the chaos as ideal training for his newest recruit. *"I want Tom*

---

95   ibid, p243
96   Hughes, p34
97   Hawarden correspondence Moss to J Gladstone 10.9.1836
98   Hawarden correspondence Moss to J Gladstone 14.11.1836
99   Andreades, p266
100 Hawarden correspondence Moss to J Gladstone 10.9.1836

Moss to see the real duties of a banker in a storm. I would rather he got into a few scrapes now that he may profit by them when I can no longer be consulted." [101] Having a *"perfect recollection of 1810, 1819 and 1825"*[102] Moss regarded the current crisis and the Bank of England's poor management of it, with horror.[103] In November, the joint stock Northern and Central Bank of Manchester stopped payments. This company, in fairness the exception rather than the rule, adopted all the worst aspects of malpractice that the delegation of country bankers had complained of in 1832. Among its many failings was the fact that not one of its board of directors had any previous knowledge of banking.[104] Ignorance was one shortcoming but dishonesty was another. Between them these directors owed the Northern and Central Bank in excess of £200,000, and the principal security for these advances consisted of shares in that same Northern and Central Bank which they had allotted themselves at below market price.[105] Despite its incompetence and crookedness, this bank operated branches in 39 towns, and its failure would have proven so disastrous that the Bank of England, which had at first refused it assistance, was eventually forced to make advances totalling £1,370,000 to save it.[106] This further depleted the Bank's gold stocks. It was, by now, spectacularly failing in its duties; its gold reserves, which should have equated to one third of its liabilities, stood at £3,640,000 as against liabilities of £30,941,000.[107]

In January 1837, the Bank came to the assistance of London's American houses which, it transpired, were solvent but unable to meet the demand made upon them at that

---

101 Hawarden correspondence Moss to J Gladstone 14.11.1836
102 ibid
103 *"But the Bank of England is more to blame than any of them. The Bank of England instead of acting like a prudent nurse, and keep them from harm, took them to the edge of the precipice and is now doing all she can to push them over."* ibid
104 E Victor Morgan, p19
105 Francis, p248
106 Andreades, p266 & Francis, p241
107 Andreades, p265

particular time. It boldly advanced them £6m, a move which not only averted a terrible crash but which brought an influx of gold after the Americans made swift repayments. [108] On 26 April, Moss noted that things were decidedly better and that confidence was beginning to be restored. *"I have so far escaped as a Banker without making a single bad debt. If I am equally fortunate for the next 2 months I think you will say I understand more things than rail road making."* [109] By March 1838, the Bank of England's correct ratio of coin and bullion to liabilities had been restored, (£10,527,000 to £31,573,000)[110] and the crisis appeared to be over…it was not. The harvests that year were very bad, and imports of £10m of corn led to a great outflow of gold. Towards the end of 1838, the Bank of Belgium suspended payments, the Bank of France turned to London for money to withstand a run on it, and American currency reform caused a further drain on English gold. By July 1839, with its reserves down to £2,987,000 the Bank of England was staring insolvency in the face.[111] However, having now recovered from its own near demise, the Bank of France stepped in to save the day.[112] Moss wrote that *"The directors of the Bank of England are very nervous. They do not understand the management of such a bank as theirs."* [113] By the end of October, despite the continuing crisis, once again Liverpool's private banks remained robust. There had not been a single banking failure.[114]

---

108 ibid, p266
109 Hawarden correspondence Moss to J Gladstone 26.4.1837
110 Andreades, p267
111 ibid, p268
112 To facilitate the exchange, Baring Brothers drew bills of exchange in a sum of £2m on twelve Parisian bankers, and a further £900,000 was secured from Hamburg in a similar way. ibid
113 Moss could sense that the tide had turned and the private banks were now *"the favourites."* Hawarden correspondence Moss to J Gladstone 26.8.1839
114 Reports said they had £600,000 under discount. *"Their chairman wanted to persuade me that they were ill used. I told him that if I was at the heart of the bank that I should be much more restricted, that I thought all Country Banks ought to take in sail when the Bank of England did. In confirmation of which I told him I had not sent the Bank of England one Bill in since they altered the rate to 6%."* Hawarden correspon-

The Hawarden correspondence from the closing months of 1839 until John Gladstone's death in 1851 is, in relation to the subject of banking, almost non-existent, and therefore only the briefest of details of subsequent developments must suffice.

There was another panic at the end of 1839. A growing body of economists was of the opinion that notes issued in the provinces, and the Bank of England's own circulation, ought to correspond at all times to the amount of gold in the Bank. As it stood, the fluctuations in provincial circulation did not correspond with the fluctuations of either the gold or of the notes of the Bank of England, and it was assumed that this was the cause of the latest panic. Joint stock banks continued to proliferate at the expense of the private banks. By 1842, they numbered 117 as against the 311 private country banks whose numbers had fallen from 554 in 1825.[115] The economy lurched from crisis to crisis and, between 1839 and 1843, sixty three country banks (including 29 note issuing ones) had to suspend payments.[116] The joint stock banks were made the whipping boys for the economy's ills when the Bank of England's Charter was reviewed. The intention of the Bank Charter Act of 1844 was that the Bank of England should eventually become the sole bank of issue. The Act decreed that any *new* notes the Bank issued would have to be backed by a corresponding increase in its gold reserve. There were to be no new banks of issue. Any country bank now converting itself into a joint stock would lose its right to issue. If two issuing banks were to merge then one of them would lose its issue and if, for any reason, any bank ceased to issue, it would not be permitted to resume. Before the Act was passed, 42 banks, by virtue of agreements struck with the Bank of England, had ceased to issue their notes - Moss & Co among them.[117] This

---

dence Moss to J Gladstone 29.10.1839
115 Crick, W F & Wadsworth, J E - A Hundred Years of Joint Stock Banking, p21
116 Andreades, p268
117 At some indeterminate stage in the past, Moss & Co commenced issuing their own notes as their name appears in Section 23 of the Act as one of the 42 banks which

Act ensured that, for the next 13 years, only a small handful of new joint stock banks opened, and the restrictions it placed on them helped arrest the demise of the country banks until 1857, when it was repealed.

No doubt, had the Act of 1844 not been passed, the blame for the wildly speculative Railway Mania years of 1845 to 1847 would have been heaped upon the excessive issue of the joint stock and country banks. Annual investment in railway stock increased from £60m in 1845 to £132m in 1847.[118] The failure of the 1845 and 1846 potato crop both here and in Ireland added fuel to the fire. In the hope of averting starvation, great quantities of bullion left the country in exchange for foreign corn.[119] By January 1847, Moss could foresee another disaster looming. Nonetheless, he was confident Moss & Co would ride the storm. *"A Banker does require more eyes than other men. Still we find our profits very ample, more than I ever expected and seldom any losses."*[120]

The 1844 Act had restricted interior note circulation in exact proportion to the export of bullion, so that it now became virtually impossible to convert bills into cash. Many merchants speculated on the high price of grain, but the vast quantities imported, together with the prospect of a good harvest of corn and potatoes for 1847, led to a spectacular fall in the price of cereals, which had reached a high of 131 shillings in May.[121] In August, 13 businesses related to the corn trade failed. By October, the price of corn was just 49 shillings, 6 pence[122] bringing ruin to the speculating firms,

---

received compensation for their loss of issue. James William Gilbert - A Practical Treatise on Banking, p475

118 Andreades, p132

119 Between 1845 and 1847 imports of wheat increased from 3.7m cwts to 11.5m cwts, of wheat meal and flour from 945,000 cwts to 6.3m cwts, and of maize from 241,000 cwts to 15.4m cwts. ibid, p331

120 ibid

121 Andreades, p335

122 ibid

which failed with total liabilities of £15m.[123] On 2 October, the Bank of England raised its discount rate to 5½ % and announced that no advance would be paid on Exchequer Bills. This caused a panic on the stock exchange, and the public began withdrawing notes and coins from the banks to hoard them. On the back of failures on the Liverpool Stock Exchange running at three or four a day,[124] the banks began to buckle and the joint stock Royal Bank of Liverpool failed on 18 October.[125] Moss expressed surprise that the Royal, along with other *"reckless"* joint stocks, had held out that long.[126] Its failure pulled down more businesses and caused a run on the other banks, a situation Moss was more than ready for, *"having collected very large amounts of cash for some time previous"*[127] to cope with the over-inflated demand. Once again, his knowledge of all the previous crises stood him in good stead. This crisis, he thought, resembled 1793 (which his father had told him all about) more than any other period, except that the private banks then were far more involved with the circulation of paper money.

On 23 October 1847, the Bank of England's reserve of notes fell to just £1,176,000. There was a clamour for the Act of 1844 to be suspended so that notes could be issued in excess of the limit stipulated in it. Sir Charles Wood, Chancellor of the Exchequer, wrote to the Governor of the Bank of England on 25 October authorising the increase in discounts and loans. In the Commons, on 30 November, Wood said *"Let us have notes... We don't mean, indeed, to take the notes, because we shall not want them; only tell us that we can get them, and this will at once restore confidence."* [128] His words proved prophetic. The Bank prepared £400,000 of additional notes which were

---

123 ibid
124 John B Neilson, a Liverpool stock broker, to Robertson Gladstone 18.10.1847 – Hawarden miscellaneous correspondence
125 Barclays Bank - 150 Years of Banking in Liverpool (1831-1981), p4
126 Hawarden correspondence Moss to J Gladstone 22.10.1847
127 ibid
128 Andreades, p336

never needed, but the effect was an immediate restoration of confidence. Notes and bullion came out of their hiding places so that the Bank's own reserves of both soon reached adequate amounts. The panic ceased, but the events of October and November had caused the failure of 334 businesses, 54 of them Liverpool houses.[129]

Others may have considered this latest crisis a tragedy, but more tragic for Moss were the deaths of his daughter Margaret in April 1846 and of his brother James in September 1847.[130] By now his banking partnership had swelled to five family members, with the admission of his third born son William Henry.[131] Having survived the financial tempest of 1847, 1848 dealt the Moss family another two savage blows. The seeds of Henry Moss's demise were sown in the Irish Potato Famine, which resulted in Liverpool's native population being swamped by the arrival of 296,331 Irish refugees (of whom 116,000 were half naked and starving)[132] between January and December 1847.[133] A major typhus epidemic spread with lightning speed through the huddled masses living in the city's damp cellars.[134] Although Dale Street was, in the 1840s, the

---

129 George Chandler - Four Centuries of Banking, p278 & ibid
130 James was born 20 March 1783, died 24 September 1847. Burke, p1046
131 Banker's Almanac 1846
132 The *Liverpool Mercury* of 10 January 1846 reported that *"at no former period of dearth and destitution have such multitudes of naked and houseless wretches been seen on our streets imploring relief from the inhabitants as at present."*
133 Frank Neal - 'Liverpool, the Irish steamship companies and the famine Irish', *Immigrants and Minorities*, V (1986), p34
134 "(Typhus) attacks the small blood vessels of the body, especially those of the skin and brain, and the patient becomes all but unrecognisable; the circulation of his blood is impeded, his face swells, and he turns the dark congested hue which gave typhus its Irish name of 'black fever'. The patient's temperature rises, in a severe case his limbs twitch violently; he raves in delirium, throws himself about; as the fever becomes intense and his body burns he is apt to jump out of the window, or plunge into a river in search of coolness; the rash appears from which typhus derived its former name of 'spotted fever'. Meanwhile the patient is in acute pain - he vomits, develops agonising sores and sometimes gangrene, followed by the loss of fingers, toes and feet. A loathsome symptom is the odour from the typhus patient, described by William Bennett of the Society of Friends, as 'an almost intolerable stench'." Cecil Woodham Smith - The Great Hunger, p189 Reproduced by kind permission of Penguin Group

main road into the town and, on the face of it, most elegant, behind it lay dreadful slums. In the Dale Street sub district alone, typhus claimed 804 lives in the second quarter of 1847, and 747 in the third.[135] In the whole of Liverpool 5,239 people died of the fever that year. For Henry and Cottingham, there was no alternative but to brave the diseased throngs on their way to work at the bank. Although, by the end of the year, the death rate was on the decline, the epidemic rolled into 1848. On 24 February, Cottingham's sudden and unexpected death, at the age of 35, was unsatisfactorily explained by his physician as *"Spasm of the muscles of larynx. 3 days"*. [136] Henry was, by this time, living a long way from home at *"Severn Bank, Severn Stoke, Worcestershire"*[137] having been transported, no doubt in serious ill health, to take the waters of nearby Malvern. While great advances had been made in the field of hydrotherapy[138] Henry, weakened by a chronic heart condition,[139] was in need of much stronger medicines yet to be discovered. He finally succumbed to the horrors of typhus fever on 8 March, at the age of 57.[140]

Moss's correspondence concerning his banking activities ceases here and, regrettably, the HSBC's London archives hold

---

(UK) - Penguin General Division

135 Frank Neal – Black '47, p138

136 Death certificate DYA 322802 (COL183949) The *Liverpool Mercury* revealed that he died "*at his residence, Aigburth*" The *Liverpool Mail* Obituary on 26 February stated that "*Mr Moss caught cold in returning from hunting on Monday last, which, although not considered of any serious nature at first, resulted in acute inflammation of the windpipe, which medical aid could not subdue…The deceased gentleman was universally respected by all who had the pleasure of his acquaintance, and there were few of the leading, enterprising and rising men in Liverpool who had so many admirers and friends.*"

137 Codicil on 27 February 1848 amending original will of 25 November 1837

138 not least at Malvern where, in 1842, Doctor James Wilson began to advertise his self proclaimed "water cure" at a cost of between £4 and £5 a week. The curative properties of the waters of England's spa towns were somewhat overestimated by the Victorians.

139 Hawarden correspondence Moss to Gladstone 14.11.1836 "*Henry Moss is absent having gone to London to consult some MD respecting some very unpleasant feelings about the heart*"

140 Death certificate of Henry Moss DYA 325084 (COL183083) Henry was born 17 May 1790. Burke, p1046

no relevant records of Moss & Co prior to the 1860s, so it is not known how the bank reorganised itself following the loss of two such important partners. It would be safe to assume that Moss, although in his mid 60s, played a major role in steadying the ship. After all, he had successfully navigated his independent family House through 40 of the most turbulent years in British banking history. No "run of the mill" banker would ever have risen to Moss's position as lobbyist for the nation's country bankers. In so doing he had helped shape key banking legislation. Throughout the 1850s, despite his incessant banking avocations, Moss would probably have delegated ever more responsibility to his sons, so that, by the time of the next major financial crisis in 1857, (which caused widespread failures on both sides of the Atlantic) they may have coped without too much reliance on their 75 year old father. In that year the Bank Charter Act was repealed and new measures were introduced, which resulted in the rapid expansion of joint stock banks with vast nationwide systems of branches. The country banks simply could not compete with the wide range of services on offer, and they began to disappear. Such was the fate of Moss & Co. After Moss's death in October 1858, and that of his 34 year old son William Henry,[141] two months later, his remaining sons Thomas and Gilbert assumed joint control of the bank. They converted it into the joint stock North Western Bank in April 1864, and Thomas became its first chairman.[142] So it was that the internationally renowned banking name of Moss disappeared for ever. The North Western was swallowed up, in October 1897, by the giant London and Midland Bank which we know today as HSBC.

---

141 Burke, p1046
142 Hughes, p200

James Loch

William Huskisson

Sir John Gladstone

Henry Moss by T Hargreaves (1820)

The Bank of Moss, Dale, Rogers and Moss on Dale Street, Liverpool (1811)

John Moss by Charles Baugniet (1856)

Otterspool House by Isaac Shaw (1847)

Otterspool House by Isaac Shaw (1847)

CHAPTER 7

THE LIVERPOOL AND MANCHESTER RAILWAY

"When I come to look at the difficulties we had to encounter at the first commencement...I am astonished how 3 insignificant merchants (for there was but 3 planned all the work) without influence or experience, succeeded in carrying a measure against what we had to contend with."

John Moss to James Loch – 21st April 1836

In July 1821, William James of West Bromwich, a wealthy and influential London based land agent, was introduced to Liverpool corn merchant Joseph Sandars. James had harboured plans to build railways since 1799,[1] and Sandars told him of his own desire to establish a rail link between Liverpool and Manchester. Having already laid down short roads to haul iron and coal at his Warwickshire mines,[2]

---

1 E.M.S Paine – The Two James's and the Two Stephensons, p19. James first opened his mind to the idea of forming a railroad from Liverpool to Manchester in around 1803

2 Samuel Smiles - The Story of the Life of George Stephenson, Railway Engineer, p148 (1860)

James was able to convince Sandars of the feasibility of his railway scheme, and offered to survey the route. Sandars, after conferring with his friend John Moss,[1] authorised James to proceed, for a fee of £300.[2] Sandars, Moss and James appeared as advocates of the measure at public meetings in numerous towns along the way to Manchester.[3] Theirs was a revolutionary idea. Previously, railways had only been in operation at mines, where wagons were pulled very slowly along short stretches of track by ropes attached to horses or to fixed steam engines. James, though, had seen one of George Stephenson's primitive locomotive engines[4] pulling coal wagons at 6 miles an hour, and proposed that locomotive power be the means of traction on the Liverpool to Manchester road. Nobody, not even Stephenson, could possibly have foreseen the huge economic and sociological benefits which locomotives and railways would bestow upon Britain and the rest of the world.

At a meeting in the summer of 1822, a Provisional Committee of the Liverpool and Manchester Railway was established, and Moss was elected chairman. The merchants of these two rapidly expanding towns were incensed by the exorbitant charges levied by canal companies and by the lavish profits they made from inefficiently ferrying freight. Of greatest concern was the Bridgewater canal - the main artery between the towns. The industrialization of the Midlands and North West England had resulted in ever increasing quantities of goods from all over Britain and the Americas pouring into the port of Liverpool, where bottlenecks caused unacceptable delays to inland conveyances. The Bridgewater transported raw materials upstream to the factories of Lancashire and, via the Trent and Mersey (or Grand Trunk) Canal and other connecting

---

[1] Samuel Smiles - Lives of the Engineers, with an Account of their Principal Works, p184
[2] Smiles - Life of Stephenson, p148 (1860)
[3] ibid, p149
[4] at Killingworth Colliery, Northumberland in the summer of 1821.

waterways, to the Potteries and the Midlands.[5] Merchants had already petitioned Robert Haldane Bradshaw, the despotic Superintendent of the Bridgewater Trust, to reduce rates of carriage on the canal, but to no avail. Bradshaw's role was to sustain the enormous income which his master, the Marquis of Stafford,[6] drew as owner of the canal. Without hope of conciliation, the railway committee announced their intention to approach Parliament with a Bill for the building of the rail road the following year.[7] James tried to press ahead with his survey but was hampered, not only by formidably wealthy canal proprietors but also by turnpike operators, coach operators, landowners and farmers. He was further impeded, in November 1822, by a 3 month prison sentence,[8] and was later diverted by his involvement with the Bolton & Leigh Railway and another being planned between Portsmouth and Chatham.[9] He found himself incarcerated again between May and October 1823.[10] Although he insisted his plans and the survey were complete, they were never received by the committee, who now strove to distance themselves from him. Jesse Hartley, Engineer to the Liverpool Docks Board, was asked to resurvey the line, and submitted his report in the spring of 1824. It was only then that the committee, all busy businessmen in their own right, began to invest the necessary time and effort to undertake their highly complicated task. In early May, they appointed George Stephenson as James' replacement.

At a meeting on 20 May 1824, Moss was appointed chairman of the Permanent Committee of the Liverpool &

---

5 Manufactured goods were sent back down stream for consumption and eventually to Liverpool for export

6 The Marquis of Stafford, George Granville Leveson-Gower, had become the owner of the Bridgewater canal upon the death of the Duke of Bridgewater in 1803. The old Duke's will decreed that control of the Bridgewater canal's affairs be placed in the hands of three Trustees, but in practice it came under the command of only one – Bradshaw

7 RHG Thomas - The Liverpool & Manchester Railway, p15

8 arising out of a financial dispute with his brother in law. ibid, p17

9 ibid

10 ibid

Manchester Railway. The new committee members, some of whom had seen Stephenson's steam engines at work at Hetton colliery, near Sunderland, and examined his Stockton & Darlington Railway under construction, declared themselves unanimously in favour of employing locomotives on the proposed railway.[11] Four days later, they resolved to form a joint stock company to construct the line as soon as government authorised it. The estimated £300,000[12] cost of the project was to be funded by the sale of 3,000 shares at £100.[13] To dispel any suggestion of profiteering, it was announced that no subscriber would be allowed more than 10 shares.[14] The full £100 was not to be paid at once, but in "calls" (or instalments), and the first call of £3 per share, to cover the expense of obtaining an Act of Parliament, was made immediately. The committee began the task of canvassing support nationwide.

On 1 June, Moss wrote seeking the support of the Common Council of the Borough of Liverpool. He complained that the port's merchants had, for many years, experienced great difficulties and obstructions in carrying out their business, not just because of the canals' high charges but also due to their inability to supply vessels at all – frequently for days on end. These problems were a direct result of the monopolies enjoyed by two carrying companies - the Old Quay and the trustees of the late Duke of Bridgewater.[15] Moss claimed that a railway would reduce conveyance charges by 25% and that the time which goods spent in transit would reduce by almost 75%.[16] Goods could no longer be damaged by water, nor would there

---

11 So far Stephenson's unparalleled engineering feats included the construction of several colliery wagon-ways, almost 40 stationary steam engines and around 16 steam locomotives. Frank Ferneyhough - The Liverpool & Manchester Railway 1830-1980, p16
12 £21,885,031 in 2008 using the Retail Price Index
13 £7,295 in 2008 using the Retail Price Index
14 T Baines - The History of Liverpool, p600
15 Robert E Carlson – The Liverpool and Manchester Railway Project 1821 to 1831, pp266-268
16 ibid

be delays caused by floods, droughts, frosts or storms. He stressed that railways would bring *"incalculable advantages to the country; and to this town in particular, and to the revenue of the corporation, the benefits will be immense."* [17] When the *"great public benefit"* railways brought about became apparent, he believed that canal proprietors would *"submit without resistance."* [18] The council, whose opinion was evenly divided, met on 2 June to discuss the proposal. The Tory mayor Charles Lawrence informed Moss that, when his plans were more advanced, the council might be more receptive to them and would give the general subject further consideration.

Upon receipt of this response, the committee reconvened and Moss decided to relinquish the chairmanship. His obituary states that he did so *"in order that the advantage and the influence of the Liverpool Mayoralty, then filled by Mr. Charles Lawrence"* [19] might enhance its chances of success. Thomas, the railway biographer, considered that Moss felt temperamentally unfit to guide the committee through the stresses and strains which lay ahead,[20] while Carlson suggested that Moss was becoming acutely nervous, that he was particularly disturbed in a crisis, and sometimes lacked the tact and discretion necessary to advance the cause.[21] Perhaps there are elements of truth in all these views, but Moss confided to John Gladstone that he gave up the chair because it would have been *"too much like a job and I purposely absented myself when the Bankers were chosen."* [22] The appointment of Moss, Rogers and Moss as the company's bankers [23] ensured that he remained far from idle. Gladstone played a significant part in the early days of the Liverpool and Manchester Railway, even selling his allocation of 10 shares in order to demonstrate that he was acting in

17 ibid
18 ibid
19 Liverpool Mail, 9 October 1858
20 Thomas, p19
21 Carlson, p69
22 Hawarden correspondence Moss to J Gladstone 19.1.1825
23 Carlson, p81

the public interest, and not in his own.[24] His knowledge of Parliamentary procedure and commercial matters in general, greatly aided the measure.

Shares in the Mersey & Irwell Navigation Company, (commonly called the 'Old Quay Company' and the 'Old Navigation Company') originally purchased at £70, were selling, in early 1824, at £1,250[25] and paying an annual dividend of £35.[26] That year the Marquis of Stafford netted a profit of £80,697 from the Bridgewater canal alone.[27] However, by October 1824, the Old Quay's shares had fallen to £1,000 "*from the apprehension of this railroad scheme*" [28] and Bradshaw led the fight against the railway on Lord Stafford's behalf. His cause was aided by two wealthy Lancashire landowners - Lords Sefton and Derby, across whose estates it was hoped to run the line. They did all they could, by fair means and foul, to prevent Stephenson and his team from completing a survey of the route. He was watched day and night, fired at, threatened with a ducking, arrest and violence, and twice turned off the Marquis's land. A propaganda campaign was conducted against the locomotive, which was described to farmers as "*a most frightful machine, emitting a breath as poisonous as the fabled dragon of old* (and) *that if a bird flew over the district where one of these engines passed, it would inevitably drop down dead.*" [29] The railway committee offered Bradshaw an opportunity to take shares in the enterprise, but he refused, and retorted that their surveyors "*in the middle of the night, trespassed on these lands and considerably injured the growing crops of the Trustee's tenants.*" [30]

---

24 Hawarden correspondence Moss to J Gladstone 13.11.1824 & 20.12.1824
25 C R Fay - Huskisson & His Age, p24. Letter from Gladstone to Huskisson 14.10.1824
26 Carlson, p27
27 FC Mather - After the Canal Duke, Appendix A, p358. Carlson's figure of an average of £100,000 (p,53) for the previous 20 years is based upon the exaggerated claim of Joseph Sandars
28 Fay, p24. Letter from Gladstone to Huskisson 14.10.1824
29 Smiles - Life of Stephenson, p237 (1860)
30 Carlson, p72

On 19 October, Stephenson complained to his friend Joseph Pease about his *"sad work...the ground is blockaded on every side to prevent us getting on with the survey....We are to have a grand field day next week... Lord Sefton says he will have a hundred men against us."*[31] Stephenson and his men had no option other than to press on in the face of their intimidators.

Published on 29 October 1824, the first prospectus of the Liverpool & Manchester Railway confirmed Charles Lawrence as chairman with Moss, Lister Ellis, Robert Gladstone and Joseph Sandars (all Liverpool men) as deputy chairmen. Following his survey, Stephenson proposed a route from Liverpool's Princes Dock, *"to Vauxhall-road, then through Bootle, Walton, Fazakerley, Croxteth, Kirby,* (sic) *Knowsley, Eccleston, Windle, Sutton, Haydock, Newton-in-Mackerfield,* (sic) *Golborn, Lowton, Leigh, Pennington, Astley, Irlam, Worsley, Eccles, Pendlebury, Salford, Hulme"* terminating near Water Street in Manchester.[32] The estimated cost of the project had risen to £400,000,[33] an amount to be raised by the sale of 4,000 £100 shares.[34] To dispel any suggestion of them acting out of excessive self interest, the company announced that the maximum dividend payable per share would never exceed £10 per annum. While Moss understood the reason for them not *"acting as the canals have done"* he questioned whether the proprietors would be *"equally anxious to please and benefit the public if they have no interest beyond 10%? Will not their exertions to lower the rates etc be paralysed if the benefit is not to go into their pockets?"*[35]

In early December, Richard Harrison and Thomas

---

31 JGH Warren - A Century of Locomotive Building by Robert Stephenson, p162
32 Carlson, p82
33 £29,180,042 in 2008 using the Retail Price Index
34 Article: Timothy Robson - The Liverpool & Manchester Railway. From The Journal of the International Bond & Share Society, May 1997
35 Hawarden correspondence Moss to J Gladstone 30.11.1824

Headlam[36] were despatched to Ireland to canvas the support of Irish members of the British Parliament. It was argued that the railway would hasten the movement of, for instance, Irish corn, flax and linen to the Yorkshire markets, and that Irish labourers would find work in England's great manufacturing centres. Moss proclaimed, on 4 December, that *"Harrison and Headlam are carrying all Ireland before them"*[37] and, one month later when the pair returned to England, that they *"secured us 29 Irish members and 9 Irish peers all promised. No one that they saw refused them."* [38] Petitions in favour of the Bill were obtained from the Chambers of Commerce of Waterford, Dublin, Drogheda and Belfast as well as the merchants of Cork and Galway. [39]

The measure of limiting shares to ten per subscriber seems to have been abandoned by this stage. A "secret committee" of Moss, Sandars and Lawrence were given licence to dispose of a number of shares in a manner they thought *"most beneficial to the undertaking."* Moss complained that *"The Manchester Committee, who, by the bye, have done nothing to help us, have questioned our right to dispose of shares."* [40] The secret committee had intended to take 20 shares each, but the Manchester men and Messrs Hibberson and Garnett[41] *"objected and talked of law"*. In the opinion of the company's solicitor George Ashby Pritt, the shares could be given to anyone but the secret committee members themselves. Therefore they divided them so that each of the original 2,000 proprietors got an increase of 1/3. *"In general the persons have returned them to the gentleman who nominated them and thus we shall get our 20 shares each*

---

36   Headlam was Moss's neighbour from Barkhill in Aigburth. He was a merchant and one of the original committee members of the Liverpool & Manchester Railway

37   Hawarden correspondence Moss to J Gladstone 4.12.1824

38   Hawarden correspondence Moss to J Gladstone 1.1.1825

39   Carlson, p106

40   Hawarden correspondence Moss to J Gladstone 4.12.1824

41   Joseph Hibberson and John Garnett were members of the Liverpool Provisional Committee of 1822. Carlson, p46

without the committee doing it." [42] Unfortunately, this did not prove to be the case, and Moss's total holding later increased by only around 15 shares to about 28.[43]

In mid December, talk turned to determining who would be suitable to go to London to carry the Bill through Parliament. Moss deeply resented the involvement of Lister Ellis, a member of the railway's finance committee, who was not only a banker prominent in local financial circles, but also an accursed Whig. In late December and early January, the secret committee spent some time in London canvassing the support of MPs in readiness for the day the Bill would first be presented to a Parliamentary Committee. This deputation was the source of jealousies, which boiled over at the L&M's committee meeting on 26 January 1825. Ellis commenced proceedings by finding fault with the secret committee. Moss retorted that he would answer no questions and, if Ellis and others were not satisfied with the work they had done, then he would resign after *"first burning all my documents. Sandars and Ellis had some warm words, and all would have been in flame had not…Robert,* (Gladstone) *stepped forward to moderate matters"* [44] When eventually the matter of the London delegation was raised, Ellis was *"pointed at and objected to"* [45] Affronted, he announced his intention to go to London, if not appointed, at his own expense to keep a close eye on Sandars and Moss *"who he knew were determined to concede too much."* [46] At the

---

42   Hawarden correspondence Moss to J Gladstone 11.12.1824
43   *" The nominees do not generally do so. For instance only two of mine have as yet consented. I expect several of them will do it only I am resolved not to ask it as a favour. I think I shall have in all about fifteen shares."* Hawarden correspondence Moss to J Gladstone 20.12.1824. By early 1825 his holding had increased by one third to 13&1/3 shares, a subscription of £1,333 6 shillings and 8 pence. The "Liverpool & Manchester Rail Road Subscription List" which was incorporated in the Prospectus presented to parliament in early 1825, reveals that 13 &1/3 was the maximum number of shares ascribed to any individual, and many others held this amount. Moss's brother, Henry, held 11& 2/3. Manchester Central Library. B.R.F.385.81, L1
44   Hawarden correspondence Moss to J Gladstone 26.1.1825
45   ibid
46   ibid

conclusion of the debate, Lawrence, Sandars and Moss were confirmed as a secret committee and, assigned to them as a London committee, were *"Harrison, Booth, Adam Hodgson, Bailey and Kennedy of Manchester, Headlam, Ellis and Brandreth, the latter three only to go when the Bill is in Committee...The events of today have sickened me of public business."*[47]

January was a hectic month for Moss. On New Year's Day he wrote, from Grafton Street, London, that he and his fellow directors were busy signing share certificates. *"It takes more time than I should have imagined to sign a name 4,000 times."*[48] On 14 January, so soon after his excursion to the South East, Moss commenced the long trip to Newcastle in the North East, *"to see some experiments made by the loco motive engine. So much has been said pro and con that I wish to judge for myself."*[49] He traveled in the company of three engineers, and met a further three from the Birmingham railway company on arrival (see The Grand Junction Railway)."[50] The purpose of his journey was not only to gather technical information, but to also secure the backing of influential parties. *"On our way to Newcastle we went by appointment to Chatsworth to see the Duke of Devonshire"*[51] The Duke pledged his *" best consideration"* and felt inclined to support the railway *"on public grounds. Private considerations shall not influence me."*[52]

On 19 January, from Newcastle, Moss reported that the trials undertaken at Killingworth Colliery *"which took us from day light until dark, succeeded beyond my most sanguine expectations...I came from home not a little prejudiced against the loco motive engine but I return quite satisfied."*[53] He met

---

47 ibid
48 Hawarden correspondence Moss to J Gladstone 1.1.1825. Although misfiled at Hawarden in 1824 the letter is franked 1825
49 Hawarden correspondence Moss to J Gladstone 8.1.1825
50 ibid
51 Hawarden correspondence Moss to J Gladstone 19.1.1825
52 ibid
53 ibid

people from all parts of the Kingdom[54] as well as agents of the Old Quay and the Leeds & Liverpool canals. "*Instead of being vexed to see them we invited them to go with us and they took notes of all that was done. They at first rode on horseback close to the engines and will be good evidence to prove that horses are not alarmed with them.*"[55] Moss was now confident of proving to Parliament:

"*1st that these engines have worked 10 years and the only accident was one man scalded and confined to his house a short time but now quite well.*

2nd that land through which they go is not deteriorated either in quality or price.

3rd that it can be done at half the expense of horses.

4th that they are stopped easier than a carriage"[56]

There were 6 trials held that day involving an 8 horsepower locomotive pulling anything between 1 and 15 wagons up and down a 1¼ mile stretch of track. They ran at speeds of between 3½ and 4 miles an hour, drawing loads of between 48 and 64 tons.[57] Moss took a particularly close interest in the last trial:

"*No.6*

Engine wheels 4 foot diameter 8 horse power.

1 empty wagon attached to it. 20 persons rode in it. I sat on the engine near the fire place. Some wagons prevented us taking the exact time but it made 65 strokes in a minute up hill and 80 strokes returning which is equal to a speed of 10 or 12 miles. I

---

54 "*Present Mr Wakefield of London, 5 engineers, 3 gentlemen from Liverpool, 6 gentlemen from Birmingham, Several persons from canals.*" ibid
55 ibid
56 ibid
57 Mather, p28

assure you I felt a little nervous and appeared to go faster than I rode in any carriage." [58]

By mid January, the survey and plans for the L&M were completed, and the estimated cost of the project, including £50,000 for *"cutting through Knowsley where the greatest elevation is"* remained at £400,000. [59] On 21 March, the Bill was first presented to a Parliamentary Committee. However, by the end of March, Moss was harbouring grave doubts about its prospects.[60] By 4 April, he conceded that the Bill was now *"more than doubtful... The fact is that we shall lose it by the folly of our own people. Sandars, Ellis, Booth, Benson, Brandreth etc etc are very good men to conduct an opposition but totally unfit to carry any measure."* Moss intended to stay in London until 1 May *"to assist in the committee provided they will listen to reason. I have some doubts and I shall act accordingly."* [61]

It was not until 25 April that the company's engineer, George Stephenson, was called. His first day's testimony concerning the general principles of steam operated railways was unerring, and delivered with confidence by the world's greatest authority on those matters. On the following two days, however, Stephenson was cross examined on his survey and estimates about which, it soon became apparent, he knew little. He had trusted a largely inexperienced team to survey the line in the summer of 1824 and had not properly checked their findings. His nemesis was Edward Alderson, counsel to the canal owners, who took delight in exposing his errors and omissions, describing the railway as *"the most absurd scheme that ever entered into the head of a man to conceive."* [62] Stephenson's woeful estimate of the height of a bridge over the

---

58   Hawarden ref GG1205
59   ibid
60   He complained that he had *"not felt very sanguine in the cause since our committee decided that Ellis and Brandreth were proper persons to send to London - I have seen much to find fault with..."* Hawarden correspondence - Moss to Gladstone 26.3.1825
61   Hawarden correspondence Moss to Gladstone 4.4.1825
62   Ferneyhough, pp20-21

River Irwell led Alderson to query whether he was *"so ignorant of his profession, as to propose a bridge not sufficient to carry off the flood water of the river, or to permit any of the vessels to pass, which of necessity must pass under it, and to leave his own Railroad liable to be several feet under water."* [63] Fun was made of his Geordie accent. Someone asked if he was a foreigner, and another hinted that he was mad. [64] In Moss's mind, at least, the cause was lost by 19 May, when he left London. Headlam told him that, with the exception of Harrison and himself, the committee would feel *"relieved"* by his absence. *"I was, I assure you, most happy to hear it, for all my habits and comforts are totally at variance with London and Great people."* [65] It was not long before all concerned realised the hopelessness of their cause. The last day of Parliamentary dealings was 31 May, when the vote was taken and the Bill thrown out.

Little time was wasted in licking wounds. Within a fortnight, Moss announced *"We have decided to go on with the Railroad"* [66] Recent events had proven a humbling experience for certain committee members. Moss found *"Ellis & Co quieter in temper than what they were and I hope to see things very differently managed in our Company."* For the next Bill to stand a better chance of success, a number of human impediments had to be removed. At a meeting on 1 July, it was decided to dismiss Stephenson. Moss had expressed a preference for replacing him with Thomas Telford,[67] but he was heavily engaged in the schemes of canal companies. John Rennie accepted the positions of engineers-in-chief on behalf

---

63 Anthony Burton - The Rainhill Story, p57
64 According to Edward Pease, Stephenson *"spoke in the strong Northumbrian dialect of his district."* Smiles - Life of Stephenson, p183 (1857) Stephenson said in a speech at Newcastle on the opening of the Newcastle & Darlington Railway *"Someone enquired if I was a foreigner, and another hinted that I was mad. But I put up with every rebuff, and went on with my plans, determined not to be put down.' "* ibid, p226
65 Hawarden correspondence Moss to J Gladstone 19.5.1825
66 Hawarden correspondence Moss to J Gladstone 16.6.1825
67 *"I want very much to have him as our Engineer...I think I could get him the appointment if he would assist us hand on heart and it would be a good thing for him."* Hawarden correspondence Moss to J Gladstone 16.6.1825

of his brother George and himself. The Rennies' first task was to make a new survey of the line, and they appointed Charles Blacker Vignoles to conduct it. Meanwhile, Stephenson busied himself with the Stockton & Darlington railway and other projects. Moss, Lawrence, Sandars, Robert Gladstone and Henry Booth were appointed a secret committee and given *"full power to get the Act."* [68] An attempt was made by Robert Benson [69] to bring in Lister Ellis *"but it was not seconded."* [70]

On 13 July, Moss, ever the diplomat, assured the sacked and discredited William James that the committee intended to push through another Bill in the next session of Parliament.[71] On the same day, he wrote to the sacked and discredited George Stephenson expressing his regret for the loss of the first Bill. *"No-one can be more satisfied than I am that you deserved very different treatment than you met with from Mr. Alderson. Your talents are of a very much more valuable nature than that of a witness in the House of Commons."* [72] Stephenson replied from Newcastle, on the 18th *"I assure you the trouble and anxiety of mind I met with in London still gives me much grief… The Darlington Railway will be opened out in a short time. I wish I could get Alderson along with me on that day. I would run his hounds into a corner more than he could do an Engineer's in a Witness Box."* [73] Stephenson estimated that to build Moss a small locomotive engine to carry *"8 to 10 people on a circular Road about 30 ft diameter"* [74] would cost between £200 and £250.[75] He even offered to manufacture a miniature engine which could *"run on a table"* for £20. [76] Moss intended to get a locomotive to Liverpool *"to show to the public"* and then remove it to

---

68 Hawarden correspondence Moss to J Gladstone 2.7.1825
69 Robert Benson, Liverpool committee member since 1824
70 Hawarden correspondence Moss to J Gladstone 19.7.1825
71 Liverpool Record Office. Ref 385JAM/1
72 Liverpool Record Office. IMS 135/3
73 Liverpool Record Office. Ref 385 STE/16
74 ibid
75 ibid and Hawarden correspondence Moss to J Gladstone 27.7.1825
76 ibid

London when Parliament next met.[77] It has been suggested that Stephenson stayed with Moss at Otterspool while constructing a model railway on the dry bed of the "River Jordan", a Mersey tributary on the estate.[78] While there is no reason to doubt that this did happen, it was at Charles Lawrence's Wavertree Hall that the *Liverpool Mercury* first recorded a section of track as having been laid down.[79]

The committee tried conciliatory measures to get the obstructive Lords Sefton and Derby (AKA Lord Stanley of Knowsley) on their side but, as ever, met with resistance. Sefton had responded to one letter *"in a way that shows that he has neither the feelings nor manners of a Gentleman."* [80] In the hope of nullifying their opposition, Vignoles directed the line further away from Sefton's and Derby's estates. Sefton and Stanley carried on grumbling a while longer.[81] The new, more direct route ran through the parishes of Liverpool, Walton, Childwall, Huyton, Prescot, Winwick, Warrington, Leigh and Eccles, before terminating at Salford.[82] By not venturing over the Irwell into Manchester, where most of the factories the railway hoped to serve were situated, the Mersey & Irwell canal company's objection was negated. Despite the railway's partial encroachment over Bridgewater land, even Bradshaw consented with a rhetorical *"Am I not a Liberal?"* [83]

---

77   Hawarden correspondence Moss to J Gladstone 27.7.1825
78   Griffiths, p113
79   The 35 lb per yard rails were laid *"on large blocks of stone, whose area and solidity, combined with the massive rails...impress the idea of a structure which is intended to last for ages."* Liverpool Mercury – 27 September 1827
80   Hawarden correspondence Moss to J Gladstone 21.6.1825
81   Hawarden correspondence Moss to J Gladstone 10.9.1825. *"On Thursday Lawrence and myself went to Knowsley by appointment to see Lord Stanley. This latter person had always said that if we went South of Highton* (sic) *Church it would be unobjectionable to him, but now that we have altered our line to meet his wishes, he says that what he meant by 'South' was that we should carry the line between Roby and Childwall Hall in front of the finest properties in the neighbourhood."* Then, on 15 September, an exasperated Moss wrote *"I am told that he says our present line is more objectionable than our former one was – Lord Sefton is also by his conversation equally decided against us"* Hawarden correspondence Moss to J Gladstone 15.9.1825
82   Carlson, p145
83   Stafford correspondence Bradshaw to Loch, 27.9.1825. Mather, p38. It should

On 27 September, Moss attended the opening of the Stockton and Darlington Railway, an occasion on which he marveled at the sight of an engine beating the Mail Coach for pace. While some on the L&M's committee still advocated the use of horses, and others of fixed engines pulling the carriages on ropes,[84] Moss was left in no doubt that *"loco motive engines may be had that will do the work for half the price of horses and double the speed and equally safe."* [85] Back at home, three days later, Moss delighted in the news that Lister Ellis had resigned from the railway, believing he would *"meet with no more trouble from that Gentleman."* [86] However, when, at a meeting on 13 October, the committee announced its regret that *"any circumstances should have arisen to induce Mr. Ellis to resign."* Moss was furious. *"I have a declared objection to telling a person I am sorry for that which everyone is pleased...since the majority present did not regret his retirement. Four of the committee have retired before and yet this is the first person deserving of notice. The fact is, however bad the conduct of the Whigs, that Party are always ready to excuse it...but no Whig ever excuses the smallest error we commit."* [87] Apart from Ellis's political crimes, Moss may well have begrudged his holding of 56 shares. [88] Moss held no more than 30.

---

be borne in mind that the Trustees had, up to this point, spent nearly £10,000 in the fight against the railway and would have been keen to avoid further confrontation and expense

84 Hawarden correspondence Moss to J Gladstone 8.10.1825. Moss was adamant *"that it will not do to permit any clause in our Bill to prevent the use of loco motive engines...I therefore got Pritt (the company's solicitor) to draw a clause prohibiting the use of any engines that do not consume their smoke, and putting in the power for any person to summons before the Magistrates the owner of any engine that had not a smoke burner and fining him £5 - or for using any engine that should be considered a nuisance. This clause will satisfy all reasonable people (and) ...tell Parliament at once our intention without putting us to the necessity of proving what the engines will do."*

85 Hawarden correspondence Moss to J Gladstone 30.9.1825

86 ibid

87 Hawarden correspondence Moss to J Gladstone 14.10.1825

88 By February 1826 Ellis was the company's sixth largest shareholder with 56 shares. Harold Pollins - The Finances of the Liverpool & Manchchester Railway - Economice History Review, 2nd Series, Vols 4-15, (1951-53)

Marquis of Stafford	1,000	
J B Pilkington	107	Liverpool
Charles Tayleur	98	Liverpool
Thomas Richardson	75	London
R G Long	75	Rood Ashton, Wilts
Lister Ellis	56	Liverpool
Richard Dawson	47	Liverpool
Jos. Christopher Ewart	45	Liverpool
Thomas Murdoch	35	Portland Place, London
R B Phillips	31	Middle Temple, London
	1,569	

Pollins, p92

Having again failed, during the summer of 1825, to win over Bradshaw with the offer of shares, Moss, Lawrence and Robert Gladstone entered into prolonged negotiations directly (and in secret) with the Marquis of Stafford, George Granville Leveson-Gower. During the French Revolution the Marquis had been ambassador from the Court of England to the French Government, and William Huskisson had been his secretary. Only now did Huskisson begin to fully exploit that relationship for the benefit of his constituents. Stafford's marriage to Elizabeth, the 19th Countess of Sutherland resulted in the amalgamation of vast estates in Shropshire, Staffordshire and Sutherlandshire in the Scottish Highlands, the income from which made the Leveson-Gower family one of the most wealthy and powerful in Britain. The Bridgewater canal accounted for only a small part of that enormous wealth. While Bradshaw controlled the Marquis's Bridgewater interests, the overall management of the Sutherland-Stafford estates fell upon his principal agent James Loch, a Scottish Whig who, despite his role as caretaker of an aristocratic fortune, was in favour of the principle of free trade. It was he and Huskisson who managed to talk Stafford round to considering a compromise.[89] Moss now fully appreciated that "*something more than a good case is necessary to secure a Bill*

---

89   Mather, p40

passing." [90] On Boxing Day, he proudly informed Gladstone that *"We commenced* (negotiations) *by offering 1,000 shares to the Marquis...I think we have not shown ourselves bad negotiators when I announce to you that the Marquis of Stafford accepts the 1,000 shares and that his name appears in our Prospectus"* [91] In addition to those shares, Stafford would be entitled to appoint three directors to the 15 man board. This arrangement was entered into *"contrary to Mr. Bradshaw's advice and opinion and in direct opposition to his feelings..."* [92]

Lord Stafford, like all the other subscribers, had made a promise by accepting the shares that he would make full payment on any "calls". This brought the L&M a potential investment of £100,000,[93] although Stafford committed £40,000 to pay for improvements on the Bridgewater canal at the same time.[94] He was perfectly entitled to sell his railway shares at any time but, in fact, entered into the agreement *"in the spirit in which it was made"* [95] Thus had Moss helped, not only to overcome the railway's most powerful foe, but had also extracted from Stafford what amounted to the canal interest's suicide note - a slow death, which Moss never lived to see. Given the unknown potential of railways, Stafford could never have foreseen the dire consequences of his actions. He appointed Loch, James Sothern and Captain James Bradshaw (RH Bradshaw's son) as his railway directors, but more often than not they were absent from the board meetings. Moss communicated with Loch on behalf of the L&M almost exclusively by letter. Captain Bradshaw complained that he

---

90   Moss to Huskisson 26.11.1825. Carlson, p154
91   Hawarden correspondence Moss to J Gladstone 26.12.1825 Moss intimated that *"The negotiations were not made through Bradshaw and I will thank you not to mention the subject to him."*
92   Mersey & Irwell Navigation Company, Order Book, 1821-8, p142 - Mather, p41
93   Mather cites one source, 'The Journal of Mrs Arbuthnot 1820-32', Vol ii, p388 which suggests the Marquis paid the prime cost - i.e. - only half the price the shares were worth
94   Mather, p41
95   Henry Booth - An Account of the Liverpool & Manchester Railway, p24. Booth was the railway's treasurer.

"felt hampered in his exertions in favour of the Canal from having some knowledge of what were the views and objects of the Railway Directors." [96] The Bridgewater opposition collapsed as its L&M directors, emasculated by having to represent a master with two conflicting financial interests, saw their purpose as being to make the Marquis as much money as possible out of his railway holding. Loch's mission was to balance **all** the interests of the Stafford-Sutherland family, and he had to be ever mindful of the fact that, on Stafford's death, the canal would become the sole inheritance of his second son Lord Francis Leveson-Gower. The remainder of the Leveson-Gower fortune would pass to his eldest son, Lord George Sutherland-Leveson-Gower.

A Second Prospectus of the Liverpool & Manchester Railway Company was drawn up in December 1825, and the capital was increased from £400,000 to £510,000.[97] A Further call of £3 was made, the remittances to be sent to Moss's bank. [98] Lawrence was confirmed as chairman and Moss as a deputy chairman along with Robert Gladstone and Sandars. Of the 27 man committee, 18 were Liverpool men and only 9 Manchester. [99] The list of subscribers presented to Parliament for the 1826 session demonstrated that £423,333 of the £510,000 had been pledged, and that although both cities stood to benefit enormously by the railway, this was predominantly a Liverpudlian venture.

	Number of names	Shares subscribed
London	96	844
Liverpool	172	1,979
Manchester	15	124
Other	24	286 & 1/3
Marquis of Stafford	1	1,000
	-----	--------------
	308	4,233 & 1/3

Pollins, p92

96 Stafford correspondence J Loch to W W Currie. 30.9.1831. Mather, p45
97 £35,308,941 in 2008 using the Retail Price Index
98 or Barclay, Tristen, Bevan & Co, London. Carlson, p153
99 Booth, p25

Moss traveled to London at the start of February to help see the Bill through. He was far more confident of its prospects this time, given the backing of numerous powerful allies.[100] On 10 February, the Bill was read for the first time, having passed the Standing Order Committee without a single objection. *"It is surprising how quickly we go on"* Moss enthused,[101] before returning to Otterspool at the end of the month to be with his pregnant wife. He explained that *"at such a time no man of proper feeling could think of leaving home."*[102] Hannah gave birth to a girl in early April.[103] Then, Moss travelled back down to London to carry on the fight. He was most fearful of Lord Derby's vigorous opposition in the House of Lords.[104] Having championed the cause in the Commons, Huskisson was once again called upon by Moss, on 12 April, to exert his influence over the upper chamber.[105] With Huskisson's assistance, the remaining Parliamentary opposition was overcome and, on 5 May, the Act was given royal assent. At a meeting on 29 May, a board of 12 directors was appointed (in addition to Lord Stafford's three appointees). [106] The following day, Charles Lawrence was elected chairman, and Moss his sole deputy chairman.[107]

Throughout June, the position of principal engineer was hotly debated, and a committee of Lawrence, Moss and William Rotheram rejected the terms proposed by George and

---

[100] Other than the Stafford family, Lord Lowther was on side, as was Lady Glengale. *"I am afraid that her zeal for the cause is almost too strong...Mr. Huskisson is apparently more for us than he was last year."* Hawarden correspondence Moss to J Gladstone 7.2.1826

[101] Hawarden correspondence Moss to J Gladstone 9.2.1826

[102] Hawarden correspondence Moss to Gladstone 26.2.1826

[103] Hawarden correspondence Moss to Gladstone 6.4.1826 This child was either Margaret or Harriet Eliza. Burke does not reveal the year of the four daughters' births (only their deaths) and neither does the Moss mausoleum at St Anne's.

[104] Hawarden correspondence Moss, in London, to J Gladstone 11.4.1826

[105] Veitch, pp 46-47.

[106] Robert Benson, Adam Hodgson, James Bourne, Charles Lawrence, Thomas Shaw Brandreth, John Moss, Lister Ellis, William Rathbone, Robert Gladstone, William Rotheram, Richard Harrison and Joseph Sandars. (Carlson, p180)

[107] ibid - It was agreed that each director would receive one guinea for every meeting attended, subject to a maximum of 52 meetings in any one year.

John Rennie for remaining as principal engineers. The name of Stephenson again began to be whispered. The Rennies stipulated that they would not be associated with him except in some capacity in the locomotive department. On 3 July, with the backing of Lawrence, Sandars, Booth and Moss,[108] Stephenson, who had more experience than any other man in the building and operation of railways, was appointed principal engineer on what was, at the time, the biggest engineering project ever to be carried out in Britain. The Rennies, *"after having with so much labour and anxiety carried the Bill through Parliament"*,[109] had fully expected to have been appointed executive engineers. As it was, they were left to lament that *"The Executive Committee of the Railway behaved extremely ill to us."* [110]

The works, which would take more than 3 years to complete, commenced in earnest. These included the construction of 63 bridges over and under the line, a 2,200 yard tunnel under Liverpool, a 2 mile cutting through solid rock at Olive Mount adjoining the tunnel, a 60 foot, nine arched viaduct at Sankey and the draining of a five mile expanse of deep bog at Chat Moss, over which the line was to float. Of these projects, the Chat Moss scheme proved the most problematical. Stephenson always insisted that, if enough spoil were poured into the bog, the bottom would eventually be found and the land made firm enough to support railway lines on a raft of wicker hurdles, branches, heather, hedge cuttings and the like. Over a course of weeks, hundreds of thousands of tons of material disappeared into the bog, as Stephenson said, *"without the slightest apparent effect."* [111] The directors considered it a hopeless task, and even Stephenson's assistants

---

108 Carlson, p186
109 Autobiography of Sir John Rennie, FRS, Comprising the History of his Professional Life, Together with Reminiscences Dating from the Commencement of the Century to the Present Time, p238
110 ibid
111 Smiles - Life of Stephenson, pp253-254 (1857)

began to doubt his scheme. A board meeting was held at Chat Moss, in March 1827, to decide whether to abandon the works and take another route. The directors were being transported at speed along temporary rails in a little three feet gauge wagon, which came off the track, and Moss *"was thrown out in a soft place, from which, however, he was speedily extricated, not without leaving his deep mark."*[112] Stephenson referred to this incident as *"the meeting of the Mosses."* [113] Because a massive amount of time and money had, by now, been invested in the works, the thought of writing off such a large loss compelled the directors to carry on with the existing works, *"the ultimate success of which"* Stephenson (with the benefit of hindsight) *"never for one moment doubted."* [114] By the second half of 1827, his plan appeared to be working, and a temporary line floated over an embankment was found capable of supporting loads of 10-12 tons without difficulty. By April 1830, a train weighing 45 tons was able to cross the moss at more than 15 mph without damage to itself or the track.[115]

At the beginning of 1828, the L&M's directors took the first step towards resolving the problems raised by the unsatisfactory situation of the railway's terminus at Salford. They purchased a site for a new terminus in Liverpool Road next to the Bridgewater Canal's wharves at Castlefield. Had any of the Bridgewater directors bothered to attend the L&M's meetings, they would have been fully aware of these plans. Moss wrote to Loch on 29 February seeking assurances from Bradshaw that the Bridgewater Trustees would raise no objection to the river being crossed. In June, he wrote again recommending that an agreement be made to divide the Manchester and Liverpool traffic between the two concerns at that point, on the basis that *"there are goods which we might*

---

112 Smiles – Lives of the Engineers: with an account of their principal works, p223-224
113 ibid
114 Spoken at a dinner in Birmingham on 23 December 1837. Smiles - Life of Stephenson, pp253-254 (1857).
115 Thomas, p49

advantageously spare for each other." [116] Then, in September, he went as far as to suggest meeting up with Bradshaw in order to explore *"the best mode of making the two properties productive without sacrificing the interest of either."* [117] Moss assured Loch that he was *"<u>individually</u> anxious that our connection with the Stafford family should be encouraged."* [118] Loch, acting purely in the financial interests of the family, proposed that a connection be made by either extending the canal into the railway premises or by permitting the railway to extend into Castlefield. Plans were at an advanced stage when Bradshaw raised his objections. His fear was that, once the railway had established itself in Manchester, it would then move eastwards to deprive his canal of its trade with Yorkshire and the East Midlands. Loch facilitated a meeting between Bradshaw and Moss, (in the company of his fellow director Gilbert Winter of Manchester) in late October, at Bradshaw's Worsley Hall abode.

Moss was acutely aware of Bradshaw's formidable reputation for intransigence. *"I hear from all quarters that he is not content to have a fair share of the contract, but that those who deal with him must prepare to concede more than he has a right to demand, that even those who are notorious for the zeal with which they protect their own interests, always find, after an arrangement with Mr. Bradshaw, that they have nothing to boast of."* [119] At the interview, in October, it became apparent that the Bridgewater canal was Bradshaw's sole raison d'etre. He explained to Moss that *"the old duke had made him promise twenty-six years ago to attend to the interests of the Canal, from which day, he, Mr. B., had not once dined out."* [120] After a diatribe against those who came to do him no good, those who attacked him, the constant abuse he took from Manchester and other remarks, which lasted for nearly a quarter of an

---

116 Stafford Correspondence Moss to J Loch 30.6.1828 D593/K/1/3/16)
117 Stafford Correspondence Moss to J Loch 19.9.1828 (D593/K/1/3/16)
118 ibid
119 Stafford Correspondence Moss to J Loch 30.9.1828 (D593/K/1/3/16)
120 Stafford Correspondence Moss to J Loch 22.10.1828 (D593/K/1/3/16)

hour, Bradshaw eventually enquired *"Now what your wants?"* (sic) Moss replied that it was intended for the railway to cross the Irwell, and enquired whether Bradshaw would oppose it? *"Certainly I must."* Bradshaw said, and asked for copies of the plans for the bridge, a request Moss refused on the grounds that Bradshaw should have no interest in the manner of the crossing. *"Not interested? When you come into my very premises and are taking levels for another branch to cross my canal, wharfs etc and which will take my trade from me."*[121] Despite this rather unpromising start, the meeting was a success, of sorts, for both sides. Loch had previously commended Moss and Winter to Bradshaw as *"gentlemen whose opinions and declarations I may place dependence upon.*[122] The pair managed to extract from him an assurance that he would not object to the railway bridging the Irwell. He also agreed to Moss's proposals for an interchange of railway and canal traffic. In return, Bradshaw secured Moss's assurance that the railway company would make no play for the Bridgewater's Yorkshire trade - a pledge which the Liverpool & Manchester Railway honoured until 1844. They left Bradshaw *"...apparently in good humour after 3 hour's conversation - during which time he never asked us to partake of even a sandwich."*[123]

The L&M's directors had hoped to raise an Exchequer loan of £125,000 to meet the additional expense of the extended route and mounting construction costs. The Exchequer Loan Commissioners consulted Thomas Telford, the country's greatest pre-railway engineer, to report on the suitability of the railway for the loan. After his inspection, feeling the company had been at best uncooperative and at worst rude, Telford filed an unfavourable report, early in 1829. He estimated that the L&M would actually need £200,000 to complete its line. An undignified slanging match ensued. Moss observed that Telford was engineer to both the Old Quay and

---

121 ibid
122 ibid
123 ibid

the Weaver Navigation companies and was, as such, *"the paid advocate of canals"*[124] His report merely *"confirmed rather than injured the good opinion we previously had of the works and the undertaking…I was warmly in favour of his coming down because I wanted to know from our warmest opponent what fault he could find with the work."* [125] Symbolically, Moss immediately sold his 20 shares in the Macclesfield Canal, declaring *"I am more than ever confident that Railroads will be most formidable rivals of Canals."* [126] Telford's opinions apparently worried John Gladstone into selling 20 Liverpool & Manchester shares. Moss reassured Loch that Gladstone had always intended to sell his stake once it had realised a gain of 50 per cent. *"He is one of those prudent north Country Gentlemen who is always ready to make money and would sell for a profit."* [127] Although a loan of £100,000 was authorised at the end of the year, in the interim, the company had to seek alternative means of raising funds. Moss proposed a new share capital of £127,500 through the issue of 5,100 shares at £25 each[128] for the establishment of a carrying department and to pay for wagons, warehouses and depots. His proposal was approved by Act of Parliament on 14 May 1829.[129]

Still the means of traction over the Liverpool & Manchester's tracks had not been decided upon. The idea of propulsion by horses had been completely discarded, but the committee's previous unanimity for the locomotive had been unsettled by the rejection of the first Bill, and the fixed-engine faction, led by James Cropper, was very strong. Even though Moss was among Stephenson's greatest supporters, he remained open-minded on the question.[130] In October 1828 Moss, along with Cropper and Booth, had surveyed all the rail

---

124 Stafford Correspondence Moss to J Loch 16.2.1829 (D593/K/1/3/17)
125 Stafford Correspondence Moss to J Loch 11.2.1829 (D593/K/1/3/17)
126 Stafford Correspondence Moss to J Loch 21.2.1829 (D593/K/1/3/17)
127 Stafford Correspondence Moss to J Loch 16.2.1829 (D593/K/1/3/17)
128 £1,838 per share in 2008 using the Retail Price Index
129 Carlson, p204
130 Thomas, p63

roads of Yorkshire and Durham, an experience which prompted him to remark "*I must say I think Thompson's stationary engines are way superior to loco motives.*"[131] The committee canvassed the opinion of two highly respected engineers and, in January 1829, James Walker and John Rastrick filed a report which recommended the use of 21 stationary engines, at stages of 1½ miles, to haul the trains by cable. George Stephenson and his assistant engineers Robert Stephenson (his son) and Joseph Locke, understandably alarmed, submitted their own report to the directors on 20 April, making a powerful counter argument in favour of the locomotive. This raised the spirits of many on the committee, who were still hopeful about the locomotive, but only if a significantly superior one to those that they had yet seen, could be developed.

Intending to establish the locomotive's potential once and for all, the directors proposed a competition to find the best one, and put up prize money of £500 for the winning entry. The conditions[132] which governed the now world famous Rainhill trials were framed by Sandars, Cropper, Moss, Benson and Rotheram.[133] Each entrant was required to travel 70 miles (the length of the return journey between Liverpool and Manchester), pulling various combinations

---

131 Stafford Correspondence Moss to J Loch 22.10.1828 (D593/K/1/3/16)

132 "The engine must effectually consume its own smoke. If of six tons weight, it must be able to draw, day by day, twenty tons weight (including the tender and water tank) at ten miles an hour, with a pressure of steam on the boiler not exceeding fifty pounds to the square inch. The boiler must have two safety-valves, neither of which must be fastened down, and one of them be completely out of the control of the engineman. The engine and boiler must be supported on springs, and rest on six wheels; the height of the whole not exceeding fifteen feet to the top of the chimney. The engine, with water, must not weigh more than six tons; but one of less weight would be preferred, on its drawing a proportionate load behind it; if only four-and-a-half tons, then it might be put on only four wheels. The company to be at liberty to test the boiler, etc, by a pressure of one hundred and fifty pounds to the square inch. A mercurial gauge must be affixed to the machine, showing the steam pressure above forty-five pounds per square inch. The engine must be delivered, complete, and ready for trial, at the Liverpool end of the railway, not later than the 1st October 1829. The price of the engine must not exceed £550."

133 Thomas, p65

of loads backwards and forwards over a 1¾ mile length of track, at an average speed of not less than 10 mph. Other than the Stephensons' *Rocket*, there were five entrants - *Sanspareil, Novelty, Perseverance, Cyclopede* and the *manumotive*. The latter two were not locomotives at all, but were powered by two horses and two men respectively. On 6 October, the opening day of the trials, crowds of between 10,000 and 15,000 people were drawn from all over the country; the vast majority having never seen the likes of these fire breathing machines before. *The Times* reported that *"the scenes presented were similar to those which roads leading to racecourses usually present during days of sport."* [134] A grandstand had been erected halfway along the course, for the benefit of ladies. *"Never, perhaps, on any previous occasion, were so many scientific gentlemen and practical engineers collected together at one spot as there were on the rail-road yesterday. The interesting and important nature of the experiments to be tried had drawn them from all parts of the kingdom to be present at this contest of locomotive carriages, as well as to witness the amazing utility of railways in expediting the communication between distant places."* [135]

Of the four serious contenders, the favourite to win had been the London built *Novelty*, which was supported by James Cropper and others.[136] On 14 October, the last day of the trials, with *Perseverance's* previous performances short of the mark and *Sanspareil* withdrawn, the final test, between *Novelty* and *Rocket*, brought spectator attendance almost as high as on the opening day. Unfortunately, *Novelty's* exhausting fan gave way and it came to a halt, never to recover. At this point, Stephenson turned to his assistant Locke, and was overheard saying *"Eh mon, we needn't fear yon thing, it's got no goots."* [137] The problem of assessing a winner had been removed as *Rocket* was the only entrant which fulfilled all the tasks set. Cropper

---

134 The Times, 8 October 1829. CRH Simpson - The Rainhill Locomotive Trials, p14
135 ibid, p28
136 Ferneyhough, p64
137 Olinthus Vignoles - Life of Charles Blacker Vignoles, p 130

held up his hands and exclaimed *"Now has George Stephenson at last delivered himself."* [138] Had *Rocket* failed, as all the others entrants did, the locomotive would have been condemned. The Rainhill Trials established, beyond all reasonable doubt, the superiority of locomotive engines over any other means of traction. The L&M bought Rocket for £550 and abandoned all notions of employing stationary engines for general traffic. Now, schemes to construct locomotive powered railways proliferated nationwide and, indeed, worldwide.

Regrettably, all of Moss's correspondence from December 1828 to June 1830 has disappeared from Hawarden, presumably removed for private research. With it may have been lost the tales that would help explain the high esteem in which he held Stephenson. The only relevant piece of correspondence from around this time is a letter, from the Stafford correspondence, in which Moss stated he had *"been over the whole line of our rail road and inspected every part of it with a determination to see it with my own eyes and judge as impartially as possible. I am perfectly satisfied and much pleased with the work, which will obtain for Stephenson as high a name as ever an Engineer obtained in England."* [139] What prophetic words.

On 23 October 1829, Moss took his wife and a party of ladies for a trip on the railway. *"We went all speeds from 12 to 30 miles an hour, without any unpleasant feeling on the part of the ladies and children."* [140] With the opening of

---

138 Smiles - Life of Stephenson, p294 (1857)
139 Stafford Correspondence Moss to J Loch 26.1.1830 (D593/K/1/3/18). It was Moss who proposed, on 26 August 1844, that John Gibson be commissioned to erect a marble statue of Stephenson. (Thomas, p225). Then, in 1846, after congratulating John Gladstone on the baronetcy bestowed upon him by Queen Victoria and Robert Peel, Moss added *"I wish they had included George Stephenson in their list. In any other country but England services like his are noticed."* (Hawarden correspondence Moss to J Gladstone 29.06.1846). Stephenson remained unacknowledged by the British establishment. By September 1848, when Gibson's statue was delivered to St George's Hall in Liverpool, he was already dead. Smiles - Life of Stephenson, p491. (1857) From the minutes of the Liverpool Board of the London & North Western Railway 6 September 1848
140 Stafford Correspondence Moss to J Loch 24.10.1829 (D593/K/1/3/17)

the railway still 11 months into the future, Moss put forward to Loch an hypothesis, which must have seemed absurd. He was convinced that a railroad could be built from the L&M's Rainhill station to Runcorn, where a tunnel would take it under the Mersey, and then on to Northwich, the Potteries and to London. *"I think you will suspect me of Castle Building beyond probability and almost possibility when I ask:*

If power and wagons can be found on rail roads to convey goods at the speed of 8 to 10 miles an hour for one halfpenny per ton per mile

If power and coaches can be found to convey coaches on rail roads at a safe speed of twenty miles per hour at the rate of two pence for each passenger for twenty miles…

May it not be worth while at some period for those interested in the Duke of Bridgewater's canal to make the canal into a rail road?." [141] Loch doubted that engines could or should travel at this *"racing speed"*, but Moss assured him that such a pace was easily attainable. *"I do not calculate upon what the Liverpool & Manchester did on the Experiment days but what I see it do on the days when no one is looking on but Engineers and Directors."* [142]

On 28 October, Moss's fanciful thinking began to take a more concrete form, when he received a deputation of three gentlemen proposing a railway from London to Birmingham. He asked Loch whether the Marquis of Stafford would assist or take any interest in such an undertaking. *"If the Duke's, Liverpool & Birmingham and Ellesmere would co-operate I am confident it would be a good thing for all."* [143] The shares in the L&M, for which Lord Stafford had so far paid £115,000, were now worth £188,750,[144] so, surely he would recognise

---

141 ibid
142 Stafford Correspondence Moss to J Loch 28.10.1829 (D593/K/1/3/17)
143 ibid
144 Eric Richards - The Leviathan of Wealth. The Sutherland Fortune in the Industrial Revolution, p92

the potential for similar returns from any new railway? No. Loch and the Marquis wished to see the results of the L&M's first year of trade before making any further commitment to railways. In actuality, he never invested another penny in them, and any suggestion that the Bridgewater canal be converted into a railway was rejected. Loch believed that, with improved facilities and better management, it could still prove highly competitive in moving heavier goods. Besides, £60,000 had recently been spent on improvements,[145] and the Bridgewater was certainly in better shape than most other canals to meet the challenge of the railway.[146] Robert Bradshaw had already warned Moss that he intended to slash rates of carriage in order to demonstrate the superiority of the canal. He threatened that *"he would count the railway wagons from his window and if they got much trade he would lower his price."*[147] Bradshaw predicted it would be on the carriage of goods, rather than of passengers, where the canal would exert its superiority, but he assured Moss, he would give warning of any reduction in his rates of carriage.[148]

From hereon in, Moss's attentions were largely centred upon seeing through the plans for the Liverpool & Birmingham Railway, (see 'The Grand Junction Railway') although he remained a director of the L&M until 1845 and its chief representative in negotiations with the canals until 1837, when the new railway opened.

While the Liverpool & Manchester railway was under construction, numerous trial trips were taken on short stretches of track, and Moss took a special interest in these. He informed Huskisson, on 14 December 1829 that *"Lords*

[145] ibid, p88
[146] Profits would, no doubt, be reduced and *"a very material alteration in the mode and rate of conveyance of goods etc on canals"* but *"the practice of railroads will not be found so overpowering as its friends so sanguinely anticipate."* Stafford correspondence James Bradshaw to J Loch, 6.12.1829 & Mather, p56
[147] Stafford Correspondence Moss to J Loch 22.10.1828 (D593/K/1/3/16)
[148] Richards, p88

Derby and Sefton...admit their surprise and admiration" and that *"The very decided success which has attended that measure has so opened the eyes of the canal people, the landowners and public that almost everyone is desirous to get in a rail-road."* [149] He added, brimming with pioneering spirit *"Provided our Liverpool and Manchester Railroad answers our expectations, that is, if goods and passengers CAN be carried at less than half the present prices - no one can doubt but a railroad will be made between Liverpool and London.'* [150] However, railways should be constructed so as *"to injure as little as possible and to protect as much as lies in our power the canal interest."* [151] He confessed to feeling daunted by the magnitude of future works. *"No less than 10 new schemes are announced to come into the Liverpool & Manchester line. I am one of those who fear that we shall have more to do than we can do well."* [152]

On 14 June 1830, a full three months before the official opening, Moss and 12 fellow directors made the first journey from Liverpool to Manchester, in a carriage pulled by the *Arrow* locomotive. About 30 other gentlemen were carried in a second coach, attached to which, were seven wagons filled with stone. It took two hours and 21 minutes, including stops, to get to Manchester.[153] The same trip by canal would have taken 36 hours, and 4½ hours by road.[154] A special meeting was held at the home of Moss's *"very particular friend, Gilbert Winter Esq. of Manchester"*[155] after whom Moss had named his third son.[156] While there, exhilarated and justifiably triumphant, the

---

149 Stafford Correspondence copy letter Moss to Wm Huskisson 14.12.1829 (D593/K/1/3/17)

150 ibid

151 ibid

152 ibid

153 Carlson, p229

154 Rocket 150. 150th Anniversary of the Liverpool & Manchester Railway 1830 – 1980 Official Handbook, p8

155 Hawarden correspondence Moss to J Gladstone 19.2.1824

156 Gilbert Winter Moss was born in 1828. John Gladstone, in honour of his friend and fellow Scot, William Ewart, named his fourth son, born in 1809, William Ewart Gladstone. It was a local custom in the latter part of the 18th and the early 19th

directors passed a resolution *"expressing their strong sense of the great skill and unwearied energy displayed by their engineer, Mr. George Stephenson, which have so far brought this great national work to a successful termination."*[157] On the return journey, a top speed of 27 miles an hour was achieved over Chat Moss. [158]

Moss received a letter from a once bitter opponent of the L&M, on 12 August. This was as close to an apology as Lord Derby could dare commit himself. *"Allow me to assure you and the committee that although at the commencement of their fine work, I thought myself fully justified in opposing it, I am now so well satisfied of the Public Benefit likely to accrue from its progress as sincerely to congratulate the committee on the accomplishment of their object and to offer them my best wishes for its complete success."*[159]

It was the committee's intention for the official opening day of the railway to be a momentous national occasion, and invitations to attend it were sent out in July. Moss had met the Prime Minister (the Duke of Wellington) on 24 July *"and he promised to honour our Rail Road with his presence on 15 September."*[160] The Freedom of the Borough of Liverpool should have been bestowed upon the Duke in 1815 in recognition, principally, of his leadership in the great victory over Napoleon Bonaparte at Waterloo, but on numerous previous occasions the official presentation had been postponed. Now, it seemed, the moment had finally arrived. The Duke was to be granted his Freedom in the evening at a grand dinner to be held in the Wellington Rooms on Mount Pleasant. Moss, anxious that the event might be over subscribed, complained *"We are plagued to death almost by the demands of the Great who imagine that they*

---

centuries to use surnames, often the mother's maiden name, as part of the forenames of offspring.

157 Carlson, p229
158 ibid
159 Stafford Correspondence Lord Derby to Moss 12.8.1830 enclosed in letter from Moss to J Loch 21.8.1830 (D593/K/1/3/18)
160 Hawarden correspondence Moss to J Gladstone 24.7.1830

only have to ask and have. Huskisson is adding to our numbers by collecting some parliamentary friends around him. It would not surprise me if we had some sparring at our dinner." [161]

As the big day approached, one reporter described how *"Liverpool was never so full of strangers....All the inns in the town were crowded to overflowing....Never was there such an assemblage of wealth, rank, beauty and fashion in this neighbourhood."* [162] On the morning of the opening day, Wednesday 15 September 1830, massive crowds descended on Edge Hill station,[163] and throngs lined the route. At twenty minutes to eleven, at the firing of a cannon, a cavalcade of eight locomotives set off from Edge Hill, destined for Manchester. However, a piece of wadding from the explosive took out the eye of a bystander - a portent of worse tragedy.[164] The procession proceeded with *The Northumbrian*, driven by George Stephenson, at its head, pulling three carriages; the first carried a military band; the second the Duke of Wellington and his guests, and the third the railway's directors and their friends. A director was designated to each locomotive, and *The Northumbrian* was under Moss's direction, although the extent of his involvement was probably limited to starting the engine at Edge Hill.[165] *The Northumbrian* departed on one line and the remaining seven trains on the other line so that all could see *The Northumbrian's* eminent occupants and Wellington's party could stop to view the various attractions en route without causing disruption.[166]

---

161 Hawarden correspondence Moss to J Gladstone 9.9.1830
162 Ferneyhough, p71
163 Edge Hill was not the Liverpool terminus. There were 2 termini – Crown Street for passengers, and Wapping for freight. 2 tunnels were constructed under the town. At Edge Hill, the carriages were detached from the locomotives and then attached to ropes and hauled into the station by steam powered stationary engines. On the return journey the carriages were moved down hill purely by gravity.
164 Ferneyhough, p73
165 Thomas, p243
166 Among the worthies under Moss's charge were *"Littleton, Peel, Holmes and Halton...with a few of less note."* (Hawarden correspondence Moss to J Gladstone 9.9.1830) Edward John Littleton (later Lord Hatherton) was a former Tory, but now Whig MP for Staffordshire. William Holmes was Tory MP for Bishop's Castle. Of Halton there is no record.

After about an hour's run, all trains stopped to take on fuel and water at Parkside, just over half the way to Manchester. Although the directors had issued strict verbal and written instructions that on no account were passengers to disembark, their advice was disregarded. Among those alighting was William Huskisson. The *Liverpool Times* observed how "*It happened that the place where the grand carriages were thus kept standing, was most unfortunately chosen, for on each side of the railroad was a deep pool of water approaching within about 3 feet of the rails; so that any person who descended from the carriages, was compelled to descend between the lines.*"[167] As guests of the directors, Tom and Robertson Gladstone were passengers in *The Northumbrian*. Robertson saw Huskisson walking along to the coach in which his wife sat *"when the Duke of Wellington, observing him, put out his arm to shake hands with him. At this moment the Rocket engine* (driven by Joseph Locke) *approached on the opposite rail to go to the reservoir. The sides of the Duke's car projected very much over the sides of the railway leaving but little room for the engine to pass without touching Mr. Huskisson. Several voices called out to him to get out of the way but he was either nervous or, from weakness, in trying to get into the car again, the door opened the wrong way, he fell and, seeing the engine coming, he tried to throw himself before it, so as to allow it to pass over him and, in doing this, his leg, the only part of his body not clear of the railway, was run over by one or two wheels (either more than enough to cause such a fracture) which literally fractured the bone from the arch with the knee to the thigh where it joins the body! He was immediately raised by one of the constables standing near him, but he uttered 'God forgive me. I am a dead man - I can never outlive this.'*"[168] It is almost certain that Moss saw the whole incident as did two people under his charge, Messrs Littleton and Holmes.[169]

---

167 Liverpool Times, 21 September 1825

168 Robertson Gladstone to John Gladstone 16.9.1830. Hawarden correspondence Glynne-Gladstone MSS138

169 Vignoles, p153 *"The perilous position of Mr Huskisson was immediately perceived. Mr Littleton… had just sprung into the car, pulling after him Prince Esterhazy; but*

Huskisson, together with two doctors, was placed in one of *The Northumbrian's* carriages and, with Stephenson at the engine, was raced to Eccles at a rate of 34 miles an hour.[170] After depositing him at Reverend Thomas Blackburne's vicarage at about one o'clock, Stephenson proceeded rapidly to Manchester from where he whisked away a team of surgeons. Back at Eccles, they found Huskisson in an exhausted state, with an imperceptible pulse at the wrist. The surgeons were convinced that any attempt at amputating their patient's mangled leg would result in him dying under the knife. Instead, they administered *"large quantities of laudanum* (opium)...*as a sedative."*[171] At around four o'clock, Huskisson asked one of them for a candid opinion on his case. Mr Whatton replied *'It is a very bad one and I fear, Sir, you cannot survive.'* With, at the most, six hours to live, Huskisson began making preparations for meeting his maker.[172] Then, after warmly thanking the surgeons, he *"took an affectionate leave of the sorrowing friends who surrounded his bedside, and a most tender 'farewell' of his devoted wife, and precisely at nine o'clock expired."*[173]

While Stephenson had been rushing Huskisson away from the accident scene, at Parkside a lengthy debate ensued. In view of the fact that a crowd of possibly half a million was waiting at Manchester, after initial reluctance, the Duke and

---

Mr Holmes, MP, was unable to get in, and thus he found himself standing close by Mr Huskisson and, seeing his bewildered condition, he cried out to him 'For God's sake, Mr Huskisson, be firm.'"

170 Liverpool Times, 21 September 1830

171 ibid

172 ibid. Huskisson's secretary William Wainewright drew up amendments to his will. Wainewright was Secretary of the Liverpool Parliamentary Office in London, established in 1814 and funded by Liverpool Corporation and various mercantile associations such as the African Chamber of Commerce, the British North American Association, the Mexican and South American Association and the Brazil and River Plate Association and the West India Association to which Moss was affiliated. As Liverpool's economy burgeoned so did its Parliamentary business and because Liverpool's two MPs had so much of this business to attend to "their thoughtful constituents provided them with a London Office and Secretary to assist them in coping with it." Henderson, W O - The Liverpool Office in London

173 Liverpool Times 21 September 1830

Robert Peel were persuaded to complete the journey. However, the trains' buglers were ordered to remain silent, the military band returned to Liverpool, and passengers were requested not to respond to the cheers of the crowds. They arrived at about 3 o'clock, but to unexpected booing and occasional stone throwing. One passenger, Fanny Kemble, a beautiful young actress who had befriended Stephenson, observed how *'Groans and hisses greeted the carriage, full of influential personages, in which the Duke of Wellington sat. High above the grim and grimy crowd of scowling faces a loom had been erected, at which sat a tattered, starved looking weaver, evidently set there as a representative man, to protest against this triumph of machinery, and the gain and glory which the wealthy Liverpool and Manchester men were likely to derive from it. The contrast between our departure from Liverpool and our arrival in Manchester was one of the most striking things I have ever witnessed.'*[174]

The Duke of Wellington greeted well wishers and endured hecklers until four thirty, when he and his party departed in two carriages attached to *The Northumbrian*. Hours late, the train reached Liverpool at seven o'clock - minus the Prime Minister, who had disembarked at Childwall. An Engineers' banquet, which was to have been held at the Adelphi Hotel, was cancelled. The Company's dinner at the Wellington Rooms, prepared for 219 guests, was attended by only 47 who dispersed after having drunk Huskisson's health. Yet again, the official presentation of the freedom of the borough to the Duke was shelved. Back in Manchester a farce was unfolding. *"Owing to the departure of two engines which had by mistake gone with the Duke of Wellington's carriages, the other part of the procession, consisting of 23 carriages and containing upwards of 600 ladies and gentlemen, was detained in Manchester till after 5 o'clock, when all the carriages were attached together, and drawn by 4 engines instead of 6."*[175] Robertson Gladstone

---

174 Frances Ann Kemble - Record of a Girlhood. (Volume 2), p197
175 Liverpool Times - 21 September 1830. The *Saturday Advertiser* reported, on 18 September, *"for the satisfaction of any party who may have considered that he was in some*

bemoaned the fact that *"so confused were the arrangements made by the Railway Company, and so contrary did they all act to their expectations, that Tom and I, with the rest of the party...did not reach the end of our journey until 20 minutes past ten at night, in place of half past four o'clock, as was fully intended!"* [176]

Moss was understandably reticent about this sorry incident. It was a shattering blow to have lost a man who was widely acknowledged as one of the finest politicians of his day.[177] Still in shock, the only comment he made to Gladstone on the matter was terse. *"Your sons will have written to you fully upon the melancholy event which has happened."* [178] One week on from the accident, he was more forthcoming to Loch. *"I have neither had health nor spirits, nor time to write to you since the 15th. No one who was present on that occasion could help feeling what Burke observed when the member for Bristol dropt* (sic) *down dead after getting his election:*

'Events like these tell us what shadows we are and what shadows we pursue.'

No one blames the directors but the directors have a right to blame themselves and I have very often felt that if the sole direction of that day had been left in the same cautious hands who originally got the Bill and who are in the habit of thinking more than acting, the accident may not have happened. Poor Huskisson's accident I am confident prevented many others. It made the Engineers think and the Directors prudent... I consider we are accountable for every valuable life lost if we do not exercise our best judgement in preventing the risks attendant upon swift

---

measure left in the lurch, that Mr. Moss, the Deputy Chairman, had left Mrs. Moss and several of his family to come with the trains which had been so left behind."

176 Robertson Gladstone to John Gladstone 16.9.1830 Hawarden: Glynne-Gladstone MSS138

177 Charles Greville, the foremost political diarist of the time, wrote of Huskisson *"There is no man in Parliament, or perhaps out of it, so well versed in finance, commerce, trade and colonial matters..."* Greville Diaries – 18 September 1830

178 Hawarden correspondence Moss to J Gladstone 18.9.1830

locomotive power…" [179]

Thoughts soon turned to Huskisson's vacant seat, which was of great interest to John Gladstone. Thomas Gladstone, who desperately wanted his father to become Tory member for Liverpool,[180] informed him on 17 September, that Moss, Peel and Holmes had been seen *"arm in arm and coming out of the bank."* This he saw as an act of betrayal.[181] Next day, Moss had to explain to Gladstone that he no longer believed he would make a successful candidate, owing to the opposition of *"the whole mass of Rathbones, Croppers etc etc and I do not think the Canning party would support you….I must confess I would rather see Sir Robert Peel, next to yourself, our Member for I am sure the advantage to the Town at large is very great in having a Minister our representative."* [182] Gladstone's brutal frankness and his ownership of slaves were two of the reasons for his unpopularity in the town, although he professed to be *"ignorant of any rational reasonable cause why it should be so."* [183] He proclaimed that he would not offer himself up as a candidate unless invited.[184] Even though Peel swiftly turned down the candidature, that invitation never came, despite the promptings of the *Liverpool Journal*. Its 25 September edition considered that *"the modesty of our merchants, in declining to come forward, should not be permitted to stand between them*

---

179 Stafford correspondence Moss to J Loch 22.9.1830 (D593/K/1/3/18) Moss remained ever mindful of poor Huskisson's dreadful demise, and as a mark of respect to the great man, he ensured that the opening day of his Grand Junction Railway in 1837 was devoid of all ceremony. In 1840, almost 10 years to the day after the opening of the L&M, he remembered how *"Huskisson fell a sacrifice to want of caution in railway management…His death determined me to resist, almost to obstinacy, whenever I had fears and I am gratified at the result of my exertions on the GJR…Add 6 pence to the fares if you please but let no means for increasing safety ever be delayed."* Hawarden correspondence Moss to J Gladstone 18.9.1840

180 Hawarden correspondence Thomas Gladstone to J Gladstone 17.9.1830 *"To see you member for Liverpool would undoubtedly be the proudest moment of our lives."*

181 ibid *"Surely Moss cannot promise anyone till you have refused - at least if he is a sincere man."*

182 Hawarden correspondence Moss to J Gladstone 18.9.1830

183 J Gladstone to Robertson Gladstone 5.12.1830 from Checkland, p233

184 Hawarden Correspondence J Gladstone to Moss from Leamington 20.9.1830

and their merits. There can be little doubt that one perfectly competent could be found: Mr. Gladstone and Mr. Moss have been mentioned." Though, no doubt, highly flattered by such comments, Moss consistently declared himself unavailable for high office on the grounds that, through his bank and through his wife's family he held too many Whig connections, that he thought nobody placed any great reliance on him anyway, that he was far more suited to railway work than politics, and that, *"after living 50 years without speaking in public I ought to be content for the remainder of my life to avoid it."* [185]

Regardless of the Huskisson tragedy, the wheels of industry kept turning and, on 16 September, the Liverpool & Manchester Railway opened for business. 140 passengers boarded the first train, reaching Manchester in two hours. Although the mood of the directors was undoubtedly somber, they could feel justifiably proud of their momentous achievement. There must have been many times during the previous eight years when they doubted the wisdom of their involvement but, through dogged persistence, they had established what is regarded as the world's first railway - in the truest sense of the word. The Stockton & Darlington, which opened in 1825, was essentially a mineral carrying line served by locomotives but, until 1833, its passenger traffic was drawn by horses. The Canterbury & Whitstable Railway, which opened in May 1830, was mainly worked by stationary engines. The first 15 miles of track on the Baltimore & Ohio line, which also came into use in May 1830, was worked by horses. By the end of 1830, just three months after its opening, the L&M's profits were such that the directors were able to declare a dividend of £2 per £100 share. £4 10s per share was paid for the six months to 1 June 1831.[186] Moss and his associates had proved to the world the

---

185 Moss to WE Gladstone 27.6.1835. British Library, ref Add 44354 f.201 *"Your Father knows well that I never in my life was worth any thing at an Election in Liverpool.. The knowledge of the miserable figure I made in the situation I was forced into, of seconding Lord Sandon and the Hon Mr. Wilbraham, has made me more reluctant than ever in taking any part in Elections."*
186 Carlson, p240-241

viability of their railway in terms of speed, safety and economic viability and, over the course of the next decade, he would play a significant part in bestowing its benefits upon the rest of Britain and continental Europe.

After its first full calendar year of operations, the L&M realised a net profit of £71,097 [187] and a surprising 65% of its receipts came, not from the carriage of freight, but from passenger traffic. The directors recognised that this figure was distorted by day trippers and thrill seekers, and they anticipated a greater proportion of their future income would come from their carrying department. In point of fact, in every year from its formation until its amalgamation in 1845, passenger receipts far exceeded freight. During that time the L&M's half yearly dividend never fell below £4 and never rose above £5, and the average annual yield per share was £9 10s. The value of the £100 shares rose to a record £295 in April 1836, and hit their lowest ebb of £173 in March 1842.[188] Robert Bradshaw "*thinking it better that each party should be left at liberty to exercise his own discretion*",[189] snubbed advances from the Old Quay and from the L&M to fix prices and, in terms of the total weight of traffic carried on the Bridgewater canal, his strategy succeeded. It increased its carryings from 91,793 tons in 1831 to 105,572 in 1833 but, with rising costs and reduced rates, net profits plummeted from £47,650 in 1830 to just £17,473 in 1833. [190] For that same year, the net profits of the L&M were £74,055 and 54% of these were derived from passenger traffic.[191] It was clear where the future lay, but it was not until the 1840s that most canals began to be overthrown. The Bridgewater was one of the few which continued to hold its own until the late 1850s when its business began to fall into

---

187 Thomas J Donaghy - Liverpool & Manchester Railway Operations 1831-1845 - Appendix A, p173. Profit equivalent to £5,331,558 in 2008 using the Retail Price Index

188 Thomas, p225

189 Mather, p59 - M & I.N.C. Order Book, 1828-34, pp128-9, 4 May 1831

190 ibid, p60

191 Donaghy, p173

slow decline. It was not until 1887 that it was absorbed by the Manchester Ship Canal.[192]

In 1851, *The Economist* carried an article headed *"Stupendous Progress in Locomotion"*. It said of the Liverpool & Manchester Railway that *"It opened at the modest speed of 20 miles an hour...In the days of Adam the average speed of travel, if Adam ever did such things, was four miles an hour...in the year 1828, or 4,000 years afterwards it was still only ten miles...in 1850, it is habitually forty miles an hour, and seventy for those who like it. We have reached in a single bound from the speed of a horse's canter, to the utmost speed comparable with the known strength and coherence of brass and iron."* [193] Changed forever was a whole way of life virtually unaltered for centuries. Fresh agricultural produce, coal and a plethora of other goods now became available to all. In this 'Age of Reform', railways enabled the different social classes to mingle more freely and, in so doing, helped bring British society a giant step nearer to true democracy. *The Economist* queried whether it was the rich, the middle classes or the poor who had benefited most from *"this vast invention"*, and concluded that it was *"Clearly the latter. The rail road is the Magna Carta of their motive freedom. How few among the last generation ever stirred beyond their own village? How few among the present will die without visiting London?...The number who left Manchester by cheap trips in one week of holiday time last year exceeded 202,000."* [194]

Drawing on her massive coal reserves, which fuelled the steam engines, not just of locomotives but of factories and of ships, Britain forged ahead as the world's leading industrial nation and built the greatest empire ever seen on the back of that industry.

---

192 Richards, p119
193 Richard L Tames - Documents of the Industrial Revolution 1750 - 1850, p43
194 ibid

CHAPTER 8

THE GRAND JUNCTION RAILWAY

"It has fallen to the lot of this Company to be the first to exhibit to the country the practical working of a railway nearly a hundred miles in length and forming the main route through the heart of the kingdom to Scotland and Ireland, and to the populous manufacturing and commercial districts of the north."

John Moss. Annual General Meeting of the Grand Junction Railway,

September 1837

Three enterprising Birmingham men, Messrs Spooner, Sparrow and Foster,[1] met in 1823 to discuss the proposal that a railway be made between their town and Liverpool. Shortly after, a united committee was formed of talented individuals from both towns and, the following year, an application was made to Parliament for a line commencing at Birkenhead, passing through Chester en route to Birmingham. The Bill

---

1   Grand Junction Railway Companion by Arthur Freeling, p8. Published in 1838 Freeling's book had been authorised by Moss, Locke and one N.D. Bold. He dedicated the book to *"Mr John Moss, Esq."* who had *"at some personal trouble, enabled me to acquire facts which, otherwise, could not have been obtained."* A rival publication under a very similar name written by a Mr Cornish had not been so sanctioned.

was thrown out following violent opposition from canal owners, [2] and Moss, along with the other Liverpool men, then became preoccupied with their work on the Liverpool & Manchester Railway. The ongoing efforts of the Birmingham men were viewed with disdain in Liverpool.[3] Delegates from Birmingham, whom Moss met at the Killingworth Colliery Trials in January 1825, calculated that they could construct a line 100 miles in length for £150,000; whereas the 33 miles of the Liverpool & Manchester were estimated to cost £400,000.[4] Regardless, the two parties did continue to collaborate, and it was proposed that a bridge be built to carry the railway over the River Mersey at Runcorn, thereby reducing the length of the route by 13 miles.[5] A further application was made to Parliament in 1826, [6] but this too was rejected, and there the matter rested.

By late 1829, Moss, confident of the L&M's prospects, felt inclined to dedicate more time to the Birmingham project. In mid-December, a company was formed whose proclaimed aim was to co-operate with the canal proprietors - in particular with the L&M's largest shareholder, the Marquis of Stafford. It made sense for the railway to negate its main opposition in the same way that the L&M had the Bridgewater interest. However, the Marquis, who had already invested £400,000 in the construction of the Birmingham & Liverpool Junction Canal[7] (started in 1827 but not completed until 1835) was understandably reluctant to take shares in a railway to rival it.

---

2   Thomas Roscoe - The Book of the Grand Junction Railway, pp 9-10 (1839). *"The Grand Junction Railway owes its first projection and complete establishment to the spirit, intelligence and enterprise of the town of Birmingham."*
3   Hawarden correspondence Moss to J Gladstone 30.11.1824. *"I do not think the Birmingham rail road has anything like such a case as we have, nor do they understand the subject. When we saw them not one of them knew what was the lowest price that a ton of goods would cost to go to Liverpool."*
4   Hawarden correspondence Moss to J Gladstone 19.1.1825
5   Hawarden correspondence Moss to J Gladstone 11.1.1825
6   *"varying the line by leading it across the Mersey at Northgate and proceeding through Cheshire"* Roscoe, p10.
7   Richards, p90

His business manager James Loch knew it was inevitable that one would be constructed eventually, and that it would be better for it to be built by Moss and his associates than by others over whom he and his master exercised no control. Loch tried to persuade Moss to delay putting forward a Bill until the end of the next Parliamentary session. By then, the L&M would have commenced operations and it would be apparent exactly *"what the Rail Roads are really capable of doing in terms of speed, economy and arrangement."* [1] However, the Birmingham men, who were *"not only independent of but declared to be hostile to canals"* [2] wished to forge ahead with the project without delay. The Liverpool party, headed by Moss, Charles Lawrence and Joseph Sandars considered that by *"declaring our intentions of conciliating all parties, we should keep the public from joining any wild adventurer, who might propose a new line to Manchester and one also to Birmingham."* [3] It was their will which prevailed, and no Bill was put before Parliament in 1829. Moss warned Loch that it had been *"no easy matter to keep our friends quiet and particularly the Birmingham people."* [4] The argument had only been won by him and others threatening to *"withdraw from the concern"*.[5] He declared that *"This is only due to yourself for the very candid and kind manner you act to us. If we meet with you it must be to co-operate with you, not to fight you."* [6]

While Lord Stafford dithered and weighed up his options, the owners of various other waterways, which would eventually feed into the Birmingham & Liverpool Junction Canal, emphatically rejected any notion of co-operation with the railways. These parties Loch described as *"a set of antiquated persons who sit quietly still until their concerns*

---

1   Stafford Correspondence Loch to Stafford 20.11.1829. Mather. p69
2   Stafford Correspondence G Pritt (Solicitor to the Liverpool & Manchester) to J Loch 19.12.1829. Mather, p74
3   Stafford correspondence Copy letter from Moss to W Huskisson 14.12.1829 (D593/K/1/3/17)
4   Stafford Correspondence Moss to J Loch 26.1.1830 (D593/K/1/3/18)
5   Stafford Correspondence Moss to J Loch 21.11.1829 (D593/K/1/3/17)
6   ibid

are swept away from under them." ⁷ With far-sightedness, he proposed that the Bridgewater Trustees should fund the construction of a railway and turnpike bridge over the Mersey at Runcorn. In recompense they would levy tolls on all goods crossing the bridge in perpetuity. Moss agreed to the plan, but Loch presented it to the Trustees' Superintendent Robert Bradshaw on 25 May 1830 as a fait accompli. Stung by Loch's inconsiderate double dealing, Bradshaw rejected the scheme out of hand. Moss continued to press for cooperation from the waterways and implored Loch to exert his influence and *"bring to as speedy a conclusion as you can the decision of the canal interest."* ⁸ It had already been determined that a Bill would be sought with or without that consent. The railway's capital of £750,000 would be made up of 7,500 shares of £100 each. Of these, it was proposed that 1,500 be given to the Marquis, who would also be entitled to appoint 1/5th of the directors. 1,000 shares *"or the Runcorn Bridge on terms to be fixed"* were to be offered to his heir Lord Francis Leveson-Gower or the Duke of Bridgewater Trustees.⁹ Moss was adamant, too, that the railway's projectors would be fairly rewarded for their hard work. *"In proposing the new scheme I must admit that pecuniary advantages form no inconsiderable part of our expectations. The Liverpool & Manchester Railroad was a struggle for the public; the few shares taken by those who fought the battle ill paid us for the time we gave it. We must now take care of ourselves."* ¹⁰

In the continuing absence of a decisive response from the Marquis, Moss warned Loch, on 15 June, that the canals

---

7   Stafford Correspondence. Loch to W Lewis 18.12.1829. Mather, p72
8   Stafford Correspondence Moss to J Loch 9.6.1830 (D593/K/1/3/18)
9   Stafford Correspondence Moss to G Pritt 14.5.1830 (D593/K/1/3/18)
"2400 are taken by 80 original subscribers, 1200 given to the public in Liverpool, 1200 for influential persons (700 are already given), 500 are reserved for the committee." This left 2,200 for canal proprietors, including Lord Harrowby, who had a substantial holding in the Trent and Mersey Canal, Lord Clive and his friends on the Birmingham Junction Canal and Edward John Littleton, a significant Shropshire landowner.
10 Stafford correspondence Copy letter from Moss to W Huskisson 14.12.1829 (D593/K/1/3/17)

had *"no idea of the importance to them of an alliance with us - I do not hesitate to state that unless they join us they will be ruined by our Act."* [11] On behalf of Lord Stafford's Bridgewater interest, Bradshaw rejected the railway as being *"contrary to the spirit of the late Duke's will."* [12] The Runcorn bridge scheme was now abandoned altogether, and work began on planning an alternative route. Moss declared that he had never approved of the scheme anyway; he had gone along with it only *"to meet the wishes of the Bridgewater Trust because I heard that nothing short of that would content them."* [13] It would be a further 44 years before, on 1 February 1869, the first Runcorn Bridge opened to goods traffic.[14]

Moss begged Loch to *"not allow the opportunity of protecting Lord Stafford's interest escape, which it certainly will if longer delayed"*, [15] and made him one final proposition on 21 August: *"I send you a map. The dotted line is the Birmingham. On it I have put two other dotted lines. Will either of these please you and those you represent?"* [16] The Marquis and Lord George Leveson-Gower were offered a 1/3 stake in the undertaking, Lord Francis Leveson-Gower a further 1/3 and the rest to be apportioned to *"those persons who by their personal exertions got the Manchester Bill... they have never been equitably considered yet."* Moss intended taking *"a large slice of such a project."*[17] The Marquis need only have looked at the price of his L&M shares to appreciate the value of this proposition; they had more than doubled to £210.[18] Moss reiterated that he would still be entitled to appoint 1/5th of the board if only he would take up the offer. However, Lord Stafford, now 72 years of age, was not up for another round of acrimonious negotiations. Loch

---

11 Stafford Correspondence Moss to J Loch 15.6.1830 (D593/K/1/3/18)
12 Stafford Correspondence Moss to J Loch 5.7.1830 (D593/K/1/3/18)
13 ibid
14 Passenger trains began operating two months later
15 Stafford Correspondence Moss to J Loch 5.7.1830 (D593/K/1/3/18)
16 Stafford correspondence Moss to J Loch 21.8.1830 (D593/K/1/3/18)
17 ibid
18 Richards, p102

declared that he had been *"brought chiefly to this conclusion by his advanced time of life, he takes no share in its progress, either for or against."* [19]

By the time of the opening of the Liverpool & Manchester on 15 September 1830, the commercial benefits of railways had become apparent to other towns, and hundreds of small projects sprang up all over the country. Few of those promoters possessed the vision or the capability of the wealthy Liverpool men, who now took control of the scheme to establish a rail link between England's three largest commercial towns outside of London. They had felt it their duty *"To secure the ground and the public, both of whom were in danger of being taken possession of by persons who have not the same prudence and experience as ourselves"* [20] Progress was slow, however, and even as late as August 1832, Moss was bemoaning the fact that *"It is not yet decided whether we go with the Birmingham rail road or not, nor will it be for a month. Our friends at Birmingham are not to be depended upon"* [21] At last, on 22 September, a Liverpool newspaper, *The Saturday Advertiser*, announced that chairman Moss had received the committee's approval *"to adopt such measures as might be thought desirable to promote the intended application for an Act in the next session of Parliament."* [22]

Soon the Liverpool & Birmingham was renamed 'The Grand Junction Railway Company' in recognition of its intention to connect the Liverpool & Manchester Railway with the projected London & Birmingham Railway. In October, a committee of 21 members was formed, (13 Liverpool men, six Birmingham men and two of unknown affiliation) with Moss as chairman and Robertson Gladstone, Charles Lawrence and a Birmingham gentleman Joseph Walker as his deputies.[23] A

---

19   Stafford correspondence J Loch to Moss 20.11.1830 - Richards, p104
20   Stafford correspondence Copy letter from Moss to W Huskisson 14.12.1829 (D593/K/1/3/17)
21   Hawarden correspondence Moss to Gladstone 18.8.1832
22   Saturday Advertiser 22.9.1832
23   The other Liverpool men were James Bourne, John Cropper, Hardman Earle,

new route, incorporating the Warrington & Newton Railway's stretch of track, had already been surveyed by George Stephenson and his assistants Robert Stephenson and Joseph Locke. The proposed starting point would be at Newton Le Willows, where the Warrington & Newton joined the L&M at its mid point and ran southwards 5 miles to Warrington. The Grand Junction Railway would construct the remaining 78 miles of track from Warrington to Birmingham. However, it took two years of wrangling and the GJR's threat of pursuing an alternative route over the Mersey[24] before the Warrington & Newton consented to being absorbed. Its shareholders and directors paid a heavy price for their stubbornness.[25] Moss rejoiced that their line had been purchased for *"upwards of ten thousand pounds less than the price we offered and they refused at the last negotiation."* [26] Having settled the terms without the aid of solicitors, Moss and his colleagues saved the GJR a small fortune. Their costs amounted to less than £30. [27]

True to his word, Lord Stafford who, in January 1833, was created the first Duke of Sutherland,[28] opposed neither the Grand Junction nor the London & Birmingham lines,[29]

Richard Harrison, Joseph Hornby, William Rotheram, Joseph Sandars, Charles Tayleur and Joseph N Walker. The remaining Birmingham contingent was made up of William Chance, Daniel Ledsam, Joseph F. Ledsam, Charles Shaw and John Turner. The other 2 members were T.W. Giffard and Theodore Price. Manchester Guardian, 20.10.1832 & Donaghy, p100

24   at Fiddler's Ferry to join the L&M at Whiston,

25   The GJR obtained its Act on 12 June 1835, and bought the Warrington & Newton's 518 £100 shares at par while accepting outstanding debts of £15,503. In 1833 they had demanded £125 per share as well as settlement of their debts of £20,000. Webster - Britain's First Trunk Line, pp43-44

26   Stafford Correspondence Moss to J Loch 5.2.1835 (D593/K/1/3/23)

27   ibid

28   On 19 July the Duke of Sutherland died. His second son, Lord Francis Leveson-Gower, inherited the Bridgewater Canal interests and his first son, Lord George, was created second Duke of Sutherland. Moss wasted little time before querying *"Has Lord F L Gower altered his opinion of rail roads in consequence of coming into possession of the Canal? I am more than ever satisfied of the advantage he might derive from a junction with the line to Birmingham."* Stafford Correspondence Moss to J Loch 21.8.1833 (D593/K/1/3/21)

29   Although Moss was not directly involved in the London & Birmingham, he did

and on 6 May, Acts for both railways received royal assent. The GJR's Bill passed both Houses almost unopposed. Its directors had previously entered into negotiations with all *"parties who felt themselves to be injured or likely to be so; and thus, by tact, prudence and perseverance, brought the projected Bill through Parliament."* [30] The company was authorised to raise £1,040,000 by the issue of 10,400 shares of £100 each and to borrow £346,000.[31] The appearance of George Stephenson's name on the prospectus of any new railway scheme always ensured a full subscription list, and the clamour for GJR shares was such that all were quickly taken up.[32] It was hoped that work on both the GJR and the L&B would take no more than four years and that both lines would open in the summer of 1837. Where once there had been dogged resistance to the encroachment of railways upon the lands of the wealthy, it was now apparent that proximity to one was considered, by some at least, an asset. Before the Parliamentary Committee on the L&B, Moss had been asked:

"Have you found owners, on the line between Liverpool & Birmingham, consent to the railroad there, who, nevertheless, opposed the Liverpool & Manchester line?"

"Yes, several, among others, Lords Derby and Sefton"

"Did Mr. Heywood of Manchester oppose the Manchester railroad?"

"Yes."

"Did he afterwards complain of its not passing through his lands?"

---

subscribe to it as well as to the London & Southampton, the Great North of England and the North Midland Railways at various times. M C Reed - Investment in Railways in Britain 1820-1824, p206

30   Freeling, p13

31   Harry Scrivenor – The Railways of the United Kingdom, p32 (1849)

32   By August 1833, Moss was the owner of 100 shares for which he had so far paid around £10 each. Moss to W Wainewright 27.8.1833. Liverpool Record Office, 328PAR7/189

"Yes, he complained very much of it." [33]

With a decade of railway administration behind him, Moss now had the confidence and the ability to inspire others, and the chairmanship was bestowed upon him. In a reversal of roles, Charles Lawrence, the L&M's chairman, would act as Moss's sole deputy. The company established its headquarters in Cook Street, Liverpool, just a stone's throw from Moss's bank in Dale Street. The Birmingham quota of the GJR's 'incorporated proprietors' was dwarfed by what became known as 'The Liverpool Party'. Prominent among those named in the Act were Robertson Gladstone, Moss's son Thomas, John Cropper, William Rotheram, Joseph Sandars, James Bourne, Charles Tayleur, Hardman Earle, Richard Harrison, and Joseph Hornby.[34] The project was now in the hands of men who, through years of experience, were extremely well qualified to construct their railway scientifically and economically.

With so many common directors, an amalgamation of the GJR and the L&M was proposed but resisted by Moss, who saw danger in operating such a powerful monopoly.[35] In any case, relations between the two boards were far from cordial. One group of L&M directors was bitterly opposed to the GJR, and sneered that it was "only a branch" of the London & Birmingham.[36] There were movements to oust the original promoters - Moss, Gladstone, Cropper, Lawrence and Harrison - from the L&M board in March 1833. Moss was appalled by the view that "*no one can hereafter be a director, without the approbation of individuals who look to a man's politics in judging of his fitness to be a director*" He was so vexed that he considered handing in his resignation, but only if Lord Stafford's representative James Loch sanctioned it. He did

---

33   Smiles - Life of Stephenson, p305. (1857)
34   Webster - Britain's First Trunk Line, p26. Other names included William Chance, Joseph Christopher Ewart, Thomas Giffard, Daniel and Joseph Ledsam, Theodore Price, Charles Shaw, John Turner and Joseph Walker
35   Stafford Correspondence Moss to J Loch 12.9.1833 (D593/K/1/3/21)
36   Richards, p133

not.[37] In August, Moss began disposing of his L&M shares, bemoaning the fact that the *"shares as well as the influence of the concern are getting more and more into the hands of those who do not in my humble opinion always act with the liberality they profess…I am pretty confident that next year Lawrence and Harrison will be turned out and I am 'setting my house in order' to withdraw before my turn comes."* [38]

While Robert Stephenson was employed by the London & Birmingham as its engineer, the GJR employed three engineers. Initially, Joseph Locke looked after the construction of the northern half, and John Rastrick the southern half. George Stephenson, who brought with him his reputation as Britain's foremost railway engineer, was placed in overall control. Locke dedicated himself to his work, but Stephenson and Rastrick were already involved in other projects, which placed constraints on their commitment to the GJR. This inevitably met with the disapproval of the directors, and Rastrick resigned in September. From then on, engineering duties were split on a north/south basis between Locke and Stephenson. Some of the directors had pressed for Locke to be appointed sole engineer. While Stephenson tried gamely to attend meetings, submit reports and to progress the works, there were many frustrating delays.[39] Despite the misgivings of others, Moss felt it unfair to criticise Stephenson too harshly. His part of the railway was beset with greater engineering difficulties than Locke's and also by more disputes with landowners and canal and turnpike operators.[40]

---

37 Stafford Correspondence Moss to J Loch 1.4.1833 (D593/K/1/3/21) *"I took so very active a part in the negotiations with you, when Lord Stafford joined us that I feel that I ought to have your entire approbation before I decide to withdraw or remain… You will have to exercise the very clear head you are known to have, whether it is not advisable to dispose of the Duke of Sutherland's shares."*
38 Stafford Correspondence Moss to J Loch 21.8.1833 (D593/K/1/3/21) He sold 17 at £215 on 20th August
39 Skeat, p146
40 ibid, p146

The railway's most notable opponent was James Watt, residing at Aston Hall near Handsworth, close to its proposed Birmingham terminus. The GJR's plan for the most direct route possible into town involved the construction of a tunnel under the knoll of Aston Park, but permission had been denied. Although it was still hoped that Watt might be persuaded to change his mind, Locke was instructed, in early 1834, to find an alternative route into Birmingham. Stephenson busied himself in concluding deals with canal proprietors and the old Birmingham & Walsall turnpike road operators.[41] The Watts case, though, proved insoluble, and so in July 1835, Moss, Lawrence and George Barker of Birmingham paid £3,106 for several parcels of land in Handsworth *"in the expectation that the Grand Junction Railway Company… will obtain an Act in the present or next session of Parliament for making certain deviations through the estates of John Gough esq. and John Heathcote, Gentleman in the parish of Handsworth."* [42] At a board meeting, in December, Moss put a brave face on it, insisting that the new route, *"though longer than the original one by about a mile, was preferable in all other respects being less expensive and affording better levels besides avoiding a tunnel under the town."* [43] The diversion around Aston Hall created a curious hook at the end of an otherwise, generally straight line.

With the exception of the 1,400 foot Dutton Viaduct over the River Weaver,[44] there were no monumental engineering features on the GJR, but there was gruelling hard work for the administrators, engineers, and in particular, the labourers. In the absence of modern machinery, and in order

---

41 ibid, p149
42 On 17 July 1835 in addition to this land purchased in a deal struck with Samuel Partidge, the GJR committee proposed to purchase timber from the site to the value of £74. The grand total to be paid to Mr Partridge was agreed at £3,229 and 14 shillings. Birmingham Central Library Ref MS 3375/461032
43 Webster - Britain's First Trunk Line, p63
44 completed on 9 December 1836. Freeling, p47 states *"This magnificent work cost about £50,000. It consists of 20 arches, each of 65 feet span. The road is 27 ½ feet wide, and is 65 feet above the level of the Weaver and canal which passes under it."*

to meet the tight deadline, work was often carried out round the clock. Thomas Roscoe described the scene at the Newton excavation, which was 80 feet deep in places:

"By day and night they struggled without relaxing, at the incessant toil, and as they continued to bore through the bowels of the land, the shelving sides of the excavation arose, letting in the cheerful light upon the close pent earth. By day the bright sunbeams, broken by the numerous angles which each successive advance presented to its linear ray, lay scattered in shining fragments upon the sloping banks, cheering the toil-worn workers - by night the hill literally swarmed with moving bodies, lighted to their work by torches flickering from side to side, and from place to place. Creaking cranes, dragging by ropes and pulleys the laden barrows with their guides, and again slowly curbing their descent down the almost perpendicular banks, the clatter of continued footsteps, the heavy sound of spade and pick-axe and the busy hum of toiling men, completed a scene of unexampled animation, and long remembered interest by all who witnessed it." [45]

The balancing act Moss had been performing with his duties at the bank, on the Liverpool & Manchester Railway, the Grand Junction Railway, his West Indian estate and other projects came at a cost, both to his family and to his health. Throughout 1833 he had suffered *"a bilious headache"* and took himself to Leamington for ten days that October *"to try the waters."* [46] His innumerable business trips took him all over Britain, and the taxing workload rendered him an all too often absentee husband for Hannah. *"I am a little out of order at parting with her. At the same time I am glad to get away from the natural anxiety which a large family brings, and to which she has almost devoted herself to for 26 years."* [47] He and Hannah sorely needed a good holiday, and William Wainewright was

---

45   Roscoe, p43
46   Hawarden correspondence Moss to J Gladstone 15.10.1833
47   Hawarden correspondence Moss (from London) to J Gladstone 12.4.1831

asked to facilitate it.[48] On 21 August 1834, five days prior to this trip to the continent, confident in the knowledge that the Grand Junction was on a firm footing, Moss announced to its shareholders that *"The works are now in active progress on a distance of thirteen miles, including the great viaduct at Dutton, and others will be immediately in operation. Specifications have been tendered for two other contracts, comprising an extent of nineteen miles...and a third is also in readiness for a further portion of the line, fourteen miles in length...In the purchase of land, considerable progress has been made; the quantity bought amounts to about forty miles in length; and as railways are no longer considered by landowners and juries as detrimental to property, this has generally been effected on terms as reasonable as could have been expected."*[49]

Moss returned home from his excursion through Belgium, Switzerland and France [50] on 18 October *"improved I hope in every respect but certainly in health."* [51] During his absence, the other directors became increasingly concerned by Stephenson's perceived indifference to the GJR, his continuing failure to attend meetings, to submit reports and to reply to letters. On 18 September they resolved to write him a reminder on the subject of rails and chairs, expressing disappointment

---

48 Moss to W Wainewright 16.8.1834. Liverpool Record Office. *"I am going to the Continent on Tuesday 26th or Wednesday 27th Aug:* (1834) *- I have written to Backhouse to ask him if he knows of a good Courier - a respectable fellow - who will not be extravagant. I want to be absent 6 weeks and go by Rhine to Switzerland - just crossing the Alps to get a peep into Italy. It has occurred to me that you may know of such a person, or that you would enquire of Backhouse - as he is so fully engaged. You would perhaps have the kindness to ask about one for me. I do not want to travel extravagantly but look to real comfort. I must be back about 6th Oct - all I fear is that for 6 weeks a good man would hardly go - but you may tell him that I have a numerous acquaintance here, and perhaps might get him a better job hereafter. I have also asked Mr. B to get our passports. Can you enquire if a good boat goes from London to Ostend on Wednesday 27th inst - and what other days. I would rather embark from London. I take no servant but a Courier if we can get a good one he must be Ladies Maid as well as all other things. I am giving you a load of troubles and dare hardly read over all I have asked from you. I leave here on Tuesday morning next before which time if you are able I wish you would drop me a line. Our party will consist of Mrs. Moss, Miss Monez* (?) *a Swiss Young Lady now with us and 2 Gents."*
49 Webster - Britain's First Trunk Line, pp63-64
50 Hawarden correspondence Moss to J Gladstone 18.10.1834
51 ibid

at having received no previous reply. Stephenson ignored it, and Locke, who was achieving all the standards the directors expected of their engineer, was eventually asked to report on the matter. By 25 September, all the contracts for Locke's portion of the railway had been prepared, issued, tendered for and let. However, on the southern section, contractors were confused by Stephenson's ambiguity, and some disturbing discrepancies came to light.[52] In December, the directors took the step of appointing Locke and Stephenson as joint engineers, although it was clear from the minutes of the board meetings that Locke alone was effectively engineering the entire line. [53] Stephenson, with his services much in demand elsewhere, (he was Principal Engineer to the North Midland, the Manchester & Leeds, the Birmingham & Derby Junction and the Sheffield & Rotherham - all of which were authorised by Acts of Parliament in 1836) continued to lose interest in his GJR work. The directors unanimously lost patience but, not until 12 August 1835 did they resolve to appoint Locke as engineer and to retain Stephenson only as a consultant.[54] For Stephenson this was one humiliation too many. He wrote to Moss tendering his resignation, and this was accepted on 16 September. The Grand Junction biographer, NW Webster wrote, of the Stephenson affair, that Moss acted all along with firmness and diplomacy, leaving matters to pursue their own inevitable course. In so doing he miraculously kept on good terms with Stephenson even after the break, and continued to speak of him in the highest terms.[55] Stephenson biographer, Samuel Smiles, stated that *"An unhappy difference afterwards occurred between Mr. Stephenson and Mr. Locke...Considerable personal feeling was thrown into the affair, which had no small influence upon the railway politics (so to speak) of the time."* [56]

---

52 NW Webster – Joseph Locke Railway Revolutionary, pp65-66
53 ibid, p66
54 Locke's salary was set at "£1,200 and Stephenson's annual fee at £300. Webster – Locke, p66
55 ibid, p67
56 Smiles - Life of Stephenson, p376 (1857)

Moss ensured that the GJR steered clear of a slanging match. *"I feel we owe rail roads to George Stephenson and I should at a time when he is behaving so ill to us be sorry to say one word against him"* [57]

Long before the works were complete, the GJR began to see itself as the builder of a line which would form the first part of a great national railway route,[58] an ambition Moss first expressed in October 1835. [59] While the works continued at a pace, the GJR's share price remained static – much to John Gladstone's and William Wainewright's disappointment.[60] Nonetheless, when, in November, Gladstone received government compensation for the loss of his West Indian slaves, Moss had no hesitation in recommending a home for a sizeable portion of that £93,536 fortune.[61] By 25 November, a deal had been struck whereby the GJR agreed to take from him *"£30,000 at 4 per cent on Bond to be redeemed at six months notice. The money may be paid in to us here or to Barclay and co London any time on account of the Grand Junction Railway with Moss House...the additional sum of £20,000 we will take at 3 per cent and no commission."* [62]

---

57   Stafford correspondence Moss to J Loch 21.4.1836 (D593/K/1/3/24)
58   Webster - Britain's First Trunk Line, p28
59   Stafford correspondence Moss to J Loch 10.10.1835 (D593/K/1/3/23) *"I consider a line of railway from Preston to Glasgow would be of the greatest service to Liverpool & Glasgow etc etc as well as to the Grand Junction...I wish I could in any way be useful in promoting such a scheme."*
60   Hawarden correspondence Moss to J Gladstone 17.6.1834. In June 1834, Moss begged Gladstone to hold his nerve. *"You ask why the GJ rail road shares are at par. The only reply I can make is the Liverpool & Manchester were so for some months when first we began. I am more satisfied of its success than ever and I feel pretty confident they will sell for as much as the L & M do before 5 years are over."* Two months later Moss was called upon to assure a jittery Wainewright that he too had made a sound, long term investment. *"I am more than ever confident that it is the safest - and will turn out the best investment of money that can be made. On this account I advise you strongly to retain your shares and not to mind if the price should drop to £5 or 10 dis for they would not long remain so."* Moss to W Wainewright 16.8.1834 Liverpool Record Office, 328 PAR7/245
61   Checkland, p321
62   Hawarden correspondence Moss to Gladstone 25.11.1835

Now, while fully occupied in overseeing the timely completion of the GJR, Moss again began to question the merits of continuing with his L&M directorship. He found objectionable an attempt, in March 1836, by the L&M board to seek an alternative means of recompense for the restrictive 10% dividend limit clause. The committee proposed that more shares be issued to pay off its £400,000 Exchequer Loan debt. Moss wanted these sold on the open market, but most others wanted them offered to the *"Projectors at Par"* whereby *"the present proprietor obtains a handsome bonus if he decides to increase his stock"*[63] On 22 March, having been out voted, and furious that the Duke of Sutherland's directors had abstained, he remonstrated with Loch. *"You will recollect that clause was set by yourself and me in poor Huskisson's private room."*[64] Once more, he expressed a long held desire that he be permitted to resign from the L&M:

"You will say that having been instrumental in bringing the Duke of Sutherland into the concern, I am bound in fairness to remain in it so long as you, his representative wish it...Personally I have no longer a pleasure in attending the Board. When I go I feel that I must either take no part in what is doing, or discuss subjects in a way I do not like and is not satisfactory to me. I have not an interest in the concern to induce me to attend...I have satisfactory occupation for all my time and therefore I ask myself, as I now ask you, why do I remain a Director? I have long seen, indeed from the opening, that I was considered by some as having too much influence at the Board, and the removal of my friends Robert Gladstone, Harrison and Sandars told me plainly that I was permitted to remain only on sufferance...I am Chairman of the Grand Junction and they are in some degree dependent on the Liverpool & Manchester. Could I as an honest man... remain a Director of both? I think not...There can be no doubt of the impropriety of my being one of those to do what I perceive an

---

63 Stafford correspondence H Booth to J Loch 2.5.1835. Richards, p126
64 Stafford Correspondence Moss to J Loch 22.3.1836 (D593/K/1/3/24)

improper act." [65] Loch disagreed with Moss's interpretation of the Huskisson clause and, believing it referred to all the capital expended on the railway, was able to persuade him, both that the share issue was legitimate and that he should not climb down from the board.[66]

By 30 June 1837, calls of £90 had been paid on all the £100 GJR shares and, soon after, they were being sold for as much as £186.[67] The Grand Junction Railway was officially opened on 4 July. Over the previous four years, reports concerning the heavy engineering works on the L&B at Tring Cutting and Kilsby Tunnel had drawn the public eye away from the steady progress made on the GJR, whose opening was also overshadowed by the official mourning period for William IV. The old king died on 20 June, but his funeral did not take place until 8 July. Freeling explained that the GJR's inaugural day was *"unattended by any display. This did not arise from apathy on the part of the public, as thousands that waited at many of the stations for the arrival of the first trains which passed along the line fully testified; but out of respect to the memory of the late Mr. Huskisson, who met with the fatal accident which caused his death at the opening of the Liverpool and Manchester line. The Chairman, John Moss esq. and the Deputy Chairman, Charles Lawrence esq, having been present at that melancholy event, requested, on his account, that a public opening should be dispensed with."* [68]

A London newspaper described the scene at Birmingham that morning:

"At an early hour the town was in a state of great commotion and pleasurable excitement...Soon after 5 o'clock the streets leading

---

65   ibid
66   Stafford Correspondence Moss to J Loch 28.3.1836 (D593/K/1/3/24). *"I am still in the direction and will be glad to assist you in what your very superior judgment decides to be done.... I wish I possessed a little more of your coolness. What seems to have no effect on you would drive me mad."*
67   W L Steel - History of the London & North Western, p 98
68   Freeling, p14

in the direction of Vauxhall, [69] *where the Company's temporary station is situated, were crowded with persons of all ranks anxious to witness the first public travelling on this important line of railway communication.... The embankments of the several excavations, and even the valley through which the railway alternately 'wends its way' between Birmingham and Wolverhampton, were literally covered with dense masses of admiring spectators... Upon entering the station yard about half past six o'clock, we were, however, much struck with the thinness of the company within the Company's premises. It presented a striking contrast to the station yard on Olive Mount, at the opening of the Liverpool & Manchester Railway in 1830. It was evident, indeed, that no exertions had been made to give éclat to the proceedings of the day. There were no bands of music, no profuse display of banners, no attendance of distinguished visitors - in fact, within the precincts of the station there was scarcely anything to distinguish it from an ordinary day of business."* [70]

The far reaching consequence of the GJR's understatement and self effacement was that its great achievements slipped rapidly from popular memory. It had been completed on time and within budget at a total cost of £1,512,150 0s 4d.[71] The cost per mile of track was £18,846 as compared with the £42,000 per mile which Moss estimated the L&M to have cost. He explained that *"Making railroads is better understood than formerly."* [72] The London & Birmingham, which did not open until June 1838, was

---

69 Vauxhall is known today as Duddleston Railway Station. Curzon Street became the L&B's permanent terminus after work was completed in 1838 and the GJR's within a year of that. For passengers, it was inconveniently situated on the east of the city centre. The London & North Western Railway established New Street, two and a quarter miles west of Curzon Street, as its preferred central passenger station, in 1854.
70 Steel, pp91-92 (The newspaper's title is not stated)
71 Freeling, p16. His breakdown of income and expenditure had been supplied by the directors of the railway. In 1838 a report stated the cost was £1,607,490 10s 10d. Second Report of the Commissioners appointed to Inquire into the Manner in Which Railway Communications...by Irish Railway Commission, p147
72 *"we shall complete it for £18,000 a mile. The L&M cost £42,000."* Hawarden correspondence Moss to J Gladstone 10.9.1836

completed at an average £53,000 per mile.[73] Webster states that Moss proved a capable chairman throughout the whole period of construction. His quiet integrity contributed to the smooth running of the project. He gave the scheme an air of dedicated purpose. His object was to build on time, within budget and without extravagance a smooth and efficiently performing trunk line between Warrington and Birmingham, and that is precisely what was achieved. Locke, too, proved supremely able, often walking the whole length of the track in 3 days, supervising work, dispensing advice and ironing out problems as he went.[74] Moss praised his Engineer in Chief for having *"devoted himself to the discharge of his responsible duties with an ability, zeal, and above all, an untiring energy which have fully justified the implicit confidence which has been reposed in him on all occasions…"*[75] It was as if Moss and his colleagues were working in the national interest, and their responsible attitude far outweighed any greed.

Freeling marvelled at the railway's engineering feats, the hard physical labour and the brilliant organization, which had made it all possible:

"The reader who has accompanied us on our journey will, perhaps scarcely be aware that he has passed 100 excavations and embankments - yet such is the fact. In the formation of these 5,500,000 cubic yards of earth and stone have been cut and removed, 3 millions of which have been employed in the embankments; the remainder has, for the most part, been laid out for spoil. In the line there are about 109,000 distinct rails, which rest on 436,000 chairs, which are supported by 436,000 blocks of stone. The railway passes under 100 bridges, 2 aqueducts, and through 2 tunnels; it passes over 50 bridges and 5 viaducts, the latter being stupendous erections. In the formation of the line,

---

73　Steel, p91
74　Webster - Britain's First Trunk Line, p56
75　ibid, pp100-101. The full report from the GJR's 5th Annual General Meeting on 7 September is quoted in Guide to the Grand Junction Railway by EC & W Osborne, 1838, p44

upwards of 41,440,000 pounds of iron have been used for rails and chairs, and upwards of 656,940 cubic yards of stone for blocks to support them. These few facts will suggest to the intelligent reader an idea of the magnitude of the work, and of the intelligence and activity necessary in the governing power which has superintended its formation." [76]

The line was just over 82 & 1/3 miles in length, and the distance from Birmingham to both Liverpool and Manchester was 97¼ miles. In the earliest timetable, the first and last trains, (both first class) departed Liverpool and Manchester at 6.30 a.m. and 6.30 p.m. respectively, and arrived at Birmingham 5 hours and 5¼ hours later. The fastest first class trains left Liverpool and Manchester at 11.30 a.m. and took 4¾ hours to get to their destination. The fastest journey of the "mixed" class (the 8 a.m.) took 6¼ hours. First class trains only stopped at the stations in capital letters: LIVERPOOL, MANCHESTER, Newton Junction, WARRINGTON, Moore, Preston Brook, Acton, HARTFORD, Winsford, Minshull Vernon, Coppenhall, CREWE, Madeley, WHITMORE, Norton Bridge, Bridgeford, STAFFORD, Penkridge, Spread Eagle, Four Ashes, WOLVERHAMPTON, Willenhall, James's Bridge, Bescott Bridge, Newton Road, Perry Bar and BIRMINGHAM. [77]

In their 'Guide to the Grand Junction Railway', EC & W Osbourne described the scene at the Newton Le Willows junction:

"The trains for Liverpool and Manchester here pass to the left and right to their respective lines; and the trains from these towns arrive at this station usually at the same minute, and proceed along their curves on to the line of the Grand Junction, the Liverpool train taking the precedence. The sight of both trains connected together, passing along the Grand Junction line, and

---
76   Freeling, pp134-135
77   ibid pp18-21

then separating right and left, and speeding away from each other at the rate of thirty miles an hour is very beautiful; but to see the trains coming from the Liverpool & Manchester line, and watch them running down the curved branches on to the Grand Junction line, is majestic... We gaze with admiration and astonishment upon it, as much the fiftieth as the first time." [78]

In December 1837, the GJR raised the subject of an alternative route into Liverpool and sought the L&M's approval to make a new junction at Huyton. Moss, Lawrence, Hornby, Sandars, Rotheram and Hardman Earle were incensed by Theodore Rathbone's suggestion that matters concerning the two companies should be discussed by a committee of which they were not members. At last, Moss carried out his threat of resigning from the L&M board, fuming that *"The L&M have refused their assent to the Fiddlers Ferry Line. I am sorry for it for I am sure the subscribers of the GJ are very anxious for a separate line and now that this vote has been given when all the GJ Directors were absent I am afraid of the consequences..."* [79] A week later, having received Rathbone's assurance that he had never intended to call into question their honour and integrity, the six Grand Junction directors withdrew their resignations. James Loch condemned the behaviour of all concerned: *"it was very unlike that of prudent considerate men of a certain time of life."* [80]

Despite its early operations having been interrupted by breakdowns, accidents and delays,[81] Moss was happy that the first few months had been *"as satisfactory as the most sanguine could desire."* [82] By 31 December, the Grand Junction had transported 232,022 passengers, and the receipts from them, parcels and the conveyance of mail were £116,740 10s 7d.[83]

---

78 Webster - Britain's First Trunk Line, p88
79 Stafford Correspondence Moss to J Loch 14.12.1837 (D593/K/1/3/25)
80 Richards, p133
81 Webster - Britain's First Trunk Line, p99
82 7 September at the 5th GJR AGM. ibid, pp100-101
83 The GJR only commenced carrying freight in the February of 1838. ibid, p97

The clear balance of profit was £56,035[84] while the L&M's net profit for the final 6 months of 1837 was £47,148.[85] Although the company's finances seemed in rude health, Moss considered its management (as well as the L&M's) highly objectionable. On 16 January 1838, he explained to Loch how *"Our Boards* (are) *governed by men who are Republicans at heart. They hear that the American President carries his own bag in the steam boat or stage coach and they cannot see why You or I should not do the same or why we should take a carriage at all. To such a pitch is this carried that although I am a director of the GJ I am entitled to go free, yet when I went to Leamington for my Health in the summer and came home expressly to attend a public meeting of the company I was told by the Board that I must pay for my carriage in which I went – it being the way I always travel – and they took the money. I am quite satisfied that our Grand Junction concern is the most splendid one ever completed and the most beneficial but the system of management is as bad as bad can be. We have not one officer fit for what he is appointed to. We have second class people with small salaries to fill places only suited to first rate abilities…I know of several cases where we act more like licenced oppressors than Gentlemen who obtained our Act to 'Benefit the Public.' "*[86]

The following day, Moss restated his intention to *"tender through Mr Cropper my resignation to the proprietors of the L&M at the annual meet next week."* [87] Yet again, he was dissuaded by Loch, who recognised that a permanent solution to the problems was an amalgamation of the two companies. A united management with one common purpose would put an end to all mistrust. Such a large concern would benefit from economies of scale and would offer greater security against attack from rival lines. There was little hope of such

---

84 Second Report of the Commissioners appointed to Inquire into the Manner in Which Railway Communications…by Irish Railway Commission. 1838, p147
85 Donaghy, p174
86 Stafford Correspondence Moss to J Loch 16.1.1838 (D593/K/1/3/26)
87 Stafford Correspondence Moss to J Loch 17.1.1838 (D593/K/1/3/26)

a settlement, though, in the foreseeable future. While Moss assured Loch that *"I am bound to you to bring about a settlement between the two railroad companies"* [88] he complained that his *"whole time is taken up trying to prevail upon our Board to alter our system of management to remedy the Evils you and others complain of, but every suggestion I make is contested in a manner that greatly distresses me and it becomes so personal that there is little prospect of my continuing a member of the Board, much less the Head of the concern. I am sure you will agree with me that I could now not enter into the consideration of so very important a subject as the settlement of the questions between the 2 companies...Every measure I recommend is contested as if I had an interest different from the Company...I am heartily disgusted and tired of such scenes as rail road Boards present, and very anxious to retire from them. I feel conscious, whatever others may say or think that no one ever exerted himself more than I have done to benefit the two concerns."* [89] Moss wrote again, on 7 March, to inform Loch that he had offered to resign as chairman of the GJR.[90] Lawrence hesitantly accepted the chairmanship, leaving Moss *"happy in thinking that they have accepted my resignation."* [91] Just three weeks later, poor Moss, like an animal tethered to two poles, announced that *"an almost unanimous request of our proprietors and committee has placed me in the GJR chair again."* [92]

A contemporary account of the GJR, by James Cornish, depicted an unprecedented efficiency in the day to day running of a railway. *"Every train is provided with guards, and a conductor, who is responsible for the order and regularity of the journey. The Company's porters will load and unload the luggage, and put it into or upon any omnibus or other carriage at any of the stations. No fees or gratuities allowed to conductors, guards,*

---

88   Stafford Correspondence Moss to J Loch 13.2.1838 (D593/K/1/3/26)
89   Stafford Correspondence Moss to J Loch 8.2.1838 (D593/K/1/3/26)
90   Stafford Correspondence Moss to J Loch 7.3.1838 (D593/K/1/3/26)
91   Stafford Correspondence Moss to J Loch 12.3.1838 (D593/K/1/3/26)
92   Stafford Correspondence Moss to J Loch 22.3.1838 (D593/K/1/3/26)

porters, or other persons in the Company's service."[93] In actuality, corruption was endemic in parts of the organisation, and Moss informed Gladstone, on 26 August 1839: *"I am sorry to tell you that our Guards have been robbing us to a great extent letting persons ride for 5 shillings to them to Birmingham. 13 out of 16 have been guilty amongst them…I fear the person whom you recommended will be one. Our pay has been too small and our system of inspectors not good. Some of our Directors could not, until now, bear to pay men to be honest."*[94] Despite such serious pilfering, the company continued to prosper. *"Our receipts are 30% more than the corresponding weeks of last year."*[95] The £100 shares had now doubled in price[96] and, by the end of January 1840, they were selling for £227. Moss insisted that, even at this price, *"These are still low and so you will say when you have read the reports. I could say sufficient to raise them £25 more. I shall not be satisfied until we divide 8% and put by each half year something handsome."*[97] Rewards of this magnitude were not permissible on the L&M, where Moss saw, at first hand, the disillusionment caused by its 10% maximum annual dividend (distributed half yearly).[98] In the absence of such constraints, he wrote of the GJR, in September, *"7% it shall pay so long as I belong to it unless some great convulsion takes place."*[99]

Moss's hard work and acumen had, by now, secured him national recognition. He declined a place on the board of the Brighton Railway *"not liking to share responsibility where I have no power of controlling, nor have I time or inclination*

---

93   James Cornish - Grand Junction Railway Companion, p13
94   Hawarden correspondence Moss to J Gladstone 26.8.1839
95   ibid
96   *"It fell in price last week… and some shares were sold as low as £192. I did not hear of it until too late to get any. I directed a purchase and could only get, in two days, five at £194. They are now £200."* ibid
97   Hawarden correspondence Moss to J Gladstone 29.1.1840
98   The *"proprietors were very sulky today at only 5% and talked of examining the accounts, as if any man could extract a drop of water from a sponge which Henry Booth had had the squeezing of."* ibid
99   Hawarden correspondence Moss to J Gladstone 9.9.1840

for new things." [100] Instead, he directed his attentions towards the amalgamation of the Chester & Crewe Railway Company, whose unfinished line was heading towards financial disaster. Once completed, the Chester & Crewe would join the GJR at its Crewe station and provide it with an important western branch – the first part of a line into Wales.[101] By May 1840, it had been incorporated and its shareholders issued with 5,000 GJR shares valued at £25 each. The news was met favourably on the Stock Exchange, and the £100 GJR shares rose to £254. *"Our receipts keep up and our expenses decreasing."* [102] Moss reaffirmed his great wish *"to pay 7% per whole share half yearly both on the old and proportionately on the new quarter shares."* [103] The Chester to Crewe line opened in October.

At the time the GJR commenced trading, in 1837, there were no more than 20 people living in the open countryside around its Crewe station, but this quiet spot had been purposefully selected.[104] In June 1840, Joseph Locke was requested to prepare estimates for the construction of engine shops at Crewe. At that time, the company's workshops were at Edge Hill in Liverpool, on ground and in buildings rented from the Liverpool & Manchester Railway. These had become so overwhelmed by repairs, modifications and maintenance operations that, without room for expansion, there was no option other than to look elsewhere. Although Crewe lacked essential raw materials like coal, timber and iron, now that the GJR was fully operational, all its requirements could be transported from the Midlands and Lancashire directly to site. Plans were drawn up for the creation of a small town of 200 houses to accommodate workers transferring from Liverpool,

---

100 He did, nonetheless, own shares in this enterprise and he recommended it and the South-western to Gladstone as *"sound concerns."* Hawarden correspondence Moss to J Gladstone 29.1.1840
101 The recently sanctioned Manchester & Birmingham as well as the Chester & Crewe were given royal assent on 10 June 1837. Webster – Locke, p83
102 Hawarden correspondence Moss to J Gladstone 20.6.1840
103 Hawarden correspondence Moss to J Gladstone 18.9.1840
104 B Reed – Crewe Locomotive Works, p11

as well as workshops for the building and repair of carriages, wagons and engines. Building work began the following year, and Moss predicted that *"this grand manufactory"* would become *"the finest and most extensive railway workshop in the world."* [105]

After a further bout of ill health, Moss took measures to reduce his workload. He pledged only to work on railways as a consulting director, and did not travel into Liverpool until 12 o'clock, leaving for home at 4 *"so that I have no time for the work I used to do…I am decidedly better and intend to keep so."* [106] Nonetheless, his services as a first class railway administrator were now in demand internationally, and his enthusiasm for new share dealing opportunities continued unabated. It was geographical detachment which restricted his involvement to that of consulting director to the Paris & Rouen Railway. (See 'Foreign Railways') [107]

Despite a national economic downturn, by December 1840, the workload of all GJR directors had become intolerable. Moss wrote that *"Rail roads are very seriously suffering from the mismanagement of some."* [108] With the complete backing of the board, he began *"quietly but gradually placing the GJ upon a very safe footing"* [109] and, in May 1841, appointed Captain Mark Huish as Secretary and General Manager. Conferring constantly with the directors, Huish became responsible for the general welfare, efficiency and overall business performance of the company. [110]

The continuing economic slowdown brought

---

105 ibid, p9
106 Hawarden correspondence Moss to J Gladstone 6.6.1840. *"I always find Leamington does me good and I can get there in a few hours. A week there sets me up. It is London that disagrees with me and the House of Commons Committee Rooms. With them I have taken leave and I already feel the benefit of it."*
107 *"I will send you on Monday or Tuesday a scheme I am embarking in…If you like any shares I have reserved some for you and I am glad to think I can now serve my friends. I feel I owe you much in every way."* ibid
108 Hawarden correspondence Moss to J Gladstone 5.12.1840
109 ibid
110 TR Gourvish - Mark Huish and the London & North Western Railway, p61

turbulence to the stock markets. In 1842, the GJR reduced its annual dividend payment to 10% on its £100 shares (5% each half year), and there it remained through 1843, 1844 and 1845.[111] Despite this, Moss held on to his shares, not seeing any real cause for the panic. He reported, in October 1842, that the reduction in the company's receipts had been attributable to various factors - *"...the fine weather has taken many by steam boats – poverty has checked much pleasure travelling and the income tax has caused numerous persons to save and economise."* [112]

Grand Junction Railway Average Share Price[113]

Year	Price Paid £	Average Share Price £
1837	70	156
1838	95	206
1839	100	204
1840	100	205
1841	100	212
1842	100	196

1843 found Moss in continuing ill health. In February, he was confined to his room by *"a severe bilious attack."* [114] He explained to Loch that *"I am too old and now idle to do any work myself...I find it very difficult to keep the L&M and GJ at peace. There are Gentlemen on each Board who are not satisfied to let 'well alone' and to blame me for advocating conciliation."* (between the canals and railways) [115] Then, in July, he complained of having had *"a smart attack of (almost) jaundice which has caused me to delay all correspondence."*[116]

By December, two engines had been manufactured at

---

111 Steel, p109

112 Hawarden correspondence Moss to J Gladstone 7.10.1842

113 William Galt - Railway Reform - Its Expediency and Practicability Considered, p110 (1844)

114 Hawarden correspondence Thomas Moss to J Gladstone 10.2.1843

115 Stafford Correspondence Moss to J Loch 17.3.1843 (D593/K/1/3/31)

116 Hawarden correspondence Moss to Gladstone 28.7.1843. *"We have just closed our Grand Junction accounts and I am quite satisfied. We shall pay 5%. without touching reserved funds...I do not think any RR will show a better dividend derived from real trade..."*

the newly opened Crewe works, and the town's population had risen to over two thousand. 1,150 were GJR employees and their families. Of these, 900 had been transported, en masse, from Liverpool in March.[117] The original plans for the town had been expanded, and there were now 250 GJR owned houses as well as gas works,[118] schools, community halls and a temporary church.[119] To celebrate the official opening of the workshops, a banquet, ball and supper was held in the coach building department on 2 December, and a reporter for the *Railway Record*, bearing the moniker 'Veritas Vincit', was there to witness it.[120] Despite being an irreverent critic of railway management, he described Moss as *"the worthy Chairman of the Directors."* Moss stood up to speak to the 300 employees in attendance at the dinner. *"Part of his address ran thus: 'I am fully persuaded that many of you (the workmen) in coming here (meaning to the new village) have deprived yourselves of many sweet enjoyments, the pleasing stir and busy hum of populous and engaging localities; the early ties of parents, kindred, love, and affection; but I and my brother Directors are most sincerely anxious to use all our endeavours in making you as happy and comfortable as possible. Time is all we require to mature what we contemplate in your behalf, and I hope before long we shall be enabled to establish for you a good library and a commodious news-room.'"*

The response of the gathering, towards certain personalities, is revealing. *"The next toast was, 'The Chairmen and Directors,'*

---

117 B Reed, p13

118 Webster – Locke, p86

119 B Reed, p14

120 Veritas Vincit – (12.12.1843) Railway Locomotive Management, pp 69-72. *"This room is capable of dining 800 persons."* At the far end *"was painted on canvas extending the whole width of the room, in large letters, 'Prosperity to the Grand Junction' and over the chair were the crown and cushion. In this place I expected to have seen the whole of the servants connected with the Grand Junction that could be spared from their duties, but in this I was disappointed, for the locomotive fitters at Liverpool and those at Vauxhall Station did not receive tickets. I know it was the design and intention of the directors that they should have tickets, but these orders did not seem to have been carried out to the strict letter… Everything having been announced ready, about 300 sat down to dinner."*

which was responded to by the Liverpool & Manchester Chairman (Charles Lawrence) in a most laughable manner, in which he said something about the flourishing state of the establishment under Mr. Trevethick." Francis Trevethick was the executive in charge of the workshops and yard (he had been stripped of control over the town in February).[121] *"Many a look was given from one to another as to what the honourable gentleman could possibly be referring to; for, as I have frequently before remarked, Mr. T is only a useless drone on the establishment."*

"The health of Mr. Locke was then proposed, and was received with the most rapturous applause by the whole assembly; the workmen continued cheering for some minutes. When this burst of heartfelt gratitude had subsided, Mr. Locke rose, which was the signal for another ebullition of prolonged cheering..."

"The next toast was 'Captain Huish and the other officers connected with the Company.' After an unsuccessful attempt by some individuals around the Chairman, to get up applause at the mention of Captain Huish's name, I heard some half suppressed groans proceeding from the body of the room, which I believe Captain H himself noticed, for when he got upon his legs he almost immediately began to allude towards obedience, and excused the necessity of punishments for what he calls insubordination (a military and naval term of course), telling them about his anxiety for their individual comforts, but at the same time that the duties of all must be attended to ..."

"The workmen of Crewe, together with their wives and families!' was next proposed by Mr. John Moss, in a speech which did him great justice as a philanthropist and a gentleman. Mr. Samuel Holmes, builder, Liverpool, returned thanks in the name of the workmen, being the building contractor... then proposed the concluding toast which was 'Prosperity to the juvenile City of Crewe'... The tea-table and ball followed. I have only time

---

121 Trevethick (1812-77) was the son of the great railway pioneer Richard Trevethick. Webster – Locke, p86

to remark, that the room had a very animated and splendid appearance, and I think there could not have been fewer than 1,300 persons present. I was sorry to observe that many of the humbler classes were not permitted to enjoy this pleasing sight. The fire-works were very gratifying to many who had never seen the like before."

Vincit Veritas concluded that *"Instead of the expense and splendour which the Directors lavished on this occasion, the same sum of money would have been by far more beneficially spent by providing each separate family with a good Christmas dinner. It would in some measure have made up for the privations which many of them were subjected to on their arrival there. Their wages were lowered; there was the expense of removing; the houses were damp, the coal dear, and all family necessaries to be brought from a distance; and yet it was expected that the whole body would extol their masters, and declare that black was white, from the getting up of this fete. The principal part of it was more gratifying to the surrounding petty aristocracy than to the workmen's families."* [122]

---

[122] Veritas Vincit, pp 69-72. Another contemporary account put a far more positive slant on proceedings. *"Several of the Directors and their families joined in the merry dance; and the Highland bagpipes finished off the ball with The Campbells are Coming… Altogether this was a joyful day. It was in truth a fascinating spectacle. The young women, of whom there were large numbers, looked charming and tripped admirably in country dances and quadrilles. All appeared to be delighted and the whole fete will be long remembered; and, doubtless, stand recorded as one of the first remarkable events in the annals of the juvenile city of Crewe."* Webster – Locke, pp85-86. Source not quoted

CHAPTER 9

AMALGAMATIONS

"It is no longer a question whether Scotland shall be connected by railway with England; and therefore it has become of the utmost moment to secure the benefits of that connection to the Grand Junction Railway. The Directors of all the other companies from London to Lancaster have taken the same view...The Directors may add, that they have reason to believe arrangements are proceeding most satisfactorily for the continuation of the line from Carlisle to Edinburgh and Glasgow."

John Moss's statement to GJR shareholders 30 January 1844.

The Grand Junction Railway's vision had, for many years, far exceeded its stated purpose of linking Birmingham with Liverpool and Manchester. At its fifth Annual General Meeting, in September 1837, John Moss declared *"It has fallen to the lot of this Company to be the first to exhibit to the country the practical working of a railway nearly a hundred miles in length and forming the main route through the heart of the kingdom to Scotland and Ireland, and to the populous manufacturing and commercial districts of the north."* [1] Following the 1834 merger

---

1   Webster - Britain's First Trunk Line, pp100-101

of the Wigan Branch and the Preston & Wigan railways, a track stretched 21 miles north to Preston from Newton Le Willows, where the renamed North Union Railway joined the Liverpool & Manchester. Cooperation of this sort would be needed on a far grander scale for Moss's ultimate ambition to be realized, but the country's two greatest railway companies – the GJR and the London & Birmingham – instead pursued the extension of their own networks. Although attempts were made to work together, over the next few years, the L&B's head was turned by many suitors; its coquettish behaviour caused Moss and his colleagues innumerable anxieties. While the GJR controlled the valuable traffic from the Midlands to the North, the fact that its **only** route to London was over the L&B's tracks, strengthened the L&B's hand. Although the GJR was the L&B's most important connection, it was only one of several companies whose lines fed into the L&B's London Euston terminus. The GJR was further undermined by a relatively minor railway - the Manchester & Birmingham (opened in 1840) - which joined the GJR at Crewe and provided a shorter route between Manchester and the South.

In 1839, belatedly recognizing the importance of a coordinated national rail network, the government commissioned Colonel Sir Frederick Smith and Professor Peter Barlow to investigate how best to connect London with Dublin, Edinburgh and Glasgow. They recommended a new line along the North Wales coast to the port of Holyhead, from where the sea crossing to Dublin was shortest. However, following the completion of the L&B in 1838, a direct line had been established between the capital and Liverpool, so the contract to ship the Dublin mails was won by Liverpool. The GJR, which received revenue from the Post Office for the carriage of the London mails on its stretch of track,[2] showed no enthusiasm for the alternative route. However, the L&B *was*

---

2   Birkenhead then won the contract in June 1841, the mails being shipped across the Mersey from Liverpool.

enthusiastic, and its chairman George Carr Glyn wrote to the GJR, in September 1843, proposing that the two companies share the expense of preliminary notices for the introduction of a Bill. When, in November, Moss traveled reluctantly to London to discuss the proposition, he was shocked to discover that the L&B was already involved in negotiations with another party - the Chester & Holyhead Railway Company. Although Parliament had not yet approved their railway, the C & H (based in London!) had already made contact with the government about the North Wales route to Ireland. The GJR felt the C&H had no right to be a party to any negotiations, but the L&B insisted on their involvement and, on 14 December, the GJR (again reluctantly) agreed to back the scheme, taking a one-third share.[1]

On 10 January 1844, the chairmen of the L&B, C&H and GJR met with Prime Minister Robert Peel, in London. A capital of £2.1m was proposed for the line to Holyhead, a cost the GJR's board considered far too high.[2] It had hoped to persuade the other parties to adopt a cheaper route via Mold. On the 16th, Moss wrote *"Our meeting with Sir Rob was anything but satisfactory to me personally... I do not take much from it. The deputation were sadly mortified... I am vain enough to think I could have met Sir Robert alone and made a satisfactory arrangement for all parties. I would not have attempted to make it a one sided contract. I doubt now if any party will in the end be pleased."* [3] William Rickford Collett, the C&H chairman, had initially argued that a government contract worth £80,000 per annum to carry mails would be necessary to justify the cost of the line. However, as negotiations continued, Moss watched while the C&H gave ground and proposed *"£40,000 in lieu of £80,000 first asked. If this is refused I think there will be some*

---

1 M.C. Reed, p32
2 ibid
3 Hawarden correspondence Moss to Gladstone 16.1.1844. By 1843 Gladstone held GJR shares to the value of £95,400. Checkland, p339

alteration in the partnerships." [4] Before the government had made any decisions, sensing uncertainty, the C&H wrote to the GJR, on 31 January, seeking confirmation that it still intended subscribing to one third of the scheme's capital. In the same day's post, Moss received a separate letter in which the C&H announced it intended to purchase the Chester & Birkenhead Company, thereby establishing for itself and its L&B partner, Chester as the starting point for the line to Holyhead. It could also link into the national network (and therefore the Post Office mail contract) via the GJR owned branch from Chester to Crewe. Outmanouevred and wounded by this bombshell, the GJR withdrew entirely from the scheme. [5] The London & North Western Railway biographer Malcolm Reed emphasized how, as dealings became strained, the GJR made every effort to compromise, and Moss in particular, sought to avoid confrontation. In February his conciliatory hand was behind a circular to GJR shareholders which endorsed George Carr Glyn's recent statement that the interests of the GJR and L&B were closely identified. Assurances were given that the GJR would not impede the C&H (and vice versa), but they would offer each other every assistance. Within weeks these mutual expressions of good intent were found to have been misplaced.[6]

The proposed Trent Valley Railway was part of a scheme to establish a more direct route from Manchester to London. Rather than present rival promoters with a foothold into this traffic, the GJR supported the TVR's plans for a 50 mile track between Stafford and Rugby. Moss approached the Manchester & Birmingham and the L&B urging them both to participate, but found himself perplexed by the latter's reluctance. *"New lines are threatening them on every side yet they will not join us in an alliance defensive to both."* [7] Recognising the seriousness of that threat, the GJR's board gave Moss and Charles Lawrence

---

4   Hawarden correspondence Moss to Gladstone 16.1.1844
5   M.C. Reed, p32
6   ibid, p33
7   Stafford correspondence Moss to J Loch 25.4.1844 (D593/K/1/3/32)

full licence *"to discuss, arrange and settle the various important matters now to be considered."* [8] The L&B was persuaded to agree to the proposal by the end of April but, all too soon, Moss was complaining to James Loch about more of their treachery. *"You will be surprised to hear that on Tuesday 10 May the L&B Board without a word with us decided to support a line from Birmingham to Shrewsbury!!"* [9] He insisted *"I am not difficult to deal with if met fairly – sometimes hasty but never I hope unjust…I have purposely avoided all discussion with lines hostile to the L&B hoping to see our two companies interest in a defensive alliance. I shall be glad to talk matters over with Mr Glyn. The L&B have not one opponent at the GJ Board. I wish I could say the same at theirs. But we cannot mend people and must keep peace if possible. I am resolved to try."* [10] In the event, the Trent Valley proposal failed to secure authorisation in the 1844 session of Parliament,[11] although the Chester & Holyhead did, on 4 July.[12]

To the North, things were running a lot more smoothly. By 1836, at the expense of the GJR, Joseph Locke had undertaken a survey of the land between Preston, Carlisle, Glasgow and Edinburgh for a "west coast" route into Scotland.[13] In 1837, Parliament authorised the Lancaster & Preston Junction Railway, thereby extending the existing network a further 25 miles northward. By then, however, a rival "east coast" scheme linking London to Edinburgh via Rugby, Newcastle and Berwick, was being championed by the "Railway King" George Hudson. Smith & Barlow produced four reports for the government between 1840 and 1841 - all favouring the GJR's west coast scheme, but dependent upon what progress could be made with a projected route

---

8   Stafford correspondence Moss to J Loch 18.4.1844 (D593/K/1/3/32)
9   Stafford correspondence Moss to J Loch 13.5.1844 (D593/K/1/3/32)
10   Stafford correspondence Moss to J Loch 9.5.1844 (D593/K/1/3/32)
11   M.C. Reed, p34. It was revived the following year
12   ibid, p32
13   Webster – Locke, p68

from Lancaster to Carlisle. However, these reports only made recommendations, and Hudson's scheme was not ruled out entirely. In January 1844, with the east/west dispute still unresolved, Moss sought John Gladstone's assistance:

"I wish you and other parties of real influence could induce, as in the case of the line from London to Dublin, all parties to concur in an application to government, to send Mr Walker or some other eminent engineer to decide upon the best line and let all parties be bound by it. If not we shall have a parliamentary contest of the most serious and expensive nature, such as was exhibited in the Brighton and Trent Valley schemes. In the latter the Grand Junction were assistants and I know that no less than £70,000 was expended by the two parties in parliament. I dread a repetition of such things and I should be highly gratified if you or any one could give a helping hand to prevent it. I shall advise an application to the Board of Trade and to Sir Rob Peel. If those fail there is nothing left but to arm and fight." [14]

On 30 January, in a statement to shareholders, Moss recommended that the GJR make a sizeable investment in the Lancaster & Carlisle Railway as a *"desirable defensive measure"*. He added that *"It is no longer a question whether Scotland shall be connected by railway with England; and therefore it has become of the utmost moment to secure the benefits of that connection to the Grand Junction Railway. The Directors of all the other companies from London to Lancaster have taken the same view... The Directors may add, that they have reason to believe arrangements are proceeding most satisfactorily for the continuation of the line from Carlisle to Edinburgh and Glasgow."* [15] Gladstone was of the opinion that the traffic to Scotland was insufficient to generate a decent profit and, in March, curtly dismissed Moss's plans. *"I am inclined to think your Board of directors have been rather premature in deciding in favour of the Scottish rail road which the Government Surveyor recommended, which is proposed*

---

14 Hawarden correspondence Moss to Gladstone 16.1.1844
15 Webster - Britain's First Trunk Line, p146

to fork off to both Edinburgh and Glasgow…I do not mean to be a party in it and, as a GJ shareholder do now and will when called upon protest against it." [16] Moss pressed on regardless, and the GJR became the driving force behind the project. The Bill for the 70¼ mile Lancaster & Carlisle Railway gained royal assent on 6 June. While the GJR committed to subscribe £250,000 towards the authorised share capital of £900,000, the L&B pledged only £100,000. Lesser sums were subscribed by the North Union, the Lancaster & Preston Junction and the Liverpool & Manchester.[17] Construction began apace on 18 July, and the opening ceremony took place on 15 December 1846. The Bill for the Caledonian Railway (the line from Carlisle to Glasgow) was passed on July 31 1845, and the same group of companies collaborated in its planning, financing and implementation.[18] Mercifully, there had been no expensive Parliamentary battle; Hudson's east coast scheme also gained approval in the same session.[19]

In 1844 'Railway Mania' set in. Like the South Sea Bubble before it and the dot com share boom of the 1990s, this was an extraordinary era in which ordinary members of the public plunged their savings into what seemed like an ever rising stock market. The market bestowed entirely unrealistic values upon the railway companies, and it was to be only a matter of time before it crashed, bringing financial ruin to many investors. In 1844 alone, 48 Bills were passed for the construction of 797 miles of railway with a total authorised capital of £14,793,994.[20] Moss remarked *"The present plethora in the money market would induce subscribers to any scheme."* [21] The multitude of new main line and local railways threatened

---

16   Hawarden correspondence J Gladstone to Moss 25.3.1844
17   M.C. Reed, p29
18   George Larmer and S B Worthington were appointed engineers for the Lancaster & Carlisle on the basis of a north / south divide. Locke was employed as engineer of the Caledonian Railway.
19   Steel, p 105
20   Smiles - Life of Stephenson, p416 (1857)
21   Hawarden correspondence Moss to J Gladstone 16.1.1844

both the GJR and the L&B. To protect their interests, a treaty was drawn up on 3 July whereby it was agreed that *"the two concerns shall remain separate and distinct, as at present, but shall unite for mutual protection... That if the Holyhead line is made, the Grand Junction Railway shall not, either by a disproportionate reduction of rates to and from Liverpool, or by arrangements with the Irish steamboat proprietors thence, compete for the Irish traffic, but leave it to take its natural course. That neither Company, except as above, shall engage in any new enterprise without the previous consent of the other; that they shall mutually co-operate and assist each other for the accommodation and increase of the joint traffic; and that each shall, as far as possible, direct over the line of the other all its legitimate traffic."* [22] Birmingham was defined as the boundary of each company's 'territory'.

Moss, although complaining of feeling old at the age of 62,[23] was sufficiently energized to boast *"Already we have made the canals almost ruinous concerns. The new Birmingham* (Birmingham & Liverpool Junction Canal) *is so bad it cannot pay the interest on the sum borrowed from the government and Lord Powis writes me they have ordered a report upon its capability of being converted into a railway. Under these circumstances, as we can well afford it, is it not better to leave them a little traffic? They cannot compete with us, but they may (to injure us) drop prices on articles (such as pigs etc) which pay us well. They now complain sadly of us and I can not deny them justice."* [24] Carrying on in confident vein, Moss wondered whether *"the time is arrived when the GJ may, if she pleases, decide to be independent. We can without injuring ourselves spare the sum it would require to give us a good home of our own. The Liverpool & Manchester directors are fully aware of it."* [25] The threat of losing the tolls paid by the

---

22   Steel, pp 105-107
23   Hawarden correspondence Gladstone to Moss 8.4.1844 *"You say you are getting old. What do you say of me who had I fancy 15 or 20 years the start of you - 79 on the 11th of last December"*
24   Hawarden correspondence Moss to J Gladstone 25.7.1844
25   ibid

GJR for the use of its lines set the L&M's board thinking. *"They are all very desirous of an amalgamation, a thing I have long had hinted to me and as often declined even considering it. Now that we have got through our more important troubles I have thought of the situation of these two concerns and I do see some advantages in an amalgamation on terms such as would make it worthwhile for both to agree to."* [26] It would require unprecedented levels of tact, diplomacy and mutual respect for such an outcome to be arrived at. Loch observed that relations between the two companies were *"at an irritable and unsatisfactory state"* and that *"we have most slippery and unscrupulous people to deal with on both sides."* [27]

On 10 December, the L&M's shareholders unanimously passed a resolution to amalgamate their company *"with its projected Branches and Engagements (including the Bolton & Leigh and Kenyon & Leigh Junction Railways and the North Union Railway with its Branches and Engagements) and the Grand Junction Railway Company into one consolidated Company."* [28] Clay, Swift & Company were appointed to prepare the legal content of the Bill, which was to be put before Parliament the following April. On 8 January 1845, Moss complained bitterly to Robertson Gladstone about the additional work this caused him. *"I annex a statement of what I have done the last few days of which neither Cap Huish nor the Board have any knowledge. These matters must be done by some one. In making your arrangements you can and ought to stipulate that the Chairman does not work "gratis"- when there is a fund to pay Directors. There is much to be done."* In the preceding few days, he had visited *"Mr Booth's to see stats of the amalgamation case…discussed with Mr Swift – 6 hours in all."* [29]

The GJR's uneasy alliance with the L&B was now

---

26 ibid
27 Richards, p144
28 Ferneyhough, pp136-137
29 Hawarden correspondence Moss to Robertson Gladstone 8.1.1845

dangling by a thread. Moss's mistrust of Glyn is exemplified by an almost comical letter from George Stephenson to the L&B's secretary, Richard Creed. Stephenson, an intermediary trusted by all, wrote:

"I beg to acknowledge the receipt of your letter of 9th instant enclosing a minute of the London & Birmingham Board, expressive of their satisfaction at an arrangement about to be made for me and my son to arrange various points of difference between your Company and the Grand Junction as proposed by Mr. Moss, but stating it to be the conviction of your Board that no permanent arrangement could be secured without the concurrence of the Manchester & Birmingham Board and the Committees of the Shrewsbury Company, the Chester & Holyhead Company, the Chester & Shropshire Company, together with the Manchester & Birkenhead Company, of the Trent Valley Company and Churnet Valley Company. At the time when I communicated with Mr. Glyn I considered myself fully authorised by Mr. Moss to make the proposal of reference which I did, but from a letter which I have since received from him it appears to be doubtful if he intended to go so far and at all events there is a decided objection on his part to include the Churnet Valley and Birkenhead parties in the reference and I am therefore afraid that the negotiation must be considered at an end." [30]

By early 1845, the joint Trent Valley scheme had been resurrected and a new route (the Churnet Valley Railway) had been proposed, linking Manchester to the south of England via Leek and Uttoxeter, east of the GJR. Although Leek and Uttoxeter fell within the GJR's 'territory', a suspicious amount of interest was shown in the scheme by the L&B, even though it was not actually engaged in its promotion. The full extent of the L&B's deception only became apparent at its general meeting on 12 February when Glyn announced that terms had been concluded for the proposed amalgamation of the L&B,

---

30 Letter dated 21 November 1844. Skeat, p218

the Manchester & Birmingham, the Trent Valley and Churnet Valley Companies. Thereby the L&B would secure its own route to Manchester, independent of the GJR. Furthermore its backing of a revised scheme for a line from Birmingham, proceeding northwest to Shrewsbury, would bring closer the possibility of a connection (again independent of the GJR) to Chester and, from there to Birkenhead and Holyhead. *The Railway Times* commented *"In the present instance we feel satisfied that the London & Birmingham Board will rue the day when it suffered itself to be tempted by the opportunity (too gratifying to the personal feelings of some of its members to be resisted) to wound a rival and gain a temporary triumph at the expense of good faith and fair dealing."* [31] In the face of this never ending duplicity, aside from making formal protests and increasing the cost to the M&B for the exchange of traffic at Crewe, the GJR had no choice other than to seek new alliances in order to secure its own connection to the south, independent of the L&B.

On 28 April, the prospectus for the Birmingham & Oxford Junction Railway[32] was issued; Moss and three of his GJR colleagues were listed on its provisional committee alongside Charles Russell, chairman of the Great Western Railway. It was proposed that the GJR would link on to the Birmingham & Oxford, and from Oxford its trains would run along the Great Western's tracks before terminating at London Paddington. This enterprise was supported by many Birmingham iron-masters, merchants and manufacturers who had become disillusioned with the L&B's extortionate rates and general abuse of its monopoly.[33] In exchange for the Great Western's backing of this scheme, the GJR supported the Great Western's own hopes of obtaining two routes from the south to the midlands - the Oxford, Worcester & Wolverhampton Railway and the Oxford & Rugby Railway.

---

31   Railway Times of 10 May 1845. Webster - Britain's First Trunk Line, p164
32   authorised in 1846
33   Webster - Britain's First Trunk Line, p163

These lines were to be of the "broad-gauge", with their rails spaced 7 feet apart, as opposed to the "narrow-gauge" of 4 feet and 8½ inches, which was used on all the lines the GJR and L&B were involved in. Thus the GJR had a foot in both camps in what became known as the "Battle of the Gauges." Although most of the line so far laid throughout the country was of the narrow-gauge, the advantage of broad-gauge was that it facilitated larger locomotives with bigger boilers, which generated greater power and, therefore, faster journey times. On 11 June, the GJR announced that it was prepared to consider incorporating broad-gauge into its own lines (the combination of the two called "mixed-gauge") to combat the considerable inconvenience of passengers and freight having to be moved onto a separate train wherever narrow and broad gauged tracks adjoined. It seems unlikely that the GJR was serious about such a costly solution to the problem; it was more likely a ruse designed to unnerve the L&B and bring it to the negotiating table.[34] If that was the intention, it failed; this despite all parties being further threatened by the authorisation, in 1845, of 120 more new railways covering 2,883 miles with a capital of £43,844,907.[35] Rumours of amalgamations were rife, but Moss opposed any alliance with the L&B, and John Gladstone, as a major GJR shareholder expressed his *"determination to oppose it to the utmost if persevered in, by every legal means within my power."*[36]

In June, the GJR paid dividends of £73,144 despite having only made a half year profit of £68,514.[37] Such seeming malpractice was common in business at that time. A high rate of dividend gave the impression of a successful company, and so, a higher share price. In this way companies

---

34   ET MacDermot & CR Clinker - History of the Great Western Railway, Volume 1, p116
35   Smiles - Life of Stephenson, p416 (1857)
36   Hawarden correspondence J Gladstone to Moss 5.5.1845
37   George Robb-Law - White Collar Crime in Modern England: Financial Fraud & Business Morality, 1845-1929, p44

helped stoke the Railway Mania,[38] a phenomenon Moss took every opportunity to profit from. A Parliamentary Return of June 1845 revealed that, during that session of Parliament alone, he had personally subscribed for shares to the value of almost £158,000.[39] The GJR's practices were positively prudent compared with the criminally imprudent dealings of new railway companies who, having no income from passengers, paid out dividends before their lines had even been built. The shareholders actually received dividends out of the very capital with which the companies planned to build their lines. Throughout all this under regulated lunacy, the names of the GJR and its chairman, unlike that of George Hudson and many others, were left untarnished. A plethora of deceits resulted in Hudson's financial downfall, social disgrace and eventual exile. He was made the scapegoat for the entire Railway Mania, and his legitimate achievements were ignored by vengeful shareholders.[40]

At a board meeting on 1 August, Moss declared that receipts for the half year to June, from passenger traffic and

---

[38] Railway Mania reached its peak in 1846. That year an incredible 272 new railways totalling 4,790 miles with a total capital of £121,500,000 were authorised. (Smiles - Life of Stephenson, p416 - 1857) The estimated total annual income of the whole kingdom was no more than £200,000,000. (The Economist - October 1845 quoted from Robb-Law, p47) The Times referred to the mania as "*a tale of national delusion.*" Over-subscription had taken its toll and investors now sold shares to meet calls on other shares. Hundreds of proposed lines collapsed as their scrip became unsaleable. The bubble finally burst in the 1847 stock market crash, and for twenty years after, lack of public confidence caused promoters tremendous trouble in raising capital for new railways

[39] William Arthur Thomas - The Provincial Stock Exchange, p38

[40] On the York and North Midland Railway it emerged in 1849 that, under George Hudson's chairmanship, no proper books and accounts had been kept; that he and other directors had appropriated thousands of shares for themselves; that he had overstated traffic accounts and understated working expenses so as to pay over £84,000 in unearned dividends; that, in 1845, he had made a personal profit of £14,000 by reselling 2,500 tons of rails to the Company for double the price he had paid for them. (Robb-Law, pp49-50) On the York, Newcastle and Berwick Railway he had appropriated 10,000 shares which he sold for a personal profit of £145,000. Between 1844 and 1848 the company's books had been falsified to the extent of £122,000 in order to pay higher dividends than earned. (ibid) On another of his railways, the Eastern Counties, similar extravagant inflation of dividends was exposed.

transit of the mails, exceeded £150,000 and, from freight, were almost £73,000. The Grand Junction had virtually no debts, and its estimated market value was £2,600,000.[41] Having guided his railway to success, Moss then announced his retirement, with regret. *"The state of my health has compelled me to announce to my colleagues that I can no longer sustain the mental and bodily exertions which the office of your Chairman demands... Your confidence has always been most gratifying to me...the post of working Director must devolve to a younger man... No one, I assure you, can be more sincerely, or more anxiously alive, to what ever promotes the interest of our Grand Junction Railway."*[42] Robertson Gladstone resolved *"that the unanimous and cordial thanks of the proprietors were especially due, and hereby respectfully tendered, to John Moss Esq. for his constant and untiring services in the important position he has so ably occupied as Chairman of the Grand Junction Railway Company."*[43] The chairmanship then devolved to Lawrence. Moss stayed on for the time being as a low key member of the board. Thereafter, there were *"recriminations"* between Moss and Glyn *"in which mutual charges of breach of faith have been bandied"*[44]

Unfortunately for the London & Birmingham, in its 1845 sessions Parliament rejected both its Churnet Valley and Shrewsbury & Birmingham schemes on 'standing orders'. The Great Western's two midlands routes secured royal assent on 4

---

[41]

Stations and a line of 104 miles	£1,620,660
Rolling stock	£250,000
Land, works and machinery at Crewe	£130,340
Surplus fund, undivided	£64,000
2,000 shares in the Caledonian	£10,000
5,000 shares in the Lancaster & Carlisle	£275,000
13,889 shares in the Trent Valley	£250,000

	£2,600,000

Webster - Britain's First Trunk Line, p162
[42] ibid, pp161-162
[43] ibid, p161
[44] Civil Engineer and Architect's Journal, 1847. P309

August and, four days later, the GJR's amalgamation with the Liverpool & Manchester and the Bolton & Leigh companies was approved.[45] The names of the latter two companies were dropped. Each £100 L&M share was equal to a £100 share in the increased capital and joint stock of the enlarged Grand Junction Railway. To qualify as a director of the new company each individual had to hold at least £500 of its shares.[46] Other than Moss and his son Thomas, the Act listed the names of 13 directors.[47] The Duke of Sutherland appointed George Loch (James's son) and Joseph Langton to represent his interests.[48] Thus the continuing bugbear of the payment of tolls by the GJR for the use of L&M's track (as well as all the other charges) was eliminated. The new GJR's ownership of a line stretching from Birmingham to Preston via the great cities of Liverpool and Manchester, with branches to important towns like Bolton and Chester, made it a formidable railway company. That is to say nothing of its heavy involvement in the Lancaster & Preston, the Lancaster & Carlisle and the Caledonian Railways.

Moss had been *"to the last a foremost opponent of Railway extensions and amalgamations"*,[49] but now, with him out of the way, and with its own strategy in tatters, the L&B finally recognized that the GJR was the most complementary system to its own. Discussions resumed, and *"after difficulties which might well have been regarded as insurmountable"*,[50] plans for an amalgamation were announced on 7 November. After declaring that it was to amalgamate with the London & Birmingham, the GJR performed a complete about turn by becoming vocal opponents of the Birmingham & Oxford Railway and of the

---

45 The Kenyon & Leigh had already been absorbed by the Bolton & Leigh
46 Donaghy, p171
47 Charles Lawrence, William Rotheram. Joseph Hornby, John Cropper Jr., Robertson Gladstone, George Grant, Hardman Earle, Joseph Sandars, George Hall Lawrence, Thomas Booth and Lewin Mozley
48 Donaghy, p171
49 Liverpool Mail Obituary – 9 October 1858
50 Civil Engineer and Architect's Journal, 1847. P309

broad-gauge in general.[51] From 13 December onwards, the GJR and the L&B held joint meetings, and accounts were immediately consolidated. The L&B, GJR and Manchester & Birmingham were all eventually amalgamated on 16 July 1846 under the aptly titled London & North Western Railway.[52] Glyn was elected its chairman. Two local boards, representing the North and South Divisions, were set up in Liverpool and London, with 18 and 24 Directors respectively. Moss's name was not among them. He busied himself elsewhere but, within five years, his grand vision became a reality when the line linking Aberdeen, Edinburgh, Glasgow and Holyhead to London Euston was completed.

NW Webster, who read every faded word of its board meetings, wrote that Moss's personality was stamped on the Grand Junction Railway. He ensured that shareholders' money was not squandered on grandiose architectural ventures or wild experiments.[53] Moss's 1858 obituary queries *"How many impoverished 'original shareholders' in the Manchester Line or the Grand Junction Line, or the London and Birmingham will not now devoutly wish that Mr. Moss' opposition had but been successful!"* [54] For his part *"Mr. Moss voluntarily withdrew from his prominent position on English railways* (and)... *transferred much of his enterprise to Continental railways, more justly*

---

51 A Royal Commission had been set up in July 1845 to investigate the pros and cons of each gauge and to recommend to government one, uniform gauge. While it acknowledged that greater speed and efficiency could be achieved by broad gauge engines, only 274 miles of broad gauge track had so far been laid. The narrow gauge extended over 1,901 miles. The Commission concluded that *"the alteration of the former to the latter, even if on equal length, would be the less costly as well as the less difficult operation."* (MacDermot & Clinker - Volume 1, p118) The Gauge Act of 1846 forbade the construction of any new passenger railways of the broad gauge. All Britain's public railways are, to this day, of the narrow-gauge.

52 The LNW's combined share capital of £17,242,310 was split between former L&B proprietors £8,653,750, former GJR £5,788,560 and former M&B £2,800,000. (M.C. Reed, p37) The total length of track owned was 404 miles. Charles Lawrence his deputy. The services of both company's engineers - Joseph Locke and Robert Stephenson - were retained, as were those of the 2 former secretaries - Henry Booth and Richard Creed

53 Webster - Britain's First Trunk Line, p28

54 Liverpool Mail - 9 October 1858

dealt with by Continental legislatures. But he had already won golden opinions in his railway presidency at home. And his name is now so lastingly interwoven with those great iron arteries of communication along which the commerce of the world pours into and out of Liverpool..." [55]

Moss's great friend John Gladstone wrote, upon returning to his home in Aberdeenshire, in May 1849 [56] *"I was kept very busy in London and only returned here on Saturday - 409 miles in one day, 409 miles, pretty well you will say for an old man!"* [57] And what a part Moss had played in the creation of those swift lines of communication.

---

55 ibid
56 no doubt by the east coast route
57 Hawarden correspondence Gladstone to Moss 15.5.1849. On 22 May 1849 Gladstone declined an invitation to visit Otterspool, stating *"God only knows if I may ever visit Liverpool again...."* (Hawarden correspondence Gladstone to Moss 22.5.1849) He died on 7 December 1851 just four days short of his 87th birthday.

CHAPTER 10

FOREIGN RAILWAYS

"The Liverpool & Manchester, Grand Junction, Paris & Rouen, Rouen & Havre, Birmingham & Oxford all owe their origin to me. So far that I have had the honour of sitting as chairman in starting all, the shareholders, from first to last, have made about twelve millions profit by them...and yet, I believe, some who owe their present situation in life to these rail roads give no credit to me and even doubt if I was the original chairman of the Liverpool & Manchester."

John Moss to Sir John Gladstone – 10th December 1846

French Railways

In England, by 1836, nearly 2,000 miles of railway track had been laid but, throughout France, only about 25 miles were in operation.[1] The first track built on the English model, capable of carrying a steam locomotive and stretching just over 12 miles between Paris and St Germain, opened in 1837. Even so, Joseph Locke observed that the *"line was*

---

1 Sir Edward Blount - Memoirs of Sir Edward Blount, p51

worked by English drivers at double the ordinary wages." [2] Unlike the English, the French lacked government backing, wealthy provincial manufacturing communities and a general public willing to invest sufficient money to launch their own national rail network. In 1838, the French Government resoundingly rejected a Bill for the construction of seven great state controlled trunk lines, thereby creating opportunities for private enterprise. A Paris based English banker Edward Blount offered to raise the capital in England for the spurned Paris to Rouen line.[3] He and his French banking partner Charles Lafitte travelled to London, Liverpool and Manchester seeking and receiving financial and practical assistance.

Moss first notified John Gladstone of developments on 6 June 1840 when he stated his intention to embark in *"a French railroad which will not give me any trouble."* [4] The company's capital would amount to £1,440,000 to which was to be added a £560,000 loan from the French Government.[5] 72,000 shares of £20 each were snapped up. £720,000 (half of the total capital) was quickly raised in England, and this gave courage to French capitalists who rapidly subscribed the remainder. Liverpool, as a major centre of railway capitalism, had an extraordinarily heavy involvement in the project. These shares were particularly attractive as no stamp tax needed to be paid and they could be traded just as easily on the Liverpool Stock Exchange as they could in London or Paris.[6] Moss and Charles Lawrence each subscribed for 500 following assurances from Locke (who also subscribed for 500) that this would be *"a second Grand Junction line."* [7] Moss did not intend committing

---

2   Samuel Salt - Railway & Commercial Information, p10
3   Leland H Jenks - The Migration of British Capital to 1875 incorrectly identifies Blount as an Irishman; he was not, although he was of Irish descent. He was born in Bellamour near Rugeley in Staffordshire into a staunchly Catholic house of ancient lineage. Oxford Dictionary of National Biography 2004, volume 6
4   Hawarden correspondence Moss to J Gladstone 6.6.1840
5   Manchester Guardian, 29.7.1840
6   Thomas, William Arthur - The Provincial Stock Exchange, p44
7   Hawarden correspondence Moss to J Gladstone 12.6.1840

himself to the shares long term; there was a ready market for anyone wishing to sell. *"We have applications for more shares than we can supply. I do not pledge myself to do anything with the direction. All will depend upon circumstances... Do not consider me responsible than believing the French directors to be as honest as Frenchmen can."*[1] Gladstone was, however, very wary of the French, and with good reason. France's latest (and last) king, Louis Philippe, though himself an Anglophile, ruled over an Anglophobic people, which hated the English for many reasons, but none more so than their humiliation of Napoleon Bonaparte.[2] France was perceived to be still in a volatile state, but Moss tried to offer the assurance that *"There will be no war unless it comes to a question that the people will fight, either at home or abroad and if so Louis Philippe will in all probability prefer having 100.000 Frenchmen destroyed out of France than in it."*[3] Moss had procured 200 shares for Gladstone,[4] and his son Robertson took 50.[5]

The French Government authorised the company's proposals for the line on 15 July. A company *Chemins de Fer de L'Ouest* was formed, with Blount as its first chairman. The company's president was Baron James de Rothschild, the French "Railway King". Rothschild, even then, was a great name in European banking, and this gave the whole enterprise enormous credibility. Moss wrote, on the 25th *"I think we shall have six English directors out of twelve, an English engineer and also Secretary and the power of voting by proxy. If, with all this we are cheated all I can say is we deserve it. I mean to hold 500*

---

1   ibid
2   Benjamin Perley Poore - The Rise and Fall of Louis Philippe, ex King of the French. (1848), p245

3   Hawarden correspondence Moss to J Gladstone 9.9.1840
4   Hawarden correspondence Moss to J Gladstone 12.6.1840
5   Hawarden correspondence Moss to J Gladstone 22.6.1840. Moss offered a get-out, stating that *"neither Mr Lawrence nor I would for one moment wish to keep you to the Paris Rouen RR if you would like to retire from it...I have applications for many hundreds of shares which I cannot supply and therefore if you will address a letter to me stating your wish to retire I am sure my co directors will allow me to substitute another name."*

shares as long as I can." [6] On 29 July the *Manchester Guardian* reported: *"A meeting of the shareholders of this railway resident in Liverpool was held in the Clarendon Rooms on Wednesday last. It was numerously and respectably attended. John Moss, Esq., was called to the chair. A report drawn up by the directors, Messrs John Easthope, William Chaplin, John Moss and Charles Lawrence, was read and adopted. It gave a very flattering prospect of the success of the undertaking."* Chaplin, had, in 1838, sold the largest coaching house in England in anticipation of the triumph of the railway over the turnpike. Easthope was an MP and part owner of the leading Whig newspaper, the *Morning Chronicle*. Also on the board were England's most revered merchant bankers, Francis and Thomas Baring of Baring Brothers (the House later brought down by the "rogue trader" Nick Leeson). Moss had every right to consider himself an equal in this distinguished company. Moss & Co were the bankers for two of Britain's foremost railway companies. Moss's 18 years of "hands on" experience had given him an unrivaled understanding of virtually every aspect of the railway industry - from the workings of a locomotive to the day to day running of a railway company. Furthermore, despite the rift between those two internationally respected engineers, George Stephenson and Joseph Locke, Moss had managed to remain on good terms with both. In short, it would have proved virtually impossible for the French to have found a more useful partner.

The *Guardian* article continued:

"The cost of the line was estimated at £1,740,000. Several shareholders were decidedly of the opinion, that the undertaking would prove a profitable one; for besides running through one of the first mercantile and manufacturing districts of France, its termini would rest upon Rouen and Paris. M. Lafitte (a young French gentleman who spoke English with great fluency and correctness)

---

6   Hawarden correspondence Moss to J Gladstone 25.7.1840

attended the meeting on the part of the French directors. He stated that they had been so fortunate as to engage the services of Mr. Stephenson; that the French people were anxious to benefit by the superior experience of the English in railways; that the work would immediately go on; and he had every reason to believe it would prove very profitable to the shareholders...Mr. Locke addressed the meeting at considerable length, and entered into some very important details concerning the formation of the line, its expenses and the advantages expected to be derived from it"

The English directors had appointed Locke as engineer. Having already travelled over the entire route, Locke advised the gathering that there would be no big embankments or steep gradients, and only three tunnels and four bridges. He was confident that the 85 miles of track [7] could be built cheaply. *"The motion was carried unanimously. It was then agreed by the meeting, that M. Lafitte should be the deputy from the Liverpool shareholders, to represent their interest at the general meeting, to be held in Paris on the 31st instant - In reply to an enquiry made by Mr. Coglan, the chairman announced, that the certificates would be ready for delivery as early as possible after the above meeting."*

On 9 September Moss, quite clearly holding the purse strings, assured Gladstone that he had not *"yet allowed one shilling of English money go to the Paris & Rouen Railway."* [8] He explained, on the 18th, that he had *"objected to paying the money and the consequence was, as I could not go to London, a meeting was held at my office, at which all the English directors attended with Mr Lafitte from France, Mr Locke etc. I was satisfied from the documents produced to me that war between England and France was not even probable. The line was surveying and Mr Locke promised to open 40 miles out of Paris in 18 months. In short I could find no good or even doubtful reason for delaying the payment and the English directors signed an unanimous approval*

---

7   Dionysius Lardner - Railway Economy: A Treatise on the New Art of Transport. (1850), p449. Webster states the length as 82 miles. Webster – Locke, p117

8   Hawarden correspondence Moss to J Gladstone 9.9.1840

of the money being sent and work hurried on with all speed. I should have called a meeting had I entertained any doubt of what ought to be done... Mr Reed who will be the paid director from England and reside in Paris is just come over and confirms me in the opinion I had previously formed of the line." [9]

Work now progressed at an incredible pace. Locke appointed the English contractors MacKenzie and Brassey rather than French contractors who proved expensive and inexperienced. Brassey, fresh from his work on the Grand Junction and the London & Southampton, imported 5,000 of his own English and Irish workers. A similar number was recruited locally. Locke recalled, in later years how he *"heard the exclamations of French loungers around a gang of navvies - 'Mon Dieu, ces Anglais, comme ils travaillent.'"* [10] Iron and railway material was imported from Britain or produced by the British in French workshops. Locke explained *"I at once determined on establishing workshops at Rouen; by which the Company at least might be able to rely on resources entirely under its own control."* [11] The Paris & Rouen Railway was completed well ahead of schedule in April 1843, at a cost of £23,754 per mile,[12] and opened to the public on 9 May.[13]

In early operations, the speed of French passenger trains was only about 20 miles an hour. Slower speeds caused less wear and tear on the locomotives and the tracks and, as a result, the working expenses of the Paris & Rouen amounted to only 16% of gross receipts. The savings were passed on to passengers in the form of fares which were significantly lower than Britain's. The biggest winners, though, were the promoters, who were believed to have sold their shares at 100% profit,[14] realising

---

9   Hawarden correspondence Moss to J Gladstone 18.9.1840
10 Webster - Locke, p119
11 ibid, p125
12 James Morrison - The Influence of the English Railway Legislation of Trade & Industry (1848), p176
13 The Paris terminus was at Saint Lazare, and, at Rouen, Saint-Sever.
14 Railway Register, III p359),

£2,000,000.[15] Moss enthused *"My railroad connection with France has given me an opportunity of knowing that industry is rewarded there."*[16] Assuming he had sold his 500 shares at this point, he would have made a clear profit of £10,000. It is more probable that a sophisticated investor like Moss would have been a regular buyer and seller over this period and to have held on to a significant quantity for dividend income. In July, he urged Gladstone to *"not fear Paris & Rouen. They will pay excellent dividends. We shall give you next month 4/2 per share profit on Exchanges."*[17]

In 1842, while work on the Paris & Rouen was still proceeding, Blount was able to secure, on behalf of the same group of capitalists, contractors and engineer, the contract for the 55 mile extension of the line from Rouen to Havre on the North coast.[18] Work began soon after the completion of the Paris & Rouen, although the line proved more problematical and costly, involving, as it did, a large viaduct, tunnels under Rouen and a 600 foot climb and descent back to sea level. This railway opened to the public on 22 March 1847, having cost £28,300 per mile.[19] Paris now had a direct rail link to the English Channel at Havre, from where passengers for England were ferried to Southampton. The final connection between Paris and London was made by way of the 76 mile long London & Southampton railway.

By a law of 1842, the French Government was invested with power to oversee the creation of one coherent national network of connecting railways. The idea was that the great lines should all radiate out of Paris to France's frontiers with Belgium, Germany, Switzerland, the Mediterranean, Spain, the Atlantic coast and the English Channel. Other than at

---

15   Jenks, p143
16   Hawarden correspondence Moss to J Gladstone 5.1.1843
17   Hawarden correspondence Moss to J Gladstone 28.7.1843
18   Dionysius Lardner - Railway Economy: A Treatise on the New Art of Transport (1850), p449. Webster states the length as 58 miles. Webster – Locke, p119
19   Morrison, p 176

Havre, termini were proposed at Lille on the Belgian border, Strasbourg on the German border, Lyon in the south-east, Marseilles on the south coast, and Bordeaux and Nantes on the west coast. The government gave generous concessions in order to achieve these ends and thus provided great opportunities for British capitalists and workers alike, for years to come.

By 1844, there were six foreign railways listed on the Liverpool Stock Exchange[20] but mid-Railway Mania, in September 1845, that number increased to 44.[21] In January of the following year, Moss expressed great satisfaction at having been not only *"one of the projectors of The Paris & Rouen, Rouen & Havre"* but also of the *"Great Northern"* (or Compagnie de Nord) which stretched 321 miles from Paris to Douay, from where one line forked off to the Belgian Frontier at Quivrain, and another to Calais.[22] Moss was a projector, too, of the Paris & Lyon, a 319 mile line to the south-east via Dijon. Additionally, by 1846, he had become *"one of the High Commissaries of the Dutch Rhenish in Holland"* [23] explaining that *"My experience in Rail Road matters causes me to prefer new countries to old."* [24] Moss's involvement with foreign railways was not limited to continental Europe. Along with William Chaplin, George Hudson, John Masterman and seven other Englishmen, he was briefly involved as a shareholder and member of the *"Corresponding Committee in London"* for the Great Western Railroad Company of Canada.[25]

By the end of 1846, the English had made an estimated profit of at least £5,000,000 on their investments in French railways.[26] In June, Moss intimated that he had *"been selling*

---

20 the Paris-Rouen, the Paris-Orleans, the Paris-Lyons, the Rouen-Havre, the Strasbourg-Basle and the Paris-Strasbourg. Thomas, WA, p45.
21 ibid
22 Hawarden correspondence Moss to John Gladstone 30.1.1846
23 ibid
24 Hawarden Correspondence Moss to Tom Gladstone 31.3.1846
25 An Act to Alter and Amend the Charter of the Great Western Railroad Company (Passed 9 June 1846)
26 Railway Register, III p359 and IV pp259-261

both (Paris & Rouen and Rouen & Havre) *lately. I did so because before either of them come into profitable (I mean good dividend) operation I think the present king of France can hardly be expected to live and then prices could fall."* [27] Like Britain, France suffered an economic crisis and a stock market collapse in 1847. On 8 April, Moss informed Tom Gladstone that he had reduced all his *"English rail road stock and my foreign except Dutch Rhenish and Paris & Rouen & Havre. Those I think I know the intrinsic value of as I did the Grand Junction when I and my opinion was so little thought of."* [28]

A Revolution in February 1848 resulted in the abdication of Louis Philippe and the establishment of the Second Republic. The British were not now so welcome. At a meeting in London of the proprietors of the Paris-Rouen and Rouen-Havre Railways on 9 June, Locke rued the fact that the only return the French were now giving *"was the expulsion of these very British engine drivers who had been of such eminent service in the development of their manufacturing industry."* [29] However, their government's scheme for a national network of railways continued to depend upon foreign funding. Moss considered that *"the French people are hardly prepared for the Capital which will be required to complete them,"* [30] and he continued to invest in their railways until the end of his days. [31]

The Dutch-Rhenish Railway

In 1838, the Dutch state determined to finance a scheme for a rail link with Germany, its largest trading partner.

---

27 Hawarden correspondence Moss to Tom Gladstone 24.6.1846
28 Hawarden Correspondence Moss to Tom Gladstone 8.4.1847
29 Salt, p10
30 Hawarden correspondence Moss to Tom Gladstone 24.6.1846
31 In November 1857, to satisfy his wife's annuity, he drew up a codicil arranging to *"set apart and appropriate the sum of one million two hundred and fifty thousand francs secured by the Western Railway of France Bonds to answer the annuity of one thousand five hundred pounds."*

The route was to comprise of two branches, both around 30 miles in length, running eastwards from Amsterdam in the north-west and Rotterdam in the south-west, joining together at Utrecht. From Utrecht the line would run another 40 miles to Arnhem and terminate a further 20 miles east at Emmerich on the Prussian (German) border, close to Cologne. Progress was, however, markedly slow. While Holland's canal system was unrivalled in the world, her trade was severely restricted each year by ice in December and January. The severe winter of 1844 caused a four month stoppage on the canals, and brought work on the railway to a halt. It was not until the following year that the line reached its temporary end at Arnhem. Construction had, by then, cost more than the anticipated total spend of 9 million guilders.[32]

Just as in France, insufficient domestic capital could be raised to see the project through, and an appeal was made to English financiers. Railway Mania was, by now, almost at its peak and, with few sufficiently profitable schemes to invest in at home, British capitalists looked abroad for higher returns. The Dutch Rhenish Railway Company Ltd was registered on 3 July 1845.[33] Its capital of 24 million guilders (£2m) was divided into 100,000 shares of 240 Dutch florins (£20) each. This entire sum was pledged by just 35 shareholders, and 67% of the shares were placed in the hands of British investors.[34] Moss subscribed for 6,250 at £125,000 and later persuaded Sir John Gladstone to take a sizeable number, having assured him that he had *"very carefully gone into the question of water against Rail Road and I am confident no water conveyance can*

---

[32] Augustus J Veenendaal - Railways in the Netherlands: A Brief History 1834-1994, p12

[33] The railway had 2 official names, one English and one Dutch - Nederlandsche Rhijnspoorweg Maatscappij (NRS) ibid, p13.

[34] Dutch Rhenish Railway papers including Act of Concession, Regulations, Reports etc, 1846. The only British investors with a holding larger than Moss's were Thomas Wilson & Son - 14,000 shares, A A Gower, Nephews & Co - 14,000, Frederick Ricketts - 14,000 and William James Chapman - 12,500. John Masterman, a London banker also held 6,250 The Dutch King Willem II subscribed for only 200.

successfully compete with a railway... The Belgium directors for a long time hesitated whether to order wagons to carry goods because Belgium was like Holland (splendid in water) they were forced into it and now their goods traffic is 35% of the whole. I recollect in Paris they ridiculed our taking goods with the navigable service close to us all the way. I may say on its banks." [35]

The Union Bank of London and Moss & Co became the Dutch Rhenish's English bankers.[36] The railway's board had six directors, of whom four were English and based in London, and the others were Dutch and based in Arnhem and Rotterdam. At British insistence, Locke was again appointed engineer. Sharp, Roberts & Co of Gorton near Manchester was called upon to supply the railway's locomotives, and Thomas Brassey won the contract to construct the line. Locke inspected the work already done and, having walked the entire route,[37] was confident the remainder of the line over Holland's famously flat plains could be built cheaply and easily. With such a proficient team in place, Moss declared, in December 1846 *"I am, like most men as they advance in life, pleased with this my youngest child and I shall be sadly disappointed if it does not produce 10% when completed in two years...I am not a director* (he was a commissary) *but I attend to the business as pleasant occupation, receiving all the information and finding faults without responsibility."* [38] One major fault was that the Dutch had adopted Isambard Kingdom Brunel's broad gauge of 6 feet 9 inches, despite the fact that their Belgian, Hanoverian and Prussian neighbours had all adopted Stephenson's narrow gauge of 4 feet 8 ½ inches. At the meeting places with these countries there was going to be costly trans-shipment of passengers and goods.

---

35   Hawarden correspondence Moss to J Gladstone 10.12.1846. By May 1849 Gladstone's holding was 2,000 shares – Hawarden correspondence J Gladstone to Moss 16.05.1849
36   The Dutch bankers were Associatie Cassa of Amsterdam. At Hawarden - Letter to shareholders from Dutch Rhenish Railway, Amsterdam, 22 December 1855.
37   Veenendaal, p16
38   Hawarden correspondence Moss to J Gladstone 10.12.1846

The Dutch Rhenish's early years were far from prosperous, and communication was made difficult by the geographical detachment of the board members. At Rotterdam, work was delayed until 1847 while the company and the Rotterdam council argued over the exact location of the start and finish and whether or not to build a new station.[39] In January of that year, Moss was moved to persuade Gladstone to defer investing further in the railway, observing that *"They are very slow in their work."* [40] The directors resolved to speed up construction of the line from Rotterdam to the German border. Only by so doing could they reap the rewards from transporting goods from England and the Americas to the inner continent, and bring the railway into profitability. However, years passed with little progress. While Belgium had been quick to establish its rail link between Antwerp and Germany, the Dutch government did nothing to help the trade of its own major port of Rotterdam.[41] An English shareholder commented *"Where was now the activity, the national enterprising spirit, the classic industry of the ancient Dutch?"* [42] The Dutch Rhenish took it upon itself to begin discussions with the Prussian government in 1846. While agreement was reached on the point of connection, the Prussians would not commit themselves to a timescale for the completion of their branch of the line. The company appealed to the Dutch Government but, by the time they entered into the negotiations, in June 1847, the Prussians had already prioritised the establishment of a connection to Belgium. Crucially, the Dutch refused to consider converting their tracks over from broad gauge, and so Antwerp won much valuable German trade. There matters rested until 1851, when a treaty was drawn up whereby the Dutch Rhenish company agreed to complete its line from Arnhem to the border within three years. The Prussians determined to build a railway from Oberhausen to Emmerich in the same timescale.

---

39   JH Jonckers Nieboer – Geshiedenis der Nederlandsche Spoorwegen, p57
40   Hawarden correspondence Moss to J Gladstone 4.1.1847
41   Nieboer, p59
42   ibid

In March 1852, the Dutch Government formally agreed to convert to narrow gauge and to pay the Dutch Rhenish 1 million guilders to carry out that task.[43] Work began in earnest and, as the track grew, the railway came into profitability, paying its first dividend (of less than 1%) in 1853.[44] The connection between Rotterdam and Utrecht was established, outside of schedule, in July 1855. In the 12 months to May 1856 the railway's receipts rose to £90,100 of which 42% was absorbed by expenses.[45] Moss noted how *"Since the new line to Emerich was open the increased receipts have been about 80%, often 100%. Thus we have, before there is any communications with the lines on the Eastside of the Rhine, I believe, an income of £160,000. From this deducting 42% would leave £93,000 instead of £36,000."*[46] Significantly, 70% of receipts had come from freight, and 30% from passenger traffic.[47] Despite this apparent success, Moss urged Gladstone and other investors to exercise caution. *"I do not advise any one to embark in DR but I do not advise a sale until after the frost sets in next winter. It is wonderful how the shares have kept up – the Dutch are very slow, very prudent. I hold a large quantity – more than I shall retain if they…* (rise in price)*"*[48]

The Dutch Rhenish Railway's ambition was fulfilled when the line from Arnhem to Oberhausen was opened on 20 October 1856.[49] This should have heralded greater profitability, but dividends remained below 1% until 1858. Moss informed Tom Gladstone, in June of that year how *"Dutch Rhenish affairs have been most shamefully mismanaged in Holland. A person by the name of Hesleden (the President) has been influenced, I believe, by the promise of Ribbons and orders to*

---

43 ibid, p61. In addition a subsidy of 360,000 guilders was made for interest while work was carried out.
44 Veenendaal, p14
45 Hawarden correspondence Moss to Thomas Gladstone 7.6.1856
46 ibid
47 ibid
48 ibid
49 Nieboer, p62

sacrifice the interest of the shareholders. He retires in July when all will be remodelled. My opinion of it has not varied. You will this year see a very considerable increase of receipts and expenses reduced from 55% to 45% or less. Mr Fenton, the banker of Rochdale (?) and my son T E Moss and 2 others became commissaries. The first 2 are already in office. They propose going to Holland in July and will see all put on a new footing." [50]

The future was bright for those of the company's shareholders who survived to collect the 1866 all time high dividend of 8.8%. [51]

---

50   Hawarden correspondence Moss to Thomas Gladstone 7.6.1856
51   Veenendaal, p14

CHAPTER 11

THE END

"Events like these tell us what shadows we are and what shadows we pursue."

John Moss to James Loch, 22 September 1830, quoting Edmund Burke.

On 29 June 1858, John Moss wrote to Sir John Gladstone's oldest son Tom. *"Mr Forbes[52] the new traffic manager of the Dutch Rhenish has come over to report the result of the changes he has made. I am much pleased with our prospects and I trust this time next year our dividend will prove the correctness of his views."*[53] Moss did not collect this dividend. Having lived a life *"full of years and full of honours"*[54] he died of *"exhaustion"*[55] at Otterspool House on 3 October, aged 76. His funeral was held on Saturday 9 October at his beloved St Anne's church in Aigburth. *"The usual paraphernalia of mourning coaches etc, was dispensed with, the body being borne from the residence of the deceased, at Otterspool, to the place of interment, which is only a short distance, by a number of his old and faithful servants."*[56]

---

52 James Staat Forbes undertook the reorganisation with Daniel George Bingham
53 Hawarden correspondence Moss to T Gladstone 29.6.1858
54 Obituary. Liverpool Mail 9.10.1858
55 Death certificate of John Moss
56 A Bowker & Sons (publishers) - In Memoriam of Liverpool Celebrities. The pall bearers were: *"Messrs J.C. Moss* (Henry Moss's son) *R.* (Robertson) *Gladstone,*

Although Moss is described in his obituary as a *"liberal Churchman"*, his admiration for the evangelical Anglican Reverend Hugh McNeile (Rector of St Jude's, Liverpool) who took the service, suggests otherwise. McNeile, a fire and brimstone, militantly Protestant Ulsterman, bearing deep hostility towards Roman Catholicism,[57] had once advocated the reintroduction of slavery.[58] Nonetheless he was a brilliant orator[59] and a first rate minister with a national reputation.[60] *"The funeral service, both in the church and at the grave side, was read in a very impressive manner... The body was deposited in a new vault recently erected by the deceased in the northwest corner of the burial ground."*[61] Moss's remains and those of his immediate family lie there to this day.

The *Liverpool Mail's* lengthy obituary bears testament to the fact that the town had lost an outstanding citizen, who had conversed and worked with many great historical figures. Moss's business activities, although mainly conducted from Liverpool, had influenced the lives of thousands of Britons, Indians and Africans. His work as a railway pioneer helped bring about massive social and economic change in all countries which adopted that revolutionary invention. Was Moss a great man? From my reading of his 421 letters, the very least I can say is that he was a fundamentally decent gentleman and an honest, wise, modest and industrious human being. Few men, great or not, could hope for a more glowing epitaph than that.

RIP.

Zwitchenbart, J. B. Lloyd, F. Taylor, Professor Traill, A. Lace and J. Innes."
57   James Murphy – The Religious Problem in English Education", p10 + p230
58   "Slave labor versus free labour sugar" Speech delivered at a public meeting held at Liverpool, 13 June 1848. Liverpool Central. H338.476641 MACN
59   Rev Charles Bullock – Hugh McNeile and Reformation Truth, p15
60   Disraeli appointed McNeile Dean of Ripon in 1868. ibid
61   Bowker

Appendix A

Obituary from the *Liverpool Mail* - Saturday, October 9 1858

THE LATE JOHN MOSS, ESQ.

Our obituary of the week chronicles the decease of a leading townsman, Mr. John Moss, who gathered to his fathers in a ripe old age, full of years and full of honours. His name and his public services - much more than many suppose - have become unseparably identified with the mighty future of Liverpool. His memory, therefore, is well deserving of an ampler tribute than we have seen paid to it, - indeed, far ampler than we happen to have sufficient data at hand for fully rendering.

It is, however, unnecessary to dwell on Mr. Moss' lengthened career, private character or personal successes. Suffice it to say that he was, we believe, in early life, in partnership with his father, a well known merchant of the old school of Liverpool enterprise. The firm are understood to have held one lucrative branch of the West Indian trade almost exclusively in their own hands. Mr. Moss' father was hailed as an exemplary man of business, whose wise rule was to keep all the diversified parts of his own business immediately under his personal oversight. Mr. Moss' mother is still remembered as a perfect Lady Bountiful, and her hospitable residence was a kind of general relieving-office for the entire district; her servants were strictly enjoined never to turn the hungry and needy "empty away," and in order that they may have no excuse for hastily, or lazily, or stingily slamming the door upon any; the story runs that the kind old lady always kept in readiness a large supply of biscuit freely at the service of all beggars for bread. Such generous traits, however condemned by political economists, are worthy of recording - questionless they are not unnoticed on high.

Prosperity followed industry and enterprise. In addition to their West Indian trade, which we believe they never wholly relinquished, the family of the Mosses became Liverpool bankers. And the late Mr. Moss had for many years been at the head of the well known banking firm which bears his name. His chief eminence, however, was not mere success in trade or in finance. He quietly, almost unconsciously, achieved a lasting name for himself in the foremost roll of enterprising "Liverpool Men", by becoming one of the first and most indefatigable originators of railways in England, and one of the earliest and steadiest supporters of Stephenson, whose practical genius and indomitable perseverance inaugurated and gradually extended railway communications over the civilized world. In fact his public services were mainly devoted to fostering railway enterprise.

In politics he was a zealous and enlightened Tory, and a liberal Churchman. But it is understood that Mr. Moss systematically declined all high municipal posts, all civic distinctions, as being scarcely compatible with incessant banking avocations. But although he shrank from becoming what is called a "public man" and hence his career was a comparatively private one, still, he numbered very many and most attached friends. These delight to tell us that, while with true John Bull sturdiness he would stand out for every five-shilling piece which he believed to be his just right, within the next five minutes he would cheerfully give a five pound note, or a fifty, towards any charitable or benevolent object which commended itself to his judgment - and his judgment was more than ordinarily shrewd and sagacious. He cared little for your stereotyped guinea subscriptions and benefactions paraded in newspapers; but brother bankers of his remember with melancholy pleasure that they never asked his kindly co-operation in any good design, without meeting a ready and liberal response.

Multitudes in this great community will long remember the habitual liberality and public spirit with which the fine sheet of water within his grounds at Otterspool was opened to the public for skating and other winter amusements. He was proverbial for keeping up a sumptuous hospitality within his own extended circle. And his neighbours, from the highest to the humblest, all delight to tell how, whenever sickness and fever visited the district, the poor as well as the rich widely shared the practical sympathies of the kindly family at Otterspool, and how the graperies and hothouses and gardens were always spontaneously laid under contribution to supply choicest fruits to the humblest invalid, without stint, without ostentation, without the semblance of patronizing condescension. In an age when a Judge from the Bench had to deplore with his dying breath the want of sympathy between class and class, such trifling but expressive traits as these - traits in which the good old Lady Bountiful may be said to be reproduced in her posterity, if not yet to live in her example - seem to us not unworthy of being held in local remembrance. May there never be wanting a descendant in Otterspool mansion who shall thus worthily illustrate the kindly sympathies and similarly maintain the generous hospitalities of the GOOD OLD ENGLISH GENTLEMAN!

But to pass on to Mr. Moss' more public service to his native town: - There are perhaps no two great emporiums on the globe between which fewer engineering obstructions, or greater level facilities for economising in both land and water carriage exist, than between Liverpool and Manchester. Yet six and thirty years ago the trade of Liverpool, and especially its corn trade, keenly felt that identical grievance of extortionate freights between these two places, for which the Liverpool Chamber of Commerce have been long but too timidly seeking a permanent remedy. Both generations of complainants at first fell to work memorialising and supplicating, instead of demanding and prosecuting "according to law". Neither set of complainants seemed to be sufficiently alive to what we have repeatedly affirmed, to wit, that the great Duke of Bridgewater himself was quite of their mind, and a century ago had actually anticipated their reasonable requirements. To this hour, sufferers and complainants still overlook the pregnant fact not only reiterated again and again by us, but chronicled in McCulloch's Dictionary under the head of "Canals" and in Aiken's Warrington History, and elaborately embodied in the original Bridgewater Canal Act, to wit, that the sagacious duke to special precautions that the carrying trade between Liverpool and Manchester should never charge more than 6s per ton for freight and tolls and all possible charges put together. Nay more, a penalty of five pounds is enacted for each and every overcharge. All this remains the law of the land - unless indeed any sinister repealing clause has been smuggled into the thousand and one Railway Acts. We could never trace a shadow of repeal. Yet while trade since then has multiplied a million fold these carrying charges have long been positively nearly double the legal maximum, and are still nearly fifty per cent above it. Well, thirty six years ago - and, for once, in the local ignorance of all this, that "ignorance was bliss" - the generally recognised "Father" of the Liverpool and Manchester line - Mr. Joseph Sandars, a leading corn merchant, felicitously concluded that there was nothing else for it but to originate a railway. Doubtless he never dreamt that it and other railways would ere long combine with the Canal interest to exceed and defy the law. His own social status and financial position were not then adequate to head so novel and so vast an enterprise. He enlisted the able services of our late enterprising townsman. Mr. Moss became the first chairman of this railway movement. His disinterested magnanimity caused him to prefer and soon to take the second place - the deputy chairmanship, in order to gain for the chairmanship the advantage and the influence of the Liverpool Mayoralty, then filled by Mr. Charles Lawrence. But his ability and tact soon caused Mr. Moss to be singled out as Chairman of another important railway project, the Grand Junction between Liverpool and Birmingham. As he had been a foremost originator of our great local railways, so with characteristic foresight and sagacity he continued to the last a foremost opponent of Railway extensions and amalgamations. How many impoverished "original shareholders" in the Manchester Line or the Grand Junction Line, or the London and Birmingham will not now devoutly wish that Mr. Moss' opposition had but been successful! When he found himself outvoted and unable to carry out his well considered policy, and especially when Sir Robert Peel not only turned the first sod of the costly and unremunerative Trent Valley Line, but uttered ominous words too sadly indicative that England's railways would therefore cease to have fair play or common justice from England's legislature, Mr. Moss voluntarily withdrew from his prominent position on English railways. He is understood to have sold out very advantageously most of his English railway property and to have transferred much of his enterprise to Continental railways, more justly dealt with by Continental legislatures. But he had already won golden opinions in his railway presidency at home. And his name is now so lastingly interwoven with those great iron arteries of communication along which the commerce of the world pours into and out of Liverpool that we cannot better close this imperfect obituary notice than by quoting his lion's share of these great enterprises and the memorable recognition of his valuable services as already placed on permanent record by "the Historian of Liverpool"

"The year 1828 is memorable in the annals of Liverpool as that in which the first application was made to Parliament, for powers to construct a railway from Liverpool to Manchester. This railway was formed during the next few years, and was the commencement of the modern system of railway communication, which, in a quarter of a century, has produced such wonderful results, not only in Great Britain and Ireland, but on the continents of Europe and America.

"It was in the beginning of the year 1822 that the corn merchants of Liverpool memorialised Mr. Bradshaw, the acting trustee of the late Duke of Bridgewater, for a reduction of the rate of freight between that port and Manchester, and on 5 April he replied in a letter to the Chairman of the Corn Exchange, 'That having taken into full consideration the allegations contained in their memorial, and all the information he is in possession of on the subject, he does not feel himself justified in making any alteration in the trustees' present rate of freight.'

"At the first meeting, held at Messrs Pritt and Clays office, John Moss, esq., was formally appointed Chairman etc ... The Committee met very frequently, and, at the recommendation of Mr. Moss, Mr. Charles Lawrence, then the Mayor of Liverpool, was solicited to join the undertaking and become its chairman. Mr. Lawrence accepted the honourable office, as generously surrendered by Mr. Moss, who foresaw the parliamentary advantage of the Mayor of Liverpool appearing at the head of the committee, and especially so, as that office was then filled by a gentleman remarkable for the urbanity of his manner and the general kindness of his disposition.

In the autumn of 1839 a splendid dinner service of plate, of the value of 1,000 guineas, was presented to Mr. John Moss, the chairman of the Grand Junction Railway Company, by the proprietors as an acknowledgement of the services which he had rendered to them and the public in the progress of that great undertaking. The plate bore the following inscription: - 'To John Moss, esq., from a numerous body of proprietors of the Grand Junction Railway, in testimony of their grateful sense of his services as chairman of the board of directors from the commencement of that undertaking, being a period of seven years. 1839.'

Baines' Liverpool, pp 591-654"

Appendix B

Supplies requiring shipment from England to a West Indian plantation:

"1st. Negro Clothing; viz.

1,500 yards of Oznaburgh cloth, or German linen, 650 yards of blue bays, or pennistones, for a warm frock for each Negro, 350 yards of striped linseys for the women, 250 yards of coarse check for shirts for the boilers, tradesmen, domesticks and children, 3 dozen of coarse blankets for lying-in women and sick Negroes and 18 dozen of coarse hats.

2nd. Tools.

For the carpenters and coopers, to the amount of £25 sterling, including 2 or 3 dozen falling axes.

3rd. Miscellaneous Articles.

160,000 nails of different sizes, 2,500 puncheon rivets, 6 cattle chains, 6 dozen of hoes, 6 dozen of bills, 20 dozen of small clasp knives for the Negroes, 4 dozen of ox bows, 50 bundles of iron hoops,

2 sets of puncheon truss hoops, 2 sets of hogshead ditto, 80 gallons of train oil for lamps,

2 barrels of tar, 2 boxes of short tobacco pipes for the Negroes, 180 bundles of wood hoops,

2 sheets of lead, 6 large copper ladles for the boilers, 6 ditto skimmers for the boilers,

8 dozen of small iron pots for the Negroes, 2 puncheons of Bristol lime for temper and 4 grindstones

<u>4th. Provisions etc chiefly from Ireland</u>

80 barrels of herrings, or salted cod equal thereto, 6 barrels of salted beef, 2 barrels of salted pork,

4 firkins of salted butter, 2 boxes of soap, 2 boxes of candles, 2 hogsheads of salt, 6 barrels of flour,

6 kegs of pease and 3 jugs of groats.

To this sum are to be added the following very heavy charges within the Island; viz.

Overseer's or manager's salary, Distiller's salary, two other white servants, a white carpenter's wages, maintenance of five white servants, exclusive of their allowance of salted provisions...medical care of the Negroes...millwright's, coppersmith's, plumber's, and smith's bills, annually, colonial taxes, publick and parochial, annual supply of mules and steers, wharfage and storage of goods landed and shipped, American staves and heading, for hogsheads and puncheons, a variety of small occasional supplies of different kinds."

Quoted from Bryan Edwards - The History, Civil and Commercial of the British Colonies, pp63-64 (1791)

Appendix C

The Sugar Plantation Hierarchy

Thomas Roughley's *"The Jamaica Planters Guide"* of 1823 categorizes Negroes, steers and mules as "stock." It should not, however, be assumed that the slaves were just one mass of brawn; plantation society was far more complex than that. All had their role to play in the sugar plantation hierarchy: At the top was the **"head driver"**, whose power was derived from the white overseer, directing all the slaves' conditions and supervising each labour gang. Beneath him were the **"head cattle and mule man"**, the **"head boiler"** or manufacturer of sugar, then **"carpenters, coopers, masons, coppersmiths and watchmen"**. The **"head watchman"** reported to the overseer any losses or damage to the plantation. There then followed **"the hothouse or hospital doctor or doctress, midwives, etc"** who had *"white people, mixed, coloured and black under their care."* The **"house people"** attended to general cleaning, cooking and sewing. The **"great gang"** *"... of able men and women, sometimes amounting to an hundred"* undertook *"the field work, which requires strength and skill in the execution; such as making lime-kilns, digging cane-holes, making roads through the estate, trenching, building stone walls, planting canes and provisions, trashing heavy canes, cutting and tying canes and tops in crop time, cutting copper-wood, feeding the mill, carrying green trash from the mill to the trash-house, and repairing the public roads..."* The **"second gang"** was *"...composed of people, who are thought to be of rather weakly habits, mothers of sucking children, youths drafted from the children's gang, from twelve to eighteen years of age, and elderly people who are sufficiently strong for* (lighter) *field-work."* **The**

Third or Weeding gang" formed out of *"the rising generation, from which, in the progress of time, all the vacancies occurring in the different branches of slave population are filled up."* Then **"Negro children"** over the age of 5 or 6 performed very light duties like throwing dung into cane-holes *"...and by this they will be taught to observe the mode of planting, and putting the cane in the ground.."* **"Watchmen, invalids, and superannuated"** repaired broken fences and made *"baskets, pads, pegs, ropes, etc."* Finally, **"young children and infants"** over 3 years old would be given *"a little basket, and be made somewhat useful by gathering up trash and leaves, and pulling up young weeds..."* [1]

Unlike Moss, Roughley had to contend with a dwindling workforce:

"We have not for some years imported, neither is it ever likely to take place, that we should have a fresh supply of slaves into the British colonies. The old Africans are daily wearing out and dropping into the grave; our care is to support the present stock, encourage healthy propagation...induce them to receive Christianity...to take care that they are regularly supplied with salt provisions, comfortable clothing; that their houses are kept tenable; their time and hours to cultivate their grounds not infringed upon; those grounds kept free from trespass of cattle or otherwise; that they be not punished for every trifling fault, or unmercifully, at any time; when really sick, that they be taken into the hospital, under the care of the attending doctor, with proper medicine, nourishment etc, for them; that their infant children are provided with proper nurses when weaned, kept clean, free from insects called chegoes; a wholesome mess of stewed provisions, with a proportion of garden-stuff, made savoury by a little salt meat etc, served to these children every day, in the overseer's presence; the invalids and superannuated treated with sympathy; and their sufferings, brought on by either age or infirmity, relieved... Thus with the blessing of Providence, insuring to the proprietor a succession of healthy, well disposed, effective slaves." [2]

---

[1] M Craton, J Walvin and D Wright – Slavery Abolition and Emancipation, pp77-86
[2] ibid

Appendix D

In Defence of Henry Moss

Lest John Moss's brother, Henry, be damned as the murderer of one of the 99 slaves left on Crooked Island after the remainder had been removed to *Anna Regina*, it is fitting that a defence be mounted on his behalf. In 1995 the Government of the Bahamas commissioned archaeological research on Crooked Island.[1] This established that, during the first two decades of the nineteenth century, *Marine Farm* plantation was owned by Moss's uncle James, President of the Bahamian House of Assembly. *Great Hope* plantation *"was purchased in 1818 by Henry Moss, nephew of James Moss"* and *"Henry Moss owned Great Hope through 1847."* In 1826 *"Henry and his wife Helen were accused and convicted of the worst case of cruelty to a slave in the Bahamas as a result of an incident which took place...at Great Hope."* The circumstances were that Kate, a house slave, had steadfastly refused to carry out her work, and was also accused of theft. The Mosses had her placed in stocks, and there she remained for 17 days. She was regularly flogged for continuously refusing to carry out her duties or for being incapable of carrying them out. Red pepper (capsicum) had been rubbed on her eyes to prevent her from sleeping, and a number of different people, including her own father, flogged her. On the 17th day it was concluded that the punishment had not had the desired effect, and Kate was sent out to work, labouring in the fields. Within hours she dropped down dead.

An appeal against the prison sentence handed out to Mr &

---

[1] It was partially funded by the Bahamas National Trust and undertaken by Paul Farnsworth and Laurie Wilkie of Louisiana State University.

Mrs Moss for this crime was made to the then Colonial Secretary William Huskisson, an associate of John Moss. Huskisson found no grounds for clemency. His report concluded: *"The cruelties committed by Henry and Helen Moss are, as I have said, incontrovertibly proved; that there was a provocation to them might have been believed without evidence, for it could scarcely be in human nature to commit them from mere wantonness; but they are totally unjustified by any such provocation; they constitute an offence of an aggravated character, and for which I cannot consider the sentence of 5 months' imprisonment and fines amounting to £300 to be by any means unduly severe. I am therefore unable to advise his majesty to remit any part of this sentence."* [2]

Henry Moss of Liverpool remained married to Hannah Clegg from 1811 until his death in 1848,[3] but there is no evidence of charges ever having been brought against him for bigamy. While *"Henry Moss of Crooked Island"* was named as one of the executors of uncle James' will, he is referred to only as *"my friend"* and not as a nephew. While it may be argued that brother James' homecoming could have forced Henry to take over the role of resident manager of the estate, there is no evidence to suggest that he did so. Indeed, Hughes states that *"Henry contented himself with municipal matters, and was chosen a member of the Common Council on 6th October 1824."* [4] Further, the *Liverpool Mercury* of 26 May 1826 listed Henry's as one of 650 signatures supporting Huskisson to stand in the forthcoming general election. That election took place on 12 June 1826 and *"The Indenture of Return.... Moss alone signs and seals as Bailiff."* [5] The offences in the Bahamas took place between 26 July and 8 August 1826 leaving Henry, at a maximum, less than 44 days to leave Liverpool, arrive on Crooked Island and perpetrate the crime. In those days the outbound journey took at least 40 days by sailboat. Although the atrocity points to incompetent, poor or inexperienced management there is no evidence in the trial transcript to suggest that Henry Moss was a recent arrival on Crooked Island. Indeed, one witness, Eliza Campbell, had *"known the Defendants about 26 years"* and Captain John Pinder had *"visited them occasionally for 8 or 10 years."* Ludovic Selig who had *"resided 20 years on Crooked"* said

---

2 National Archives - Colonial & Foreign Office correspondence, ref PC1/4328
3 Hannah Moss referred to herself as a "widow" in the 1851 national census
4 Hughes, p198
5 George S Veitch - Huskisson and Liverpool, p30

"Mr. & Mrs. Moss have always treated their Negroes with humanity and kindness". [1]

Henry Moss certainly did serve a 5 month sentence at Nassau prison in 1827, but he was not John Moss's brother.[2]

---

1   Bahamas National Archives CO23/76/273-289
2   Hughes writes that when, in Liverpool *"in 1827, a motion was brought forward to enable the Town Council to erect a public building on the site of the Old Infirmary Gardens, in the minority of seven were found all the bankers, Henry Moss, Samuel Thompson and Richard Leyland. Had their views prevailed, we should have had no St George's Hall."*, p46

Bibliography

Primary Sources

Carlson, Robert E - *The Liverpool & Manchester Railway Project 1821-1831*. Liverpool Central. 1969

Checkland, S.G - *The Gladstones - A Family Biography 1764-1851*. Liverpool Central. 1971

Daly, Vere T - *A Short History of the Guyanese People*. Liverpool University. 1975

Donaghy, Thomas - *Liverpool & Manchester Railway Operations 1831 - 1845*. Liverpool Central. 1972

Ferneyhough, Frank - *The Liverpool & Manchester Railway 1830-1980*. Liverpool Central. 1980

Francis, John - *History of the Bank of England...from 1694-1844*. HSBC archives London. 1862

Green, William A - *British Slave Emancipation, The Sugar Colonies and the Great Experiment 1830-1865*. Liverpool Central. 1976

Hawarden Correspondence at Flintshire Record Office. Ref GG452-518, GG370-372 and GG2856-2880

Holt, Geoffrey O - *A Short History of the Liverpool & Manchester Railway*. Liverpool University. 1986

Hughes, John - *Liverpool Banks & Bankers 1760-1837*. Liverpool Central. 1906

Mather, F.C - *After the Canal Duke*. Bury Metro Library. 1970

Mathieson, William - *The Sugar Colonies and Governor Eyre 1849-1866*. Liverpool University. 1936

Nath, Dwarka - *Indians in Guyana*. Liverpool University. 1970

Reed, Malcolm - *London & North Western Railway.* Liverpool University. 1996

Richards, Eric - *The Leviathan of Wealth. The Sutherland Fortune in the Industrial Revolution.* Liverpool University. 1973

Sutherland Correspondence at Staffordshire Record Office. Ref D593/k/1/3/16-33

Steel, W L - *History of the London & North Western.* Manchester University. 1914

Temperley, Howard - *British Anti Slavery. 1833-1870.* Liverpool Central. 1972

Thomas, R H G - *The Liverpool and Manchester Railway.* Liverpool Central. 1980

Webster, N W - *Britain's First Trunk Line.* Liverpool Central. 1972

Other Sources:

Andrews, Alan W - *Parish Church of St Anne -A History to Commemorate the 150th Anniversary 1837-1987* (Author's personal collection) 2000

Andreades, A - *History of the Bank of England.* Liverpool University. 1909

Baines, Thomas - *History of the Commerce and Town of Liverpool.* Liverpool Central. 1852

Blount, Sir Edward - *Memoirs of Sir Edward Blount.* Manchester University. 1902

Booth, Henry - *An Account of the Liverpool & Manchester Railway.* Liverpool Central. 1830

Bowker, A & Sons (publishers) - *In Memoriam of Liverpool Celebrities.* Liverpool Central. 1876

Brady, Terence - *The Fight Against Slavery.* Liverpool University. 1975

Bryan, Michael - *Bryan's Dictionary of Painters and Engravers.* Athenaeum, Liverpool Central. 1903.

Burke, Bernard - *A Genealogical & Heraldic Dictionary of the Landed Gentry of Great Britain & Ireland.* Google Books. 1863

Butler, Kathleen Mary – *The Economics of Emancipation.* Liverpool University. 1995

Burton, Anthony - *The Rainhill Story*. Liverpool Central. 1980

Buxton, Charles - *The Memoirs of Sir Thomas Fowell Buxton*. Liverpool Central. 1849

Cameron, Gail & Crooke, Stan - *Liverpool Capital of the Slave Trade*. Liverpool University. 1992

Carter, Ernest F - *An Historical Geography of the Railways of the British Isles*. Liverpool University. 1959

Chaloner, W H - *The Social & Economic Development of Crewe 1780-1923*. Liverpool University. 1950

Chandler, George - *William Roscoe of Liverpool 1753-1831* Liverpool Central. 1953

Chandler, George - *Four Centuries of Banking* - Volume 1. Liverpool Central. 1964

Charlton, K - *James Cropper & Liverpool's Contribution to the Anti-Slavery Movement. (Transactions of the Historic Society of Lancs & Cheshire.)* Liverpool Central. 1972

Cook, Richard B - *The Grand Old Man*. Author's personal collection. 1898.

Cornish, James - *The Grand Junction and the Liverpool & Manchester Railway Companion*. Manchester University. 1837

Craton M, Walvin J and Wright D - *Slavery Abolition and Emancipation*. Liverpool University. 1976

Crick, W F & Wadsworth, J E - *A Hundred Years of Joint Stock Banking*. Liverpool University. 1936

Curtin, Phillip D - *The Atlantic Slave Trade*. Liverpool University. 1969

D'Auvergne, Edmund B - *Human Livestock*. Liverpool Central. 1933

Dawes, Margaret and Ward-Perkins, CN - *Country Banks of England & Wales*. ......Liverpool University. 2000

Fay, C R - *Huskisson and His Age*. Liverpool University. 1950

Foot, M R D - *The Gladstone Diaries, volume 1: 1825-1832*. Liverpool Central. 1968

Formby, Ann Lonsdall - *Short Sketch of the Life of the Late Doctor Formby* (from the Bickerton Papers) Liverpool Central. 1879

Freeling, Arthur - *Grand Junction Railway Companion*. Manchester University. 1838

Galt, William - *Railway Reform - Its Expediency and Practicability Considered*. Manchester University. 1844

Garfield, Simon - *The Last Journey of William Huskisson*. Liverpool Central. 2002

Gilbart, James William - *The Elements of Banking*. (fourth edition) Google books. 1860

Gilbart, James William - *The Logic of Banking*. Google books. 1859

Gilbart, James William - *A Practical Treatise on Banking*. Google books. 1856

Glasgow, Roy A - *Guyana: Race & Politics Among Africans & East Indians*. Liverpool University. 1970

Gourvish, T R - *Mark Huish & the London & North Western Railway*. Liverpool University. 1972

Gratus, Jack - *The Great White Lie*. Liverpool University. 1973

Griffiths, Robert - *The History of the Royal and Ancient Park of Toxteth Liverpool*. Liverpool Central. 1907

Henderson, W O - *The Liverpool Office in London. London: Economica*. Liverpool Central. 1933

Ishmael, Dr Odeen - *The Guyana Story (from earliest times to independence)* a collection of short essays from www.guyana.org. 2005

Jenks, Leland H - *The Migration of British Capital to 1875*. Liverpool University. 1938

Jonckers Nieboer, J H – Geshiendenis der Nederlandsche Spoorwegen. Utrecht. 1907

Kemble, Frances Ann - *Record of a Girlhood. (Volume 2)* Liverpool University. 1878

Lardner, Dionysius - *Railway Economy: A Treatise on the New Art of Transport*. Manchester University. 1850

Liverpool Mail (microfilm) - *"The late John Moss, Esq"* Obituary dated October 9 1858. Liverpool Central

Look Lai, Walton - *Indentured Labor, Caribbean Sugar* Liverpool University. 1993

MacDermot, E T & C R Clinker- *History of the Great Western Railway, Vol. 1*. Liverpool University. 1927

MacNaughton, A - *Roscoe of Liverpool*. Liverpool Central. 1996

McAlmont, Cecilia - *British Guiana's Immigration Dilemma: The Chinese Experiment*. Article in Stabroek News, 31 January 2003

McGowan, Christopher - *The Rainhill Trials*. Liverpool Central. 2004.

Millington, R - *House in the Park*. Liverpool Central. 1957

Morgan, E Victor - *The Theory and Practice of Central Banking 1797-1913*. Liverpool University. 1965

Morley, John - *Life of Gladstone. Vol. 1*. Liverpool Central. 1903

Morrison, James - *The Influence of English Railway Legislation*. Manchester University. 1848

Murphy, James – *The Religious Problem in English Education*. Liverpool Central. 1959

Neale, Frank - *Black '47: Britain & The Famine Irish*. Liverpool Central. 1998

Paine, E.M.S - *The Two James's and the Two Stephensons*. Liverpool Central. 1861

Parkinson, C Northcote - *The Rise of the Port Of Liverpool*. Liverpool Central. 1952

Pollins, Harold - *The Finances of the Liverpool & Manchester Railway* - Economic History Review, 2nd Series, Vols 4-15, (1951-53) Liverpool Central.

Pressnell, L S - *Country Banking in the Industrial Revolution*. Liverpool University. 1956

Privy Council document reference PC 1/4328 in the National Archives.

Ransom, P J G - *Locomotion: Two Centuries of Train Travel*. Liverpool Central. 2001

Reddie, Richard S - *Abolition! The Struggle to Abolish Slavery*. Liverpool University. 2007

Reed, M C - *Investment in Railways in Britain 1820-1824*. Liverpool University. 1975

Reed, B - *Crewe Locomotive Works and its Men*. Manchester University. 1982

Ritchie, J Ewing - *The Life and Times of William Ewart Gladstone*. Liverpool Central. 1900

Riley, Sandra - *Homeward Bound: A History of the Bahama Islands to 1850*. Google books. 2000

Robb, George - *White Collar Crime in Modern England*. Manchester University. 1992

Roscoe, Thomas - *The Book of the Grand Junction Railway*. Liverpool Central. 1839

Salt, Samuel - *Railway and Commercial Information*. Manchester University. 1850

Schwarz, Suzanne - *Slave Captain*. Liverpool Central. 1995

Scrivenor, Harry – The Railways of the United Kingdom. Manchester University 1849

Seecoomar, Judaman - *Contributions towards the Resolution of Conflict in Guyana*. Liverpool University. 2002

Shepherd, John A - *A History of the Liverpool Medical Institution*. Liverpool Central. 1979

Simpson, Charles, R H - *The Rainhill Locomotive Trials*. Liverpool Wavertree. 1979

Skeat, W O - *George Stephenson. The Engineer and His Letters*. Liverpool Central. 1973

Smiles, Samuel - *The Story of the Life of George Stephenson, Railway Engineer*. Liverpool University. 1857

Smiles, Samuel - *The Story of the Life of George Stephenson, Railway Engineer*. Google Books. 1860

Smiles, Samuel - *Lives of the Engineers with an account of their principal works*. Google Books. 1862

Smith, Raymond T - *British Guiana*. Liverpool University. 1962

Stephen, George - *Anti-Slavery Recollections*. Manchester Central. 1854

Stewart-Brown, Ronald - *History of the Manor and Township of Allerton*. Liverpool Central. 1911

Tames, Richard L - *Documents of the Industrial Revolution*. Liverpool University. 1971

Thomas, William Arthur - *The Provincial Stock Exchange*. Liverpool University. 1973

Touzeau, James - *The Rise and Progress of Liverpool 1551-1835*. Liverpool Central. 1910

Tywcross, Edward - *Mansions of England & Wales*. Liverpool Central. 1847

Vaughan, Adrian - *Railwaymen, Politics and Money*. Liverpool Central. 1997

Veenedaal, Augustus J - *Railways in the Netherlands: A Brief History 1834-1994*. Liverpool University. 1999

Veitch, George S - *Huskisson and Liverpool*. Liverpool Central. 1929

Vincit, Veritas - *Railway Locomotive Management*. Manchester University. 1847

Walker, Charles - *Joseph Locke (1805-1860)* (Author's private collection) 1975

Walvin, James - *Slavery & British Society 1777-1846*. Liverpool University. 1982

Webster, N W - *Joseph Locke Railway Revolutionary*. Liverpool University. 1970

Whale, Derek M - *Lost Villages of Liverpool*. Liverpool Central. 1984

Williams, Gomer - *History of the Liverpool Privateers and letters of Marque*. Liverpool Central. 1897

Woodham-Smith, Cecil - *The Great Hunger. Ireland 1845-1849*. Liverpool Central. 1980

Index

AA Gower, Nephews & Co 212 *n*
Aberdeen 83 *n*, 201
Aberdeen, Lord 60 *n*
Acton 175
Adelphi Hotel, Liverpool 150
Africa / African 5 *n*, 65-66, 74-78, 218, 228
African Chamber of Commerce 149 *n*
Aigburth, Liverpool 1, 7 *n*, 15 *n*, 52- 53, 108 *n*, 122 *n*, 217
Age of Reform 40, 155
Albion, the (newspaper) 33
Alderson, Edward 126-128,
Allerton Hall, Liverpool 86 *n*
America (North) / USA 5 *n*, 6, 17, 23-24, 60 *n*, 73, 101-103, 116, 177, 214, 223, 226,
America (South) / Latin America 9 *n*, 11, 23, 85 *n*, 89, 100, 116, 214, 223
American Revolution, the 84
Amsterdam 212, 213 *n*,
Anna Regina (Moss's West Indian plantation) 15-17, 28, 30-31, 33-34, 38, 44-48, 50-53, 55-57, 60-63, 67, 69, 77 *n*, 78, 80, 229
Anti Corn Law League 73 *n*
Antigua 49, 67,
Anti-Slavery Society / Abolitionists 6, 12, 17-19, 22, 24-25, 27, 30-32, 35, 40, 43, 45, 48, 55-58, 61-63, 69-72
Antwerp 214
Arnhem 212-215
Arrow, locomotive 145
Arthur Heywood, Sons & Co 86-88, 94
Aspinall's bank 92,
Associatie Cassa bank of Amsterdam 213 *n*
Aston Hall, Birmingham 166
Astley 121
Athenaeum, Liverpool 12 *n*
Augusta, Georgia 84 *n*
Bachelors Adventure (West Indian plantation) 21 *n*
Backhouse, John 13 *n*, 26, 49, 168
Bahama Islands, Act of the, (1784) 24
Bahamas / Bahamian 6 *n*, 11-12, 14, 18, 24-26, 52 *n*, 84, 229-230, 231 *n*

Baltimore and Ohio railway 153
Bank Charter Act (1833) 96, 99-100
Bank Charter Act (1844) 104-106
Bank Charter Act (1857) 105, 109
Bank of England 81-83, 89, 90-91, 94-104, 106,
Bank of Liverpool 15 *n*, 97,
Banking Act (1826) 95-96
Banking crisis (of 1825) 88-94, 100, 102,
Barbados 67,
Barclay & Co, London 83, 170
Barclay, Tristen, Bevan & Co, London 133 *n*
Baring Brothers 103 *n*, 206
Baring, Francis 206
Baring, Thomas 206
Barker, George 166
Barkhill, Liverpool 122 *n*,
Barkly, Henry 79
Barlow, Professor Peter 187, 190
Barton, Irlam & Higginson 75
Battle of the Gauges 197
Belgium / Belgian 103, 168, 209, 213-214
Belgium, Bank of 103
Belle Vue (West Indian plantation) 56 *n*, 63
Bengal 54 *n*, 63
Bennett, William 107 *n*
Benson, Mr (of Demerara) 28
Benson, Robert 126, 128, 134, 140
Bentinck, Lord George 65, 74-78
Berbice 15 *n*, 31
Berwick upon Tweed 12 *n*, 190, 198 *n*,
Bescott Bridge 175
Billinge's Liverpool Advertiser (newspaper) 83
Bingham, Daniel George 217 *n*
Birkenhead 156, 187 *n*, 196
Birmingham & Derby Junction Railway 169
Birmingham & Liverpool Junction Canal 157-158, 193
Birmingham & Oxford Junction Railway 3, 196, 200, 203
Birmingham & Walsall turnpike 166
Blackburne, John 7 *n*
Blackburne, Reverend Thomas 149,
Blake, George 13
Blessing, the (ship) 6 *n*
Blount, Edward 204-205, 209
Board of Trade 13, 63 *n*, 70-71, 191,
Bolton & Leigh Railway 117, 194, 200
Bolton, Colonel John 87
Bonaparte, Napoleon 146, 205
Booker, Josias 52
Booth, Henry 36, 124, 126, 128, 135, 139, 179 *n*, 194, 201 *n*
Booth, Thomas 200 *n*
Bootle 121
Bordeaux 210
Borthwick, Peter 32
Botanic Garden, Mount

Pleasant, Liverpool 2, 7
Bourne, James 134 *n*, 161 *n*, 164
Bradshaw, Captain James 132-133,
Bradshaw, Robert Haldane 117, 120, 129, 131-132, 136-138, 144, 154, 159-160, 223
Brandreth, Thomas Shaw 124, 126, 134 *n*
Brassey, Thomas 208, 213
Brazil / Brazilian 17, 35, 47, 59, 68-69, 74
Brazil and River Plate Association 149 *n*
Bridgeford 175
Bridgewater Canal, 116, 117 *n*, 120, 131-132, 136-137, 144, 154, 162 *n*,
Bridgewater, Duke of 117 *n*, 137, 221, 223
Bridgewater, Trustees of the Duke of 118, 130 *n*, 136, 159, 223
Brighton Railway 179
British Guiana 31, 36, 41 *n*, 42, 52 *n*, 56, 59-62, 65, 67, 69, 72, 75-80
British North American Association 149 *n*
Brougham, Lord Henry Peter 12, 21, 58
Brown, Thomas 84-85,
Brown, William 97,
Brunel, Isambard Kingdom 213
Buckley & Sons 90 *n*
Burke, Edmund 217
Buxton, Thomas Fowell 19, 29, 32, 35-36, 48

Caesar, Elizabeth 62
Calais 210
Calcutta 54, 56 n, 57, 61, 63, 75
Caledonian Railway 192, 199 n, 200
Canada 42, 210,
Canning, George 13-14, 19, 94, 152
Canterbury & Whitstable Railway 153
Cape of Good Hope 42
Carlisle 186, 190-192,
Castle Street, Liverpool 85
Caton, Richard 70
Ceylon 54 n
Chance, William 162 *n*
Chaplin, William 206, 210
Chat Moss 135-136, 146
Chatham 117
Chatsworth House 124
Chemin de Fer de L'Ouest 205
Cheshire Lines Railway 8
Chester 52, 156, 189, 196, 200
Chester & Birkenhead Railway 189
Chester & Crewe Railway 180, 189
Chester & Holyhead Railway 188-190, 193, 195
Chester & Shropshire Railway 195
Childwall, Liverpool 52, 129, 150
China / Chinese 77,
Christ Church College, Oxford University 9, 99
Christina, the (ship) 29 *n*
Church of England 2, 12 *n*, 46,

Churnet Valley Railway 195-196, 199
Clapham Sect 12,
Clarke, John 86 *n*
Clarke's and Roscoe's Bank 85
Clay, Swift & Co 194
Clay, Will 62
Clive, Lord 159 *n*
Coffee Grove (West Indian plantation) 34
Coglan, Mr 207
Collett, William Rickford 188
Cologne 212
Colonial Office 12, 26, 40, 45, 47 *n*, 49
Colville, Andrew 56-57, 60, 63, 68 *n*
Cook Street, Liverpool 164
Coppenhall 175
Corn Laws 73
Cornish, James 156 *n*, 178
Cort, Frederick 20 *n*
Country Bankers, Committee of 96-99
Craig Miln (Moss's West Indian plantation) 15 *n*
Creed, Richard 195, 201 *n*
Crewe 175, 180, 183-184, 185 *n* 187,189,196, 199 *n*
Crooked Island, Bahamas 11, 25, 229-230
Cropper, James 22-25, 36, 139-142,
Cropper, John 161 *n*, 164, 177, 200 *n*
Cross, James Conrad 10
Cross, William Simpson 10
Crossley, Mr (vacuum plan sugar engineer) 33
Crown Street, Liverpool 147 *n*, Croxteth 121
Cuba / Cuban 6 *n*, 17, 58-59, 68-69, 74
Curzon Street Railway Station, Birmingham 173 *n*
Custom House receipts 86-88, 93, 95
Dale Street, Liverpool 85, 101, 107-108, 164
Dale, George Edward 84-85
Dale, Roger Newton 84-85
Davidson, Barkley & Co 56-57, 60
Dawson, Richard 131
Delafons, Stipendiary Magistrate 46 *n*
Demerara Rebellion 20-22
Demerara, Demerara-Essequibo 11-12, 14-15, 17-22, 25-26, 28, 30-31, 35-37, 41, 45, 46 *n*, 48, 50, 52 *n*, 53-58, 61, 67-69
Derby, Lord (also Lord Stanley) 37-40, 42, 49, 72, 79, 120, 129, 134, 145-146, 163
Devonshire, Duke of 124
Disraeli, Benjamin 79, 218 *n*
Dominican Republic 21
Douay 210
Dublin 122, 187, 191
Duddleston Railway Station, Birmingham 173 *n*
Dutch Rhenish Railway 210-217
Dutton Viaduct 166, 168
Earl Grey (formerly Viscount Howick) 31 n, 36-38, 79,
Earle, Hardman 161 *n*, 164, 176, 200 *n*

242

East India / East Indies 22-23, 53, 58, 68, 73, 75, 80
East India Company 54
Eastern Counties Railway 198 *n*
Easthope, John 206
Eccles 121, 129, 149
Eccleston 121
Economist, the 155
Edge Hill, Liverpool 147, 180,
Edinburgh 186-187, 192, 201
Edwards, Bryan 16-17, 225-226
Edwards, Edward 7 *n*
Elford, Sir William 90
Elizabeth John (ship) 28 *n*
Ellen, the (ship) 5 *n*,
Ellice, Edward 36
Elliot, Captain Charles 36, 52
Ellis, Lister 121, 123-124, 126-128, 130-131, 134 *n*
Emancipation Act (1833) 41-42, 45, 48, 54 *n*, 60
Emancipation Bill (1833) 40-41
Emancipation Day 65
Emmerich 212, 214
English Channel 209,
Esterhazy, Prince 148 n
Eton College 9
Euston Station, London 187, 201,
Ewart, Joseph Christopher 131, 164 *n*
Ewart, Myers & Co 86-87
Ewart, William 86 *n*, 87, 145 *n*
Falkner, Mr – Receiver General 87 *n*,
Fasque, Aberdeenshire 32 *n*, 51, 202

Fazakerley 121
Fenton, Mr (banker of Rochdale) 216
Ferrand, Major Walker (Moss's son in law) 51
Fiddlers Ferry 176,
Forbes, James Staat 217
Foreign Office, the 26
Formby, Ann Lonsdall 5
Formby, Dr Richard 5 *n*
Forwood, George 8 *n*
Foster, Mr of Birmingham 156
Four Ashes 175
France / French 3, 5 *n*, 21, 25, 81, 131, 168, 203-212
France, Bank of 103
Freeling, Arthur 156 n, 172, 174-175
French Revolution 131, 211
Garnett, John 122
Georgia (USA) 23, 84 *n*,
Germany / German 66, 209-212, 214, 225
Gibson, John 142 *n*
Gillanders, Arbuthnot & Co 53 n, 54, 58
Gladstone & Co 67
Gladstone, Anne (John Gladstone's second wife) 51
Gladstone, Jack (Demerara slave) 20
Gladstone, Sir John 2-3, 9, 11-15, 17, 19-21, 23-25, 27-34, 36-60, 62-63, 66-71, 73-75, 81, 85-88, 90, 92-97, 99, 101-104, 106, 108, 110, 119-124, 126-130, 132, 134, 139, 142-148, 151-153, 157, 161, 167-168, 170, 173, 179-182,

188-189, 191-193, 197, 202, 203-210, 212-215, 217
Gladstone, Robert (John Gladstone's brother) 13 *n*, 51, 121, 123, 128, 131, 133 134 *n*, 171
Gladstone, Robertson (John Gladstone's second son) 34, 44, 47-48, 53, 67, 148, 150-151, 161, 164, 194, 199, 200 *n*, 205, 217 *n*
Gladstone, Thomas (John Gladstone's first son) 148, 151, 152, 210, 211, 215, 217
Gladstone, William Ewart (John Gladstone's fourth son) 2, 9, 39, 49-50, 70-73, 145 *n*
Glasgow 170 n, 186-187, 190-192, 201
Glenelg, Lord 55-57
Glengale, Lady 134 *n*
Gloucester 92
Glyn, George Carr 188-190, 195-196, 199, 201
Goderich, Viscount 13 *n*, 37
Golborn 121
Gough, John 166
Grand Junction Railway (GJR) 2-3, 100, 152 n 156-201, 203, 204, 208, 211, 222, 224
Grand Trunk (Trent & Mersey) Canal 116, 159 n
Grant, Charles 26,
Grant, George 30 *n*, 200 *n*
Great North of England Railway 163 *n*
Great Northern Railway (Compagnie de Nord) 210
Great Western Railroad Company of Canada 210
Great Western Railway 196, 199
Greville, Charles 151 *n*
Grey, Lord 27
Guyana 15 *n*, 80,
Haiti 21
Hamburg 103 *n*, 50
Hampton Court (West Indian Plantation) 17 *n*
Hargreaves, Thomas 110
Harman, Mr (Bank of England official) 91
Harrison, Richard 121-122, 124, 127, 134 *n*, 162 *n*, 164-165, 171
Harrogate 94-95, 51 *n*
Harrowby, Lord 159 *n*,
Hartford 175
Hartley, Jesse 117
Havre 209-210
Haydock 121
Headlam, Thomas 122, 124, 127
Heathcote, John 166
Hesleden, CW 215
Hesperus (ship) 57, 60-61
Heywood, Arthur 86-88, 94
Heywood, Mr of Manchester 163
Hibberson, Joseph 122
Hispaniola 21
Hobhouse, Sir John Cam 54, 56
Hodgson, Adam 48, 134 *n*,
Holland, Netherlands 3, 5 *n*,
Holmes, Samuel 184
Holmes, William 147 *n*, 148, 149 *n*, 152

244

Holyhead 187-189, 193, 196, 201
Hopkins, Mr (of *Anna Regina*) 28
Hornby, Joseph 162 *n*, 164, 176, 200 *n*,
Houghton, Richard 81 *n*
Howard, Edward Charles 28
Howick, Viscount (later Earl Grey) 79, 31 *n*, 36-38
HSBC 108-109
Hudson, George 190-192, 198, 210
Huish, Captain Mark 181, 184, 194
Hulme 121
Huskisson, William 19 *n*, 30, 49, 86-87, 94, 110, 131, 134, 144, 147-153, 171-172, 230
Huyton 129, 176
India (see East India / East Indies)
Indian Indentured Labour Scheme 2, 53-64, 66, 75, 79-80
Innes, J (Moss's pall bearer) 218 *n*
Ireland / Irish 24-25, 50, 66, 75, 100, 107, 122, 156, 186,188, 193, 204, 208, 223, 226
Irish Potato Famine 73-74, 75 *n*, 105, 107
Irlam 121
Irwell, River 127, 129, 138
Italy 168 *n*
Jamaica / Jamaican 14, 16, 23, 30 *n*, 49, 52 *n*, 57, 59, 69, 227
James, Mr (Moss's gardener) 9 *n*
James, William 115-117, 128

James's Bridge 175
Java 71, 78
Jenny, the (ship) 5 *n*
Kate, "Poor Black" 25, 229
Kemble, Fanny 150
Kendal, Mr (Surveyor of the Kings Dock) 29
Kenyon & Leigh Junction Railway 194, 200 *n*
Killingworth Colliery 116 *n*, 157
Kilsby Tunnel 172
Kings Locks, Liverpool 50
Kirkby 121
Kingsmill, the (ship) 54 *n*
Knowsley 121, 126, 129,
Labouchere, Henry 63 *n*
Lace, A (Moss's pall bearer) 218 *n*
Lafitte, Charles 204, 206-207
Lancaster 12 n, 40, 186, 191
Lancaster & Carlisle Railway 191-192, 199 *n*, 200,
Lancaster & Preston Junction Railway 190, 192, 200
Lancaster (Moss's West Indian plantation) 15 *n*
Langton, Joseph 200
Larmer, George 192 *n*
Lawrence, Charles 119, 121-122, 124, 128-129, 131, 133-135, 158, 161, 164-166, 172, 176, 178, 184, 189, 199, 200 *n*, 201 *n*, 204, 205 n, 206, 222, 223
Lawrence, George Hall 200 *n*
Le Resouvenir (West Indian plantation) 19
Leahy, Lieutenant-Colonel John

245

Locke, Joseph, 140,141, 148, 156 *n*, 162, 165-166, 169, 174, 180, 184, 190, 192 *n*, 201 *n*, 203 -204, 206-208, 211, 213

Thomas 21 *n*
Leamington 37, 167, 177, 181 *n*
Ledsam, Daniel 162 *n*, 164 *n*
Ledsam, Joseph F 162 *n*
Leeds & Liverpool Canal 125
Leek and Uttoxeter 195
Leeson, Nick 206
Leigh 121, 129
Leveson-Gower, Lord Francis 133, 159, 160, 162 n,
Leveson-Gower, George Granville (see Marquis of Stafford)
Leveson-Gower, Lord George Sutherland 133, 160, 162 *n*,
Leyland & Bullins bank 86-87, 94, 101
Leyland, Richard 231 *n*
Leyland, Thomas 87, 88
Light, Henry 58, 61, 66
Lightfoot & Co 29
Lille 210
Littleton, Edward John (Lord Hatherton) 147 *n*, 148, 159 *n*
Liverpool & Birmingham Railway (see Grand Junction Railway)
Liverpool & Manchester District Bank 97 *n*,
Liverpool & Manchester Railway (L&M) 2-3, 36, 96, 115-155, 157, 158, 160, 161, 162, 164-165, 167, 170 n, 171, 172, 173, 176-177, 179, 180, 182, 187, 192, 193-194, 200, 203
Liverpool City Council,
Liverpool Corporation 6, 10, 118-119, 149 *n*, 230
Liverpool Courier (newspaper) 11 *n*, 21 *n*, 23 *n*, 25, 54 *n*
Liverpool Mail (newspaper) 1-2, 8, 108, 218, 219-224
Liverpool Mercury (newspaper) 8 *n*, 23 *n*, 43, 107 *n*, 108 *n*, 129, 230
Liverpool Parliamentary Office in London 149 *n*
Livesey, Hargreaves & Co 83
Lloyd, J B (Moss's pall bearer) 218
Loch, George 200,
Loch, James 110, 115, 131-133, 136-139, 143-144, 151, 158-160, 164, 171-172, 176-178, 182, 190, 194, 217
London 6 n, 29, 32, 36, 37, 40, 41, 47, 49, 70 n, 82 n, 83, 86, 91, 92, 93, 94, 95, 97 *n*, 98, 100, 102, 103, 108, 115, 123, 124, 126, 127, 128, 129, 133, 134, 141, 143, 145, 155, 161, 168 n, 172, 181, 186, 187, 188, 189, 190, 191, 201, 202, 204, 207, 209, 210, 211, 213,
London & Birmingham Railway (L&B) 161-165, 172-173, 187-190, 192-197, 199-201
London and Midland Bank 109
London & North Western Railway 142 n, 173n, 189, 201
London & Southampton Railway 163 n, 208, 209
London Missionary Society 19
London Stock Market 85

246

Long, RG 131
Longfellow, Henry Wadsworth 60 *n*
Louis Philippe, King of France 205, 211
Lowther, Lord 134 *n*
Lowton 121
Loyd, Lewis 83
Lunatic Asylum, Liverpool 2
Lyon 210,
Macclesfield Canal 139
Mackenzie and Brassey 208
MacLean, John 30-31, 34, 38, 40 n, 41, 44, 47
Madeira / Madeiran 50, 54 n, 75-76, 80
Madeley 175
Madras 75
Malta / Maltese 66
Malvern 108,
Manchester 7, 73 n, 83 n, 90 n, 92 n, 97, 115-116, 121, 122, 124, 129, 133, 136-137, 140, 145, 147, 148, 149, 150, 153, 155, 158, 175, 186, 187, 189, 196, 204, 213, 221, 222, 223
Manchester & Birkenhead Railway 195
Manchester & Birmingham Railway 180 n, 187, 189, 195-196, 201
Manchester Guardian 206-207
Manchester & Leeds Railway 169
Manchester & Liverpool District Bank 97 n
Manchester Ship Canal 155
Manesty's Lane, Liverpool 7
Manilla 71

Marseilles 210
Martino, Mr (of Demerara) 28
Masterman, John 210, 212 n
Mauritius 42, 47, 53, 54, 55, 56, 61, 72, 78
McIvoy & Co 14
McNeile, Reverend Hugh 218
Mechanics Institute, Liverpool 2,
Melbourne, Lord 70
Mersey & Irwell Navigation Company 118, 120, 125, 129, 138, 154
Mersey Road, Liverpool 8
Mersey, River 1, 7, 129, 143, 157, 159, 162, 187
Mexican and South American Association 149 *n*
Minshull Vernon 175
Mold 188
Moore 175
Moravian Church 46-47
Morning Chronicle, the 206
Moss & Co; also Moss, Dales & Rogers; Moss, Dale, Rogers & Moss; Moss, Rogers & Moss 3, 84-86, 94, 100, 104, 105, 111, 119
Moss, Anne Jane (Moss's daughter) 7 *n*, 51
Moss, Betty nee Griffies (Moss's mother) 8 n, 12 n
Moss, Ellen (Moss's sister) 84
Moss, Gilbert Winter (Moss's fifth son) 7, 80, 109, 145 *n*,
Moss, Hannah (Moss's daughter) 7
Moss, Hannah, nee Taylor (Moss's wife) 7, 51, 134, 142,

153, 167, 211 *n*
Moss, Hannah, nee Clegg (Henry Moss's wife) 230
Moss, Harriet Eliza (Moss's daughter) 7, 134
Moss, Helen (wife of Henry Moss of Crooked Island) 25, 229, 230
Moss, Henry (Moss's brother) 6, 12, 52 n, 53, 55, 85, 96, 99, 101, 107-108, 123, 229-231
Moss, Henry (of Crooked Island) 25-26, 229-231
Moss, James (Moss's brother) 6, 12, 25, 26, 52, 107,
Moss, James (Moss's uncle) 5 *n*, 6 *n*, 11-14, 26, 84, 229, 230
Moss, John - See Contents
John James (Moss's third son) 7, 80,
Moss J C (Henry Moss's son) 217 *n*
Moss, Margaret (Moss's daughter) 7, 51, 52 *n*, 134
Moss, Margaret (Moss's sister) 84
Moss, Peter Cottingham (Henry Moss's son) 53, 96, 99, 108,
Moss, Thomas (Moss's first born son) 7 *n*
Moss, Thomas (Moss's second son) and later Sir Thomas Edwards – Moss 7 *n*, 9, 10, 33, 80, 99, 101, 109, 164, 200
Moss, Thomas of Whiston (Moss's father) 5, 6, 81, 106, 219
Moss, William (Moss's uncle) 5 *n*,
Moss, William Henry (Moss's fourth son) 7, 80, 107, 109
Mossley Hill, Liverpool 7
Mount Pleasant, Liverpool 7, 146
Mozley, Lewin 200 *n*
Murdoch, Thomas 131
Mure, Special Justice 61
Murphy's Winter 8 *n*
Murray, Lieutenant governor John 20,
Myers, William 86 *n*
Nantes 210
Neilson, John B 106 *n*
New Orleans 23
New York 66 *n*, 67
Newcastle upon Tyne 124, 127 n, 128, 190,
Newcastle & Darlington Railway 127 *n*
Newfoundland 67
Newton House, Ugglebarnby 84-85
Newton in Makerfield 121
Newton le Willows 162, 167, 175, 187,
Newton Road 175
New York 66 *n*, 67
North Midland Railway 163 n, 169, 198 n,
North Union Railway 187, 192, 194
North Western Bank 109
Northern & Central Bank of Manchester 102
Northumbrian, locomotive 147-149
Norton Bridge 175

Novelty, locomotive 141
Oaks, Mr (of Demerara) 28
Oberhausen 214-215
Old Quay Company (see Mersey & Irwell Navigation Company)
Olive Mount, Liverpool 135, 173
Otterspool Estate 1, 5-10, 52, 221
Otterspool House 7, 9-10, 51 *n*, 129, 134, 202 *n*, 217, 221
Otterspool Road, Liverpool 8
Oxford 196
Oxford & Rugby Railway 196
Oxford, Worcester & Wolverhampton Railway 196
Paddington Station, London 196
Paris 203, 204, 206, 207, 208, 209, 210, 213
Paris - Orleans Railway 210 *n*
Paris – Strasbourg Railway 210 *n*
Paris & Lyon 210
Paris & Rouen Railway 3, 181, 203, 205 *n*, 208-211
Parker, Charles Stewart 52
Partridge, Samuel 166 *n*
Pease, Edward 127 *n*
Pease, Joseph 121
Peel, Sir Robert 1, 3, 9-10, 39, 49-50, 68, 70-73, 142 *n*, 147 *n*, 150, 152, 188, 191, 222
Pendlebury 121
Penkridge 175
Pennington 121
Penzance 83 *n*
Pereseverance, locomotive 141

Perry Bar 175
Peter's Lane, Liverpool 6
Phillips, RB 131
Pilkington, JB 131
Plymouth Bank 90
Pole, Thornton & Co 90
Portsmouth & Chatham Railway 117
Portugal / Portuguese 25, 50, 66, 76, 85 *n*, 100
Powis, Lord 193
Prescot 129
Preston 170 n, 187, 190, 200,
Preston & Wigan Railway 187
Preston Brook 175
Price, Theodore 162 *n*
Prince's Dock, Liverpool 121
Pritt, George Ashby 122, 130 n, 223,
Prussia / Prussian 212, 213, 214
Purdom, Reverend William J 53
Quamina (Demerara slave) 19, 20, 21
Quivrain 210
Railway Mania 105, 192, 198, 210, 212
Rainford Gardens, Liverpool 5
Rainhill Trials, the 140-142
Rastrick, John 140, 165
Rathbone, William 134 *n*
Rathbone, Theodore 176
Reed, Malcolm 189
Reform Bill (1831) 29
Reform Bill (1832) 39 *n*,
Rennie, George 127-128, 134-135
Rennie, John 127-128, 134-135
Restriction Period, the 82, 88
Richards, Mr – Bank of

England official 91 *n*
Richardson & Co 94
Richardson, Thomas 131
Richmond (West Indian plantation) 69 *n*
Ricketts, Frederick 212 *n*
Robinson, Frederick John (see also Goderich, Viscount) 13, 14
Rocket, locomotive 141-142, 148
Rogers, Edward 84, 99
Rome & Houston (West Indian Planatation) 46 *n*, 69 *n*
Roscoe, Clarke & Roscoe, Bank of 12 *n*, 85, 86, 92
Roscoe, Jane nee Griffies 12 *n*,
Roscoe, Thomas 167
Roscoe, William 6, 11-12, 17
Roscoe, William Stanley 86 *n*
Rose, Peter 36, 41
Rotheram, William 134, 140, 162 *n*, 164, 176, 200 *n*
Rothschild, Baron James de 205
Rotterdam 212-215 208-211
Rouen & Havre Railway 3, 203, 206 208-211
Royal Agricultural Society 9
Royal Bank of Liverpool 106
Royal William (ship) 66 *n*
Rugby 189, 190,
Rugeley, Staffs 204 *n*
Runcorn 143,
Runcorn Bridge 157, 159-160
Russell, Charles 196
Russell, Lord John 39, 68, 70, 73, 78
Salford 121,129
Sandars, Joseph 115-116, 120 *n*, 121-124, 126, 128, 133, 134 *n*, 135, 140, 158, 162 *n*, 164, 171, 176, 200 *n*, 222
Sandbach Tinne & Co 52
Sandbach, Samuel 15, 30 *n*, 34, 52 *n*,
Sandon, Lord 30, 32, 35, 39-41, 63 *n*, 153 *n*,
Sanspareil, locomotive 141
Saturday Advertiser, the (newspaper) 150 *n*, 161,
Savannah, Georgia 84 *n*,
Scoble, John 56, 59, 61-63
Scotland / Scottish 12 *n*, 13, 66, 131, 145, 156, 186, 190, 191,
Sefton, Lord 120-121, 129, 145, 163
Severn Stoke, Worcestershire 108
Shand, Mr (of Demerara) 28
Sharp, Roberts & Co of Gorton 213
Shaw, Charles 162 *n*, 164 *n*
Shaw, Isaac 113-114
Sheffield 51
Sheffield & Rotherham Railway 169
Shrewsbury 190, 195, 196
Shrewsbury & Birmingham Railway 199,
Slave Registration Act (1819) 18
Slave trade, the 5-6, 17-18, 23, 25, 56, 59, 66, 70, 74, 76-77
Smiles, Samuel 169
Smith, Colonel Sir Frederick 187
Smith, Egerton 43

Smith, Reverend John of the London Missionary Society 19, 22
Smyth, Sir James Carmichael 46 *n*, 55, 57-60
Society for the Amelioration and Gradual Abolition of Slavery 22
Sothern, James 132,
South Carolina 23, 84 *n*
South Sea Bubble 192
Spain / Spanish 5 *n*, 23, 25, 85 *n*, 10, 209
Sparrow, Mr of Birmingham 156
Spooner, Mr of Birmingham 156
Spread Eagle 175
St Anne Street, Liverpool 5
St Anne's Church, Liverpool 1, 52-53, 217-218
St Domingo (Hispaniola) 21, 25
St Georges Hall, Liverpool 142, 231
St Germain 203
St Kitts 49, 67
St Lucia 41 *n*
St Thomas 46
St Vincent 84-85
Stafford 175, 189
Stafford, Marquis of (George Granville Leveson-Gower) and the first Duke of Sutherland 117, 120, 131-134, 137, 143-144, 157-160, 162, 164, 165 *n*,
Staniforth, Samuel 87 *n*
Stanley, EGS (see Lord Derby)
Stanley, Lord of Knowsley, later of Bickerstaff (see Lord Derby)
Stephen, George 36,
Stephen, James 12, 14, 40, 47-48, 55, 63, 68, 75
Stephenson, George 1, 9, 116-118, 120-121, 126-129, 135-136, 139-142, 146-150, 162-163, 165-166, 168-170, 195, 206-207, 213, 220
Stephenson, Robert 140-141, 162, 165, 201 *n*
Stewart, Patrick Maxwell 40,
Stockton & Darlington Railway 118, 128, 130, 153,
Strasbourg 210
Strasbourg – Basle Railway 210 *n*
Stuart, James 46 n, 47, 51, 60, 63, 67, 69
Sturge, Joseph 36, 59
Success (John Gladstone's West Indian plantation) 19-21, 38
Suffield, Lord 35
Sugar Duties Act (1846) 73, 75
Sugar Duties Bill 73
Sutherland, Elizabeth the 19th Countess of 131
Sutton 121
Swift, John 194
Switzerland 168, 209,
Tayleur, Charles 131, 162 *n*, 164
Taylor, F (Moss's pall bearer) 218
Taylor, Thomas of Blakeley (Moss's father in law) 7 n
Telford, Thomas 127, 138-139
Thomas Wilson & Sons 212 *n*
Thompson, George 32

Thompson, Poulett 63
Thompson, Samuel 87, 231
Thornley, Thomas 29 *n*, 30
Tinne, John Abraham 52,
Tobin, Sir John 101
Traill, Professor (Moss's pall bearer) 218 *n*
Treasury 87, 93, 100,
Trent & Mersey (or Grand Trunk) Canal 116, 159
Trent Valley Railway (TVR) 189-191, 195-196, 199 *n*, 222
Trevethick, Francis 184
Trevethick, Richard 184 *n*
Tring Cutting 172
Trinidad 14, 41 *n*, 77
Turner, John 162 *n*
Turner, Mr (of Demerara) 28
Turner, Thomas & John 92-93
Union Bank of London 213
Utrecht 212, 215
Vacuum pan 28-29, 30 n, 33-34, 43 *n*, 47, 51, 67
Vauxhall Station, Birmingham 173 *n*, 183 *n*
Vauxhall, Liverpool 121, 173
Veritas Vincit 183, 185
Victoria, Queen 142 *n*,
Vignoles, Charles Blacker 128-129
Vindex (Moss's pseudonym?) 25
Voluntary Subscription Immigration Society 67-68
Vreedenhoop (John Gladstone's West Indian plantation) 31, 38, 62
Vreedenstein (John Gladstone's West Indian plantation) 60, 62
Wainewright, William 149 n, 167, 170
Wakefield, Mr (of London) 125 n
Wales 180, 187-188
Walker, James 140, 191
Walker, Joseph N 161, 162 *n* 164 *n*
Walton 121, 129
Wapping, Liverpool 147 *n*
Warrington 129, 162, 174, 175
Warrington & Newton Railway 162
Waterloo (West Indian plantation) 63 *n*
Watt, James 166
Wavertree Hall, Liverpool 129
Weaver Navigation Company 139
Weaver, River 166
Webster, NW 169
Wellington Rooms, Liverpool 146, 150
Wellington, Duke of 1, 39, 96, 146-150
Wentworth & Co of York 90
West India Association 149 *n*, 25
West India Committee 41
West Indies 5 n, 13, 17, 23-24, 29, 33, 34 *n*, 35, 42, 47-48, 49 n, 54, 58-59, 63, 65-66, 68-69, 74, 76-77, 79
Whatton, Mr (surgeon) 149
Whiston 5 n, 162 n,
Whitby 84-85
Whitby, the (ship) 57, 60,
Whitmore 175
Wigan Branch Railway 187
Wilberforce, William 1, 11 n,

12, 14, 17-19
Wilbraham, Edward Bootle 153 *n*
Willem II, King of the Netherlands 212 *n*
Willenhall 175
William IV, King 29, 32, 39, 41 n, 172
Wilson, Dr James 108 *n*
Windle 121
Windsor Forest (West Indian plantation) 78
Winsford 175
Winter, Gilbert 137, 145
Winwick 129
Wolverhampton 173, 175
Wood, Sir Charles 106
Worsley 121
Worsley Hall 137
Worthington, S B 192 *n*
York & North Midland Railway 198